SOBER TRUTH

By Osbert Sitwell

THE MAN WHO LOST HIMSELF : A Novel
BEFORE THE BOMBARDMENT : A Novel
TRIPLE FUGUE : Stories
DISCURSIONS ON TRAVEL, ART, AND LIFE
ENGLAND RECLAIMED : A Book of Eclogues
OUT OF THE FLAME : Poems
ARGONAUT AND JUGGERNAUT : Poems
WHO KILLED COCK ROBIN ?

By Osbert Sitwell and Sacheverell Sitwell

ALL AT SEA : A Social Tragedy in Three Acts

By Osbert Sitwell and Nina Hamnett

THE PEOPLE'S ALBUM OF LONDON STATUES

By Edith, Osbert, and Sacheverell Sitwell

POOR YOUNG PEOPLE : POEMS

General and Mrs. Tom Thumb

Frontispiece

SOBER TRUTH

A Collection of Nineteenth-century Episodes,
Fantastic, Grotesque and Mysterious

Compiled and edited by
Margaret Barton and Osbert Sitwell

With a preface by
OSBERT SITWELL

and Seventeen Illustrations

DUCKWORTH
3 Henrietta Street
London

First Published April 1930
Second Impression June 1930

Printed in Great Britain

Stones have been known to move, and trees to speak.

To

MARIE AND RICHMOND TEMPLE

CONTENTS

ILLUSTRATIONS

PREFACE

In humbly offering this book to the public, it must be confessed that the aim of the compilers is more propagandist than literary. The very essence of such an anthology is that the items selected for publication should consist as far as possible of direct reports, should speak in the idiom of their dead moment and with their own words, even though these were ill-chosen; that the recital of the various murders and portents should be, as it were, straight from the horse's mouth. When necessary—where it has been impossible for one reason or another to rely entirely on newspaper-reports and the publicly-printed accounts of eye-witnesses—the editors have quoted from private letters of the time, or, in one or two instances, where descriptions of the same event have coincided in certain details, while yet each one has added this or that new point, have, in order to avoid length and monotony, decided to compress and combine them. Indeed, much compression has been necessary toward making a book of so few pages and containing such a plenitude of events.

But, above all things, the editors conceived that it was plainly their duty not in any way to intrude themselves into the labyrinths of these past mysteries. And, in order to avoid the incrustation of the text with footnotes as much as such a prolongation of present-day individuality into happenings that should appear remote and isolated, the few remarks and comments, which it seemed to them were indispensable, are incorporated in this preface, forming the last half of it.

. . . .

Any objects, it is said, however ill-assorted they may at first sight appear, will be seen eventually to go together in a room, to make a unity there, if the owner has bought, because he genuinely likes, them. They are permeated with his personality. His liking these things unites them, and makes them sink their most startling differences. So it should be with an anthology. The savour of any miscellany should reside in the point of view of those who compile it, in the individuality of the editors, filtered through the matter they choose for publication, but not thrust in solid explanatory slabs before you. There should be no need for this. But it seemed to the compilers as though some exposition of their purpose is, for once, really due to the gentle reader. For their aim is an ambitious one: no less than to undermine the current estimate of the last century and to place it in public opinion upon quite a different pedestal.

The writer of this preface has several times been accused in print of "sneering at the nineteenth century": an occupation, indeed, which would be about as useful and edifying as shying pebbles at his grandmother's tombstone. No one of any intelligence at all who remembers it, though it were only the golden glow and hush that fell upon the world in the few years that preceded the end of Queen Victoria's reign, could treat it so. This short interval, which seemed as if it might last for all time, gave colour and the appearance of truth to the pretensions of the past seven or eight decades. Never had there been so prosperous and splendid a calm, culminating as it did, in the Jubilee Celebration of 1897.

The writer remembers how, as a small boy addicted to the reading for his own pleasure of any books he could find dealing with Greek, Roman, or English history (this was a practice of which school quickly broke him a few years later), he wondered sometimes, as he looked out on the trim, well-ordered world, whether History had not for ever stopped her march . . . on the whole, he rather hoped she had . . . for she appeared to be an immane and ruthless harridan. His governess, though a strong Imperialist, always planning to marry and people the colonies, and to that purpose for ever reading how to defeat the inroads of white ants into a colonial home and collecting inedible objects, such as trunks, baths, and boxes made of a metal which would defeat their efforts, confirmed him in his newly-formed opinion. She considered History as a nice, motherly, white-haired woman, robed in a becoming Union Jack: albeit there would, she thought, always be scraps with savages in parts of an ever more far-flung empire. . . .

But soon, apart from such police-work, *an event* was at last to materialise—the Boer War. From an original over-confidence, opinion swiftly passed into an exaggerated depression. All round him, fully-grown relatives were disguising themselves in uniforms of Yeoman or Volunteer, crowning themselves, too, with enormous plumed helmets, like those of firemen; were having their swords ground and polished, and were, generally, preparing resolutely for the worst. But, being perhaps better acquainted at that moment with atlases—for one or two, open at a random continent, were thrust menacingly under his nose every day, and remained there, staring at him with their stupid, wrinkled faces for an hour or more—he could not, try as he would, take very seriously the Menace of a Boer Invasion. The Transvaal seemed such a long way off . . . and, though continually informed that children did not understand these things, he remained sanguine that, even if the Boers won, we could defend ourselves against the brutes: while if they lost—well, they lost. Not then, alas, was he aware of the diamond-strewn paths from the Rand to Piccadilly and the racecourses, not then did he understand the aching void in Park Lane. . . . But, for the rest, History, as far as it could be understood, was an affair of Jubilees and Royal Processions, when even our dusky brothers, the Indians, so greatly did they love us at this time, dashed over to help on every possible occasion; sailed over all those miles of sea, only, as the newspapers said, "to lend a touch of empery to our grey streets with the splendour of their oriental pageantry." History, even if she had not stopped marching, was marking time.

For the rest, all was quiet. In America, it was true, people were busy discovering things for our especial use; telephones, gramophones, and things of that kind . . . and it looked as though, in the future, the United States would provide a valuable field for English capital and enterprise. Otherwise, nothing stirred. . . . An anarchist or two, perhaps, threatened the less secure monarchies of Southern Europe (but then the Latin races were so unstable and excitable), and a mad Belgian fired a revolver at the then Prince of Wales. Nothing stirred; not a leaf on the Tree of Justice trembled.

But, even then, the certainty and security by which the writer was surrounded seemed to him to be oddly at variance with other aspects of the physical world and to hit it off very queerly, for example, with the only other world of which he was then cognisant: that world of superstitions, ghost-stories, and, as she would have termed it, "such-like," into which he had been inducted by his nurse. She was categorically forbidden ever to regale her charges with any of her favourite horrors or portents, but knowing, perhaps instinctively, that she would never find a more sympathetic audience, could not resist doing so. She was, unlike the others round her, a character belonging to no one age. Apart from her antipathy to bananas as "a very common fruit indeed," her intense devotion to Aberdeen granite as a divinely-ordained medium for tombstones and memorials, and her devotion to the particular Queen under whom she lived, she was, in other respects, just as true to the reign of Anne or Elizabeth as to that of Victoria; a Shakespearian character, a nurse of all time. Although, perhaps, she belonged to the age of Webster more than to any later one, for there was a certain quality about her at once robust and morbid. She loved the sea, and all its smaller fruits, shrimps, prawns, and winkles (here her aristocratic prejudices, as evinced in her horror of bananas, broke down); she loved the lanes, then fuller of wild flowers than of charabancs, and could name any flower, bird, or tree with its proper English name; she loved theatres and any form of pageantry ; but more, I think, than anything, did she love to read of a murder—though it was only in the Bible—visit a friend dying of some lingering disease, or roam at her ease in a well-ordered cemetery, observing every inscribed and floral detail. There was, further, none of the modern, scientific-nurse nonsense about her, and, were a child ill, she would give it the correct, prescribed medicine and, at the same time, indulge in some private, primeval trick or bribe for its recovery : and although, as in duty bound, she had administered the physic, in reality she attributed any amelioration that might ensue to her own practices of superstition. Yet it was this woman, with her " invincible ignorance," as those responsible for the welfare of the present writer termed it —an ignorance that yet contained a very much deeper and kinder truth than did the wisdom and education of more rational persons—together with the old house in the shelter of which he lived, that nevertheless joined every-day life for him on to that of previous ages, prevented the nineteenth century from cutting itself off entirely from the past, and provided a healthy current of red blood to that which otherwise might have seemed a dull, bloated, yet anemic age. It is then with these aspects of life, which she represented for him, that our anthology attempts to deal : for they afforded a strange contrast to the conviction of every person living during this epoch that he was in the right, the only right, and that the life of the time was the only life, and would, embalmed in the preservative of semi-education, continue for ever.

Assuredly far too much stress has been laid by recent writers upon this materialistic and dry side of the nineteenth century. To the editors of this miscellany, it has always appeared, on the contrary, as the most romantic century in recorded history : and it is to remedy the first now widely held misconception of the epoch as comic but dull, and to propagate their own view of it, that these papers are here collected together.

Part of the romance of it resides in the way in which

the prosaic and romantic lie down together, lion and lamb; part, doubtless, in the fact that everything is so fully, prosaically recorded, so strongly documented. How well we can know the century, for nearly every person who could write was so certain of the importance of his thoughts that he noted them down, so sure of the interest of his actions that he recorded them (and it is to this that we owe the plague of nineteenth-century memoirs now afflicting us). Yet such documentation did not kill the sense of things, for is not the mystery of the rarer mysteries that occur in an age given over to records and statistics by that much the more mysterious?

But—and it is because of this that the accusation of attempted disparagement is so often made against the author of this preface—to understand fully the romance of the epoch and to underline it, it is necessary to comprehend and draw attention to the arid, unpleasant side of it, too. The generation to which writers—and, one hopes, readers—belong is bound to see it as rather a cocksure and domineering century, as rather a vicious and prudish century; cannot but regard it as an era chiefly of mechanical, scientific, and material progress. In this last respect it is, as Mr. Bertrand Russell points out, a century of definite and praiseworthy achievement. There was an admirable humanitarian program accomplished during these years. But, alas, the indictment against the Victorian Age is not that it was not comfortable, or, in spite of its many cruelties, kindly; but that it left its debts, mental, moral, and physical, to be paid by a later generation. And notwithstanding that the present century still shows in Europe a greater quantity of material destruction than construction, is this not the fault of the one that bore it? For, behind the smoke screen that denoted material prosperity, under the pall of the newly-invented yellow fogs that so happily ever and again obliterated for a time the hideous, soulless squalor of industrial cities, History was preparing some of her grandest but most farcical tricks. If materialism was that which Europe valued, then she should be given a taste of it . . . material destruction on an unprecedented scale. The World War was an epilogue to the nineteenth century. History took a dangerous leap out of bed after her long rest. All the kings who had been brought up to be so sure of themselves—and had yet allowed, so great was the new regard for money, the peoples under their absolute care to be exploited—all these preposterous, puffed-up, weakly picturesque monsters were deflated and shaken down. The wicked, old, whiskered Emperor Franz-Josef, whose callous character had given birth to so many tragedies, the charlatan Emperor, with his ferocious and silly moustachios, with his withered arm hidden in the gold-braided sleeve of his pretentious, swashbucklering uniforms—this man of great descent, well-educated and of some talent, this religious man whose chief pleasure it was to listen to dirty-minded, stupid, schoolboy jokes—the weak, amiable superstitious Tsar of All the Russias, too, with his mystical, hysterical intuition that his country needed a victim to be sacrificed, the Sultan, with his vast turban and jewelled egret, that queer child-minded monster who knew of nothing outside the harem in which he had lived his life . . . the thrones of all these were blown sky high. They were replaced, in most countries, by the even less amiable and less picturesque gum-chewing ogres of Oil and Big Business, and in Russia by a set of cruel but antlike Jews. But there were others, more innocent, who had also to suffer. For if Europe had created this lust for money, now she was to be the slave of it.

Yet who could have imagined such things in the Europe of the nineteenth century, so sure, complete, and well guarded? Who, in the reign of Victoria, could have possibly believed that the young Emperor, her German grandson, would pass many years of exile in Holland or that one of her granddaughters, with all her children, would be massacred in the most horrible way in a wooden hut in Siberia, their bodies afterwards to be thrown down a mine-shaft and then burned, to avoid possible identification? And this, too, this tragic epilogue, makes the previous century romantic.

If, moreover, the twentieth century lags behind the nineteenth—at any rate in Europe—in the increase of material prosperity, is not this retrogression an advantage? Is not to unlearn sometimes as valuable as to learn, to be uncertain as valuable as to be certain wrongly? And how positive the nineteenth century was! A dull blanket of certitude hangs over it—and especially over the English, its most favoured nation—which renders the era a little intimidating, and which singles it out for us from those ages that had gone before.

And herein, perhaps, lies the difference between the best thought of the nineteenth century and the best of the twentieth (the only kind of thought, after all, and in the face of every prevailing belief, which counts). Our generation, that part of it which still survives, has begun to understand that, both for its own safety and that of Europe and the country, it must believe in nothing that is not proved; and, even when fully proved, must not hasten to believe entirely. We of the modern European—though not American—world know now how easy it is for lies to deck themselves out as the truth and deceive even the upright and earnest. We know that no nation has even yet consciously engaged itself in an unjust war: though we are inclined to think that there has never yet been a just one. We know that the enemies of every country commit atrocities—atrocities, moreover, of a hackneyed, silly, and unimaginative sort. We know, further, that every war is a war to end war. We do not believe, with the last generation, brought up on a now decayed and obsolete political economy, that any man who makes money is a good man. We deplore, in that sense, the grasping, self-made man, who still retains so strong a hold in Canada and the United States. We have gone back even to a few childish, fundamental beliefs, such as that a very ugly face is not necessarily to be pitied, but is often a warning of wickedness. Thus, when we see a millionaire with the face of a devil, even though he is a millionaire we distrust him. When we see a man put up in the House of Commons as the spokesman of Capital, and note the brutal hideousness of his appearance, the coarse lisping of his speech, we, in the face of "good-taste," question the cause that inspires such a champion. Nor do we believe, with a certain noble newspaper-proprietor, that money spells power; power, happiness: that, therefore, money spells happiness, and that, ergo, Shelley must have been a failure because he was comparatively poor, and so, of course, powerless. On the contrary, we believe that Shelley, being by now incorporated in the consciousness of any person who has heart, soul, or mind, influences the world more every day, more than all the potentates, dictators, oil-kings, cement-kings, and newspaper-proprietors in the world rolled into an unpleasant and muddy one.

Yet even in these certain beliefs we are willing not to be as certain as our grandfathers. For, hard-headed as they were then, hard-faced as they are now called, the pastors and masters wrapped themselves, it must be admitted, in gowns of very positive and rather ugly colour: that is to say, the Conservative nobleman was too certain of his rights, the Whig one too anxious to dispose of them, the religious man, of whatever denomination, knelt in joy, convinced that his God was the only God, the atheist stood, unpleasantly sure that there was no God at all, while the upright Darwinian was primly but joyously certain of the very ape from which he was descended. (This last person, in spite of all evidence, in spite of visits to the Zoological Gardens—visits which, one might have thought, would have induced an identical theory in the mind of any child of four possessed of an observant eye—had only recently been introduced to the idea, and insisted on regarding it as a great discovery.) The white man knew that the black man must for ever bear the white man's burden (no doubt the black man was soon convinced of this, too); the hangman was quite, quite sure of the wickedness of him whom he was hanging by the neck—and therefore accomplished his job with pleasure. The criminal, likewise, was expected to be grimly yet comfortingly aware of the virtues of those who had condemned him. The hunting-man, as he drove fox, stag, or otter to its bitter death, congratulated himself that the English were the only race in the world who were really kind to dumb animals. Everything was in water-tight compartments, and it was never for an instant supposed by a member of any political party (there were only two teams, as in a football match, and all nineteenth-century Englishmen worthy of the name belonged to one or other) that it might be right, and better for the country, were a man to vote Tory at one election and Radical at the next. No, principles were principles. There must be Stern Endeavour for Stern Endeavour's Sake. Nothing pertaining to authority must be questioned . . . but for the rest, God was in His heaven and all was right with the world.

The one attitude lacking, save in the supreme and lonely instance of Benjamin Disraeli, Earl of Beaconsfield, was that of scientific agnosticism. And it is this quality, so exceptional in his time, which, as he lolls, old, huddled-up, but still acting, on the front bench of the House of Commons, surrounded by a dreary, righteous, if apparently honest, mass of nineteenth-century statesmen, all speaking with never a thought of their own in well-rounded periods, gives him his queer, enviable, rakish halo of romance.

Such strictures, we think, may with some show of justice be passed at an inquest upon the dead century. But here there is not much space to spare for the examination of them—though with such an aspect of it the editors propose to deal in another anthology, more limited in the time it covers and entirely devoted to the words men spoke or wrote in those days.

But this collection of papers is devoted to deeds, in order to show that under the stream of high-minded platitudes the most extraordinary events, that should have been enough to induce in any mind that followed them both a certain scepticism and a terror and respect for the unknown and unknowable, were in progress. Part of the fascination of the epoch is to be found in this enormous divergence between opinion and the trend of events; a separation which is often—but more especially in the England of this time—to be noted. And the editors ask the reader, as he peruses the pages they have culled for him, to forgive them if he is already acquainted with the content of many of them, and not to let them be dulled by this familiarity, but to restore to the events their strange lustre by contrasting them in his own mind with the scientific progress of the time and with the certitude of the well fed and well educated: or, again, to consider them placed against the blank but impressive façade of nineteenth-century English history. He must remember, too (and some of our selections will remind him), that meanwhile in far-off countries—and all countries then seemed far away, though, owing to the constant improvement in methods of locomotion, never had they actually been so near—the most unusual incidents were occurring from time to time. And these incidents, that always appear so unusual, are, in reality, the stuff out of which history is built up and modelled into shape.

The epoch saw, among other things, the glittering tragedy of the Second Empire, just across the water; the rise of Prussia; the rise and fall of two attempts at Empire in, of all places in the world, Mexico; the end of one fantastic but bourgeois Empire in Brazil; and the conversion of Japan—that formerly hermit-country, given over to fireworks and the gentle celebration of its fruit-tree festivals—from a perplexing, lacquered dream into a modern ants'-paradise of industry.

It must be recalled, however, that though the world is the background of our stage, and a peep at it is always permissible, yet the action must chiefly be British, must always be observed from a strictly British point of view; that though it is well to know, or occasionally to be reminded of, the march of things abroad, it is upon events, portents, and episodes noticed in our own country that we ought to choose, and have chosen, to dwell. Britain was busy. She built up her second great Empire, consisting of nearly any part of the world in which the inhabitants could not defend themselves or their lands—which, therefore, needed developing for the common good of humanity. She opened up, also, a whole continent with forced convict labour. At home, too, very odd things, as we shall see, happened from year to year.

It is in this very juxtaposition of arrogant dry-as-dust realism with events so fantastic as to be impossible to imagine, or with beliefs so removed from all sense of reality as to make the mere believing in them as strange as though these creeds were justified, that, more than in anything else, the romance of the nineteenth century lies hidden. And what a romantic epoch it is that unfolds itself. The world could not be changed, as each generation trusted it would be, by a few years of gaslight and steam-engine, or telegraph and electric-light. The old wickednesses and the old pleasures, the old mysteries—or is it only the old faith in them ?—persisted. The same age which misunderstood and persecuted Shelley, produced him ; the same age that introduced child-labour on a large scale into the factories, gave birth to Dickens. The material age of certainty and comfort, and of unbelievable ugliness, was father to William Blake. A thousand false Messiahs were born into this arid, sure, and religious century. The same period which was the first, perhaps, to organise an efficient police and detective force saw towards its opening the drab, round-capped horrors of Burke and Hare, and, towards its close, watched the noiseless and remorseless operations of Jack the Ripper . . . that series of anonymous and sequent murders that is the most frightening in all the annals of English crime. Indeed, as this dim, jaunty figure of vengeance slinks down the crooked, rat-ridden alleys and through the rather beautiful courts of an older London, his murders seem to transcend crime, and to be attended by something of the monstrous and diabolic. But both these series of icy-hearted, calculating slaughters could only have occurred in the nineteenth century, in an age given over to the growing worship of science : for with

Burke and Hare (page 103) the murders were committed in order to gain money by supplying the medical market with enough fresh corpses for dissection, while Jack the Ripper (page 237) displayed an anatomical knowledge that could not have been gained in any other epoch. This fact, indeed, while it narrows down the field for enquiry, only makes the figure of the murderer more mysterious. Did he belong to the professional classes, this terrible, quiet monster; was he a doctor, a medical-student, or a student at a veterinary college, and, if so, for what purpose did he write the horrifying letters printed on page 242.

. . . .

And now it is best to proceed at once to the discussion of any points arising out of the individual items in our miscellany. This will be done in more or less chronological order, except that the writer will take the Emperor Christophe out of his place in the years, and deal with him last, for he has more to say about him than about the other persons figuring in these pages. Moreover, the dusky monarch deserves special treatment, in whatever age he lived.

Underneath the surface, then, the currents of mysticism, religious fervour, and superstition were still as strong as ever. In 1809, a schoolmaster of Thurso (page 13) admits to having seen on the rocks off Caithness a mermaid in the authentic gesture of combing her—or, in his rather rough phrase, "its"—— hair. He gives the most certain and anatomical details of her appearance, though he is in doubt whether her fingers were webbed. Furthermore, he witnessed this strange tableau in the very place where it had several times been observed before. What, then, are we to conclude . . . except that a Scottish schoolmaster really saw a mermaid?

Next the reader comes to Joanna Southcott (page 39), who provides two interesting sequels in our own time. No lack of a miracle has ever been allowed to dismay the faithful of any faith. If a miracle is expected, it either happens, is made to happen, is said to have happened, or, should it be too difficult of performance, the absence of it is then quoted as the proof of a singular sincerity and as a token that it will happen in after years. Time, we are told, is difficult to judge of in prophecy: 1788 may mean 1988, or 1840, 1940. The leader of no creed, however absurd, can ever be quite discredited in the eyes of his followers. Despite, therefore, the complete exposure of this rather unpleasant and singularly optimistic old woman a century previously, yet, during the years of the late "Great" War, an anonymous body of believers was for ever clamouring in the various agony-columns of the daily newspapers that Joanna Southcott's box should be opened and England saved. This box she had left behind her as a proof of her earthly travail, and had made it the subject of various directions and injunctions. The opening of this casket, she had indicated, would reveal many secrets, but it had to be opened, she had laid it down, in the presence of twenty-four bishops and during a period of national stress. Doubtless, the believers thought, during the stirring days of the "Great" War, it would prevent German spies—in every village, however small—from spying, would aid the passage through England of the mythical Russian hordes, and would altogether discomfit the enemy. But at that time it was not to be. . . . Perhaps the bishops were too busy recruiting to have any time for such nonsense. . . . The agitation, however, for the opening of the magic casket continued. In 1924 a monster petition was sent by Joanna's followers to the Archbishop of Canterbury, who, we regret to say, completely disregarded it. In July, 1927, excitement reached its climax, and, after having been X-rayed, the box was opened by the Bishop of Grantham. The articles found were, most of them, those more usually connected with the laying of foundation-stones . . . coins, playing-cards, ornaments, and books. Included in this small and select library was one volume entitled *The Surprises of Love ; or, An Adventure in Greenwich Park.*

Far from being discouraged, the disciples remained true ; claimed that the box which revealed these treasures was not the one she had intended for the bishops. In any case, however, it is certain that never since the examination of Dr. Bode's Leonardo-bust, some fifteen years before, had there been such a complete disillusionment. But will this discourage Joanna's followers ? Not in the least ! !

Soon we read of the strange, but no doubt always welcome, deaths of two great poets, and pass on to the case of Lady Flora Hastings, an incident as painful to the feelings as that which follows it, the extermination of the last "Great Auk" in St. Kilda. A truly pitiful story is this, but one to which it is not difficult to find an earlier parallel. For, it is recorded that during the French wars of Marlborough, the first big anthropoid ape happened to be introduced into England, and, escaping his janitors and showmen, roamed the countryside for a day or two. He was eventually arrested in a remote village, and, since no one could understand his frightened grimaces and gibberings, was at once tried by court-martial and sentenced to be hanged as a French spy. One wonders what dim consciousness of events passed in the mind of auk and ape, and what the latter, as he swung from the gibbet among the acclamations of a rustic crowd, may have concluded as to the processes of human chatter ?

Who knows, indeed, that a similar fate did not overtake several of the still bigger performing-apes who were detained in England at the outbreak of the late "Great" ? For certainly more German spies were then arrested than could ever have been in any one country at the same moment. Or, on the other hand, perhaps the "Huns" were really mean enough to indulge in such a savage and degraded disguise. These little mistakes, in any case, occur from time to time. For, to balance the adventure of that ape to which we have drawn attention, it was related not long ago in the newspapers that an English farmer, seeing the outline of a very fine female baboon on the hill opposite, at once fired on her—which apparently, if you should be fortunate enough to live in that part of the Empire and to see a lady baboon, is the correct method of salutation. The settler was now startled by the almost human cries that came from the poor, wounded creature. He first humanely finished her off by firing a second shot, and then, running to the place as quickly as he could, discovered that he had in reality shot the wife of a neighbouring Boer farmer. Apologies, we imagine, must have been difficult.

When we come to the murder of the Duchesse de Praslin, we would like to add that one of the persons to whom the Duchesse related the queer experience that befell her a year before her death was Mlle. de Montijo, later the Empress Eugénie, whom she met in the Bois de Boulogne the morning after it had occurred.

We should like to refer our readers particularly to the pages concerning the disappearance of the Dauphin (page 149), surrounded in a fog of oddly confusing accounts and explanations, and also to that surely first-rate mystery, "The Hoof-Marks in the Snow" (page 167). Concerning the fate of the Dauphin, we cannot but think that he did actually survive in obscurity (though not, we imagine, in the person of Mr. Eleazar Williams): but nobody will ever know for certain, and, as has been made obvious recently with the extermination of the Russian Royal House, the actual facts are sometimes so horrible that no one will willingly believe them, but, on the contrary, be only too eager to give credence to anything which would tend to dispose of so ghastly a truth.

Then, last in chronological order, we reach the adventures of Louis de Rougemont, many of which have, through modern discoveries, now regained the semblance of truth, though his narration of them ended his career. These tales interest the writer of this preface very much, for he remembers so well and for so many years seeing a tall, bearded figure, lank and stooping, selling matches in Shaftesbury Avenue or Piccadilly. This ghost of the streets was dressed in an old, ragged overcoat, over the collar of which the thin hair fell, and showed above it a calm, philosophical, curiously intelligent face. He was told repeatedly that this man was Louis de Rougemont. Whether this information was accurate or not, certainly with the reported death of the explorer or impostor, whichever he was, this sad, thoughtful spectre withdrew itself from the haunting of a busy world.

Now that the last item is disposed of we can approach the portentous figure of that six-foot-tall negro, King Christophe of Hayti; the monarch who provides so black and discouraging a parallel to Napoleon. Some say that Christophe was an English-speaking negro from Jamaica; others that he was a native of Hayti, employed by white men there before the Revolution. Be that as it may, when the Revolution came, it swung loose for many months: murder and theft were the everyday occurrences of coloured life there. But suddenly this very extraordinary man emerged, and directed it, restoring absolute order, and opening up the country in an unprecedentedly short time, making roads, encouraging commerce and agriculture.

This explanation is probably entirely unnecessary, for the modern reader will know much about this potentate. But the present writer recalls how interested he was in the account of that amazing man, when he first heard of him a few years ago. An American friend, who had just returned from Hayti, told him these stories that follow: stories which he had heard locally. He also showed him photographs of the châteaux as they are now. Since then, Christophe's life has been written about in *Black Majesty*, a book by an American author: but his account, if more accurate, is less picturesque. Even if they are apocryphal, these details, and the shaping of them, build up a something that is near to a tragic perfection.

First of all, then, this traveller in Hayti described the haunted beauty of the country itself. It was very difficult to persuade any bodyguard to accompany him into the jungle there, so dark was its reputation for deeds of violence, so widespread its evil fame as a land of spectres and devils. At last he succeeded in bribing a band of stalwart negroes to accompany him into the interior, but often they would have to cut their path for miles through a maze of trees and tropical undergrowth. Then, suddenly, they would find themselves standing against the door or window of an eighteenth-century French château of white stone. So overgrown and forgotten would it be that they could not see it until they were standing right up against it in this manner. The jungle had swallowed this house up since that terrible night, sequel to the French Revolution, when some tens of thousands of negro slaves, having hidden in the mountains, rushed down and massacred the French nobles who owned what were then sugar plantations and are now jungle, the French merchants who carried on the trade, and even the numerous mulattoes of the cities, and all the half-castes, whether rich or poor. No man with white blood was spared. Since that night of doom, these deserted country-houses were avoided by all the inhabitants of the island, who are intensely superstitious and afraid of ghosts, and the fact that no native could be induced to approach them, combined with the clear atmosphere of the island, accounts for their preservation. Tessellated marble floors, curving staircases with balusters of wrought iron, panelled rooms and high tiled or slated roofs, all were in more or less perfect order—though large flowers and little trees were growing out of stone walls that in places were fissured and splitting like ripe figs. Birds and serpents, inveterate enemies, shared the graceful apartments—fluttered a scintillating wing under a finely moulded cornice, or uncoiled and hissed along a black and white marble floor, stained with green mould. Each of these houses was dark as a cave, shut in by such tall trees, while tresses of parasitic growth fell entwined over the very roof, so that the light could only flicker faintly down on it, sending round discs of sunlight sometimes to quiver upon floor and ceiling.

At first, as we have seen, this American traveller had

experienced great difficulty in persuading the natives to accompany him at all, but by tact and bribery eventually contrived to have a bodyguard even as far as Christophe's Castle. This was a vast and castellated stone building which the Emperor had caused to be created in the mountains. It resembles an enormous feudal stronghold —walls many yards thick, crowned with a flat roof and a formidable tangle of high towers—and is said to have been modelled on the monarch's conception, derived from prints, of Windsor Castle. Many odd whims of the autocrat's were here realised. For example, there was an enormous well, which ran from the middle of the roof far down into the earth through the centre of the building.

In such awe and fear was this place held that no one had visited it since the Emperor's death. For one thing, it was known that all the workmen employed in building it—and it had been run up in an unprecedentedly short time by a whole army of black workmen and white slaves —had been shot or strangled wholesale after it was finished, at the Emperor's order, so that the secrets of its chambers and passages should never be revealed. And, moreover, tradition held, as will be related in due course, that the monarch had died there.

And then this American friend had seen "Sans Souci" as well, and described in detail its weedy garden, broken marble steps, and falling porticoes. Evidently from its name, the Emperor had cherished a great veneration for Frederick the Great, and this was his chief pleasure-house, though duty was sternly attended to even here. For in the garden stood, and still stands, a famous landmark—Christophe's Tree of Justice. It is now, the writer was told, of an enormous height, and in appearance somewhat resembles a monkey-puzzle tree. Standing up under its shelter, it was the monarch's wont, when in residence at this palace, to dispense justice at a certain hour every morning. The scene must have been comic, terrible, romantic to a degree.

Wearing his high crown, holding his enormous and jewelled sword of state, here the dusky tyrant would stand, surrounded by all the greatest nobles of his black realm—men of such high-sounding, and no doubt famous names as the Duc de Marmelade and the Count de Limonade. The nobility favoured white powdered wigs, of an older fashion, which contrasted strangely with their complexion—so that the effect must have been as though one were looking at the negative of a photograph—and both lords and ladies were dressed with the greatest magnificence. Gold and jewels, paste and tinsel, were used as the negro alone knows how to use them. The language of the Court was, of course, French: and before the King had entered, until the bodyguard marched in to the sound of silver bugles, crowing through an awed silence, the most high-flown compliments were flying from blue lips, and there were occasional gurgles of dark laughter. Now all was silent as the troops in their gaudy uniforms presented arms—Christophe's kingdom was famous for the splendour of its uniforms and liveries—and above all this glory a tropical sun ever flashed its golden wings. But terror there was here too: for there was only one penalty known to Christophe, whatever the crime or delinquency, and that was the death-penalty. Either the prisoner was declared innocent, or else he was condemned to have his head cut off.

In the grounds of Sans Souci, too, was a Chapel-Royal, decorated with sacred pictures and images: but all the saints represented, even the Madonna and Our Lord, were black. This man, universally feared and respected, who alone had succeeded in imposing, for a few years at least, some semblance of discipline upon his people, was deeply religious, and it was his custom, self-divested for the moment of earthly glory and clad in a simple preacher's robe, to preach there every week before the assembled Court. One Sunday, after he had reigned many years, he stood up as usual and walked down the aisle. But it was remarked that his manner was very odd. He carried his head low, like a bull; his mouth was twitching and the whites of his eyes rolled long and strangely. He mounted into the pulpit, and, suddenly seized by a fit of *folie de grandeur*, perhaps the result of some terrible illness, shook his fist at the gilded effigy of the Black Saviour, and in a loud, defiant voice challenged the Holy Image to strike him dead. There was a moment's appalling silence after he had thus blasphemed, and then the great Black Emperor crumpled up like a jack-in-the-box and lay paralysed at the bottom of his pulpit. Confusion and clamour ensued as the inanimate mass was carried out. But presently he spoke: the eyes opened, and, though he could not move, they were enough to enforce his commands. He told his nobles to have him carried to his great fortress in the hills, and when he had arrived there, to have him placed on a couch upon the vast, flat roof.

After journeying through the heat for many hours of light and darkness, they arrived, soon after sunrise, at Christophe's Castle. When his commands had been carried out, he summoned his bodyguard and all the chiefs of the army to attend him. Meanwhile, in an effort to bring back life to his dead limbs, he ordered his servants to rub his body with a mixture of hot oil and pepper. This was done, but though under this treatment the use of his arms returned to him, he still was not able to turn, raise himself, or stand up.

The picture that presented itself must have been strange—the huge roof, edged with sharp-toothed towers, the silent ranks of soldiers, bright as humming-birds in their uniforms, but motionless as the black-faced figure on the bed, which was the axle of this whole wheel of life. For several long hours they waited thus. Then at last he understood that movement would not return to him ever, and that he was a doomed man. The Emperor's dark claw of a hand crept slowly, under the purple rug with which he was covered, to his belt, and taking out of it a revolver, he fitted into it a golden bullet that he had long carried about with them, and blew out his brains. For an hour or more the Court officials, the bodyguard, the army chiefs and royal regiments, remained there without stirring, not believing that their tyrant could be dead, could really be dead. But now one or two of them, now the whole of this quiet host, so near up under the sky as it seemed, crept noiselessly, on tiptoe, the whites of their eyes rolling from fear, towards the body, poked it gently with their fingers, and found that it was in truth a stiff and helpless corpse. Then fury seized on those assembled for all the discipline, good rule, justice, and cruelty of the past decade, and, taking hold of the dead body, they mocked it, threw it hither and thither high in the air, and finally, while the solid roof trembled with their dancing, they hurled it down the huge well that pierced the centre of the building. Now, to make sure that this terrible ghost should not return to take its vengeance, they threw down after him every chair and table, every picture and object they could find in the castle, still dancing and shouting as they did so. When they had thus barricaded the dead king into his portion of the earth, absolute madness descended on them. With this unconscious gesture, they abjured for ever the European ideal which they had been driven for so long to emulate and uphold. An unparalleled voodoo continued for twenty-four hours.

. . . .

This was the story told in Hayti, and believed in so strongly that since that moment no man had visited Christophe's Castle. Little of it is to be found in the accurate but interesting account of the monarch, written by a contemporary, which we reprint. But then the whole essence of this anthology lies in its old-fashioned idiom, and in the dry, newspaper-like recording of strange facts.

1. THE MERMAIDS SEEN OFF THE COAST OF CAITHNESS

Many strange monsters were seen during the early part of the last century from the northern shores of Scotland. Sea-serpents emerged from the sea near the Orkneys, and mermaids were seen sitting on the rocks off the coast of Caithness. The first written account of one of these mermaids comes from a Miss Mackay, and was published in many of the journals of 1809.

One stormy day in the January of that year, Miss Mackay and a friend were walking along the sea-shore when they saw, floating on the surface of the water, what at first sight appeared to be a human face. But humans do not bathe in a rough winter sea, nor do they sink gently under the waves for long periods and then reappear unconcerned. This creature was in its natural element, and could be nothing else but a mermaid. Every now and then it would raise a slender white hand and impatiently toss back from its face a long mane of green hair. The two young ladies were near enough to see that the face was " round and plump and of a bright pink hue."

On reading Miss Mackay's letter, a schoolmaster in Thurso was reminded that he, too, had once seen a mermaid, very similar in appearance, and in almost the identical place. *The Times* of September 8th, 1809, published a letter from him describing his experience.

Sir,—About twelve years ago, when I was parochial schoolmaster in Reay, in the course of my walking on the shore of Sandside Bay, my attention was arrested by the appearance of a figure resembling an unclothed human female, sitting upon a rock extending into the sea and apparently in the action of combing its hair, which flowed around its shoulders, and was of a light brown colour. The resemblance which the figure bore to its prototype in all its visible parts was so striking that, had not the rock on which it was sitting been dangerous for bathing, I would have been constrained to have regarded it as really an human form. The head was covered with hair of the colour above mentioned, and shaded on the crown, the forehead round, the face plump, the cheeks ruddy, the eyes blue, the mouth and lips of a natural form, resembling those of a man, the teeth I could not discover, as the mouth was shut; the breasts and abdomen, the arms and fingers of the size of a full-grown body of the human species; the fingers, from the action in which the hands were employed, did not appear to be webbed, but as to those I am not positive. It remained on the rock three or four minutes after I had observed it, and was exercised during that period in combing its hair, which was long and thick and of which it appeared proud, and then dropped into the sea, which was level with the abdomen, from whence it did not reappear to me. I had a distinct view of its features, being at no great distance on an eminence above the rock on which it was sitting, and the sun brightly shining. Immediately before its getting into its natural element it seemed to have observed me, as the eyes were directed towards the eminence on which I sat.

I had previously heard it frequently reported by several persons, that they had seen such a phenomenon as I have described, though then, like many others, I was not disposed to credit their testimony on this subject. I can say of a truth that it was only by seeing the phenomenon, I was perfectly convinced of its existence.

Your most obliged and most humble servant,

(Signed) WILLIAM MUNRO.

2. ZERAH COLBURN, THE CALCULATING BOY

In 1812, Zerah Colburn, an American boy of seven, came over to this country to give exhibitions of his astounding powers of calculation. It is curious to read that he was abnormal in one other respect—he had more than the usual number of fingers and toes.

The Annual Register, August 20th, 1812.

"At a meeting the child undertook, and completely succeeded in, raising the number 8 progressively up to the 16th power!!! And in naming the last result, viz. 281,474,976,710,656, he was right in every figure. He was asked the square root of 106,929, and before the number could be written down he immediately answered 327. He was then required to name the cube root of 268,336,125, and with equal facility and promptness he replied 645.

"He was asked to give the factors of 36,083; but he immediately replied that it had none; which, in fact, was the case. Other numbers were indiscriminately proposed to him, and he always succeeded in giving the correct factors. One of the gentlemen asked him how many minutes there were in 48 years; and before the question could be written down he replied 25,228,800; and instantly added, that the number of seconds in the same period was 1,513,728,000

"He positively declared that he did not know how the answers came into his mind. In the act of multiplying two numbers together, and in the raising of powers, it was evident that some operation was going forward in his mind; yet that operation could not (from the readiness with which the answers were furnished) be at all allied to the usual mode of proceeding with such subjects: and, moreover, he is entirely ignorant of the common rules of arithmetic, and cannot perform, upon paper, a simple sum in multiplication or division. In one case he was asked to tell the square of 4,395: he hesitated, but said it was 19,316,025. On being questioned, he replied that he did not like to multiply four figures by four figures: but, said he, 'I found out another way: I multiplied 293 by 293, and then multiplied this product twice by the number 15, which produced the same result.'"

William Sharp, del.

JOANNA SOUTHCOTT

National Portrait Gallery

p. 39

3. JOANNA SOUTHCOTT, OR THE BIRTH OF A MESSIAH

Extract from a pamphlet, 1814.

" JOANNA SOUTHCOTT was born in the month of April, 1750, in Devonshire. Her father was in the farming line, and both her parents were professed members of the Established Church. She has recently entered her sixty-fifth year.

" Joanna opened her commission in 1792, and declared herself to be the woman spoken of in the Revelations, that is, '*the Bride, the Lamb's wife*,' and the '*Woman clothed with the Sun*.' This was at Exeter. Her profession made no small noise in the city.

" Joanna assumes to usher in the Millennium, and to seal the faithful for the enjoyment of it, to the amount of 144,000; also to chain down Satan for a thousand years, and to terminate the immense undertaking of man's redemption. When a person is to be sealed, he writes his name on a list provided for that purpose; half a sheet of paper is provided on which is written these words:

> " 'The Sealed of the Lord—the Elect, Precious, Man's Redemption—To inherit the Tree of Life—To be made Heirs of God and Joint Heirs with Jesus Christ. JOANNA SOUTHCOTT.'

" Then the person in office writes the name on it with the words, 'Not to be broken open,' and delivers it into his hands, and the person is sealed.[1]

" Joanna has for some years been stationary in London, living with an amiable lady, who (much to her praise)

[1] This industry flourished until it became known that one of the sealed, a woman, had been hanged for murder.

disposes of her income, in what she esteems the service of God. Joanna's cause in London has been, for a considerable time, in a flourishing state. She has a chapel in Duke Street, St. George's-fields, near the Obelisk, where they have preaching every Sunday, and where the Liturgy of the Church of England is also held. She has two other chapels, one at Greenwich and another at Twickenham."

Early in 1814, Joanna announced to the world that towards the end of the year, at the age of sixty-four, she would bear a son who would be the second Messiah, and unite the Gentiles and the Jews. She shut herself up, and refused to see any but her intimate friends. A few months later, her followers inserted this statement in the papers:

"Whatever mockery the announcement of such an event may cause amongst mankind, or however wonderful it may appear, there is the most satisfactory evidence that it will be realised. This proof is established upon the testimony of the three women, being mothers of children, who have all along attended her; and upon their examination by two medical men, as to the symptoms which have taken place in Joanna Southcott, from the 17th March to the 26th May, whose decision upon thereon is that, if such symptoms were in a young woman, she must be pregnant with a *living child*."

From a newspaper cutting, August, 1814.

"A letter has been published by Dr. Reece, in which, after stating that on Wednesday last he visited Joanna Southcott, and ascertained by personal examination that she is undoubtedly pregnant, he concludes thus:

"'Having thus satisfied my mind of the pregnancy of Joanna Southcott, I applied for a certificate of her age, which I received this morning. . . .

"'I regard the pregnancy of Joanna Southcott as

extraordinary only in a professional point of view. Of her prophecies I am ignorant. I should be happy to lend my aid for the purpose of detecting and exposing a species of imposture, which, of all others, I consider the most infamous.' "

Extract from Pamphlet.

" In consequence of this announcement, the followers of Joanna Southcott, in town and country, are making all sorts of necessary preparations. It is certainly true that she has literally been overwhelmed with presents—laced caps, embroidered bibs and worked robes, a mohair mantle which cost £150;—an elegant silver cup and salver—upon which is engraved, ' Hail, Messiah, Prince of Salem ! ' . . . A Magnificent Crib has just been finished by one of our first upholsterers and sent to her residence. The Crib, with its ornaments, decorations, bedding, etc., cost upwards of £200 ! ! ! "

Advertisement from the " Morning Chronicle."

" Mrs. Joanna Southcott's Accouchement.—A large furnished House wanted.—In consequence of the malicious and false Reports which have been so universally circulated, Mrs. Southcott, in order to show that she is not an Impostor, nor that her friends are dupes, has given them directions for thus advertising for a spacious and ready-furnished House to be hired for three months, wherein her Accouchement may take place, in the presence of such competent Witnesses as shall be appointed by proper authority, to prove her character to the World.

" According to applications already made by Mrs. Southcott to the Heads of the Church and the State, allowing them to send their Physicians and her invitations to the Bishops to investigate her Cause, and the permission given to the Hebrews and to others, in Conjunction with a certain Number of her own Friends, to be present at the Birth of the Child, a House capable of accommodating a large Assembly will be necessary ; and, from the Opinion of a Medical Gentleman, the time of her confinement is drawing so near that it will be necessary to have such a House provided by Michaelmas."

Michaelmas came and went, winter approached, and yet no child was born.[1] It was obvious, though, that Joanna was seriously ill. Her followers grew uneasy, but still hoped on. On November 19th they issued this report, which appeared in the *Sunday Monitor* the next day:

" *Saturday*, 3 *o'clock*.

"Last night she awaked about ten o'clock, and got no more sleep during the night; at half-past four this morning her pains came on much stronger, she said, than she had felt them before, continued near two hours, and then went off. She went to sleep, groaned much in her sleep, and awaked in great pain, but was so overpowered with sleep that she only kept awake until the pain went off; in this manner she continued until 11 o'clock, then her sickness came on, and violent retchings; in this manner she has continued since, now and then a pain, but no visible sign has appeared at present."

Sunday Monitor, *December* 18*th*, 1814.

"Mrs. Southcott continues exceedingly ill; her pulse is very feeble; the mind wandering, *with other symptoms*

[1] A popular song ran thus:

Johanna! Johanna!
Do give a poor man a
Reply, without shuffling or guile-O!
And tell me what reason,
So late in the season,
Keeps back the miraculous *Shiloh*.

Your followers, may be,
May purchase a baby,
The credulous town to beguile—O!
But yourself you should tap,
And not palm off a rap,
For we wont take a Birmingham *Shiloh*.

And so on.

indicating approaching dissolution. Her Believers suppose that her prophecy of being in a trance will be fulfilled, and in that state she will be delivered of the promised Shiloh. Should her dissolution, which we conceive to be very near, happen in the course of this day, we shall (to relieve the anxiety of many thousands of her Believers, who take our paper) publish the fact in a SECOND EDITION."

Joanna, realising at last that she was dying, dictated her will,

"in which," wrote a journalist, "she professed her conviction that she had either been visited by a *Good* or *Evil Spirit*. In the hope that she might become re-animate, which she was satisfied would be the case if she had been visited by the *Lord*, she desired she might be preserved with 'every tender care, for four days after dissolution,' the fourth being that on which, under Providence, she expected she would be restored to life, and be delivered; if that period expired without any symptoms of re-animation, she directed that her body might be submitted to skilful *operators*. Soon after she made her pleasure known, the symptoms of disease became more virulent, and she breathed her last at four o'clock on Tuesday morning, 27th December, 1814. Her friends, considering her as merely 'gone for a while,' felt no uneasiness, but proceeded to wrap her body in warm blankets, to place bottles of hot water to her feet, and by keeping the room in a state of warmth endeavour to preserve the vital spark. The prescribed period of four days and nights elapsed, and so far was the body from exhibiting appearances of a temporary suspension of animation, that it began to display a discoloration, which at once brought home to conviction the fact that the wretched Joanna was but mortal. Preparations were then made for her dissection.

"On Saturday at two o'clock fifteen gentlemen assembled, including Dr. Reece[1]. They proceeded to

[1] Joanna's medical attendant.

perform their disgusting task—the results of this examination were these:

"That there was *No Shiloh*. That the intestines were much distended by flatulency, and hence that appearance which led to false conclusions. . . . That the report of her being poisoned is without foundation. . . . The medical gentlemen present signed a certificate, stating that her dissolution was produced by natural causes."

From Dr. Reece's published account of the case.

"The disappointment of her disciples on opening the body may be better conceived than described. It was strongly depicted on every countenance. . . . The two female attendants were inconsolable. They had all pictured to themselves many happy days, the enjoyment of heaven on earth. This sad event, this unexpected change, so suddenly coming upon them was too much to bear. One of the disciples declared he would turn Unitarian. None condemned her as an impostor. . . .

"After the events that have occurred would it be believed that the blinded followers of this infatuated woman still cling to her opinions, and that their faith should not be in the least abated? They have now found that the promise of the child was *conditional*; that if the people had treated her kindly she would have produced it; but in consequence of their hardness of heart and want of faith, like the Jews to the Messiah of old, the Lord had taken the child to Heaven. . . . Some even suppose that before the 12th of this month she will rise again and produce the promised child."

4. KING CHRISTOPHE

From "Sketches of Hayti," by W. W. Harvey (1827)[1]

Christophe was born on October 6th, 1767; but respecting the place and circumstances of his birth, different accounts have been given. That he was originally a slave in Grenada, and in the early part of his life brought to San Domingo, is by far the most probable, and the most generally received account. Christophe therefore knew by experience the manifold evils of this inhuman system; and previously to his becoming one of its most strenuous opposers, he had submitted to its privations, undergone its rigours, and felt the demoralising effects which it produces on the character.

Of all the privations which Christophe suffered during this period, there was none which he more deeply felt and lamented in the subsequent part of his life than his want of education. He was not instructed even in the rudiments of knowledge. When raised to the rank of a general over the black forces, he learned to write his surname; and when afterwards he became one of the chiefs of the Island, and assumed the title of King, he learned to sign his Christian name also. More than this he never acquired.

No sooner was Christophe crowned King of Hayti, than he surrounded himself with all the appendages of royalty; and displayed all the pomp and splendour of a rich and powerful monarch. Vast sums of money were

[1] Harvey was a Cambridge don who visited Hayti during Christophe's reign (1811–1820). As a white man he was not allowed to penetrate more than three miles into the interior, but he made the acquaintance of several officers and members of the King's Household and encouraged them to talk freely. His book is the chief authority for the life of Christophe.

expended in support of an establishment such as Hayti had in no period of its history ever exhibited. The rich and splendid garments in which the sable monarch appeared on great and important occasions, could hardly be surpassed by those of the most wealthy and powerful rulers of civilised states. His palaces were prepared for his reception with all possible magnificence; the floors of the apartments were made of highly polished mahogany, or of marble; the walls were adorned with the most valuable paintings that could be obtained; every article of furniture was of the most costly kind; and whatever the most unbounded passion for splendour could suggest was procured to decorate the habitation of an uneducated negro.

His Household corresponded with the magnificence of his palaces. It consisted of a Grand Almoner, who was the Archbishop of Hayti; of a Grand Cup-bearer, the first prince of the blood royal; of a Grand Marshal of the royal palace, and a Marshal of his Majesty's apartments; of ten Governors of palaces, and the same number of Governors of castles; of sixteen Chamberlains, with a Grand Chamberlain at their head; of five Secretaries and a Librarian; of twelve Knights, fifteen pages with a Governor, and seven Grand Huntsmen; of a Grand Master of the Ceremonies, with three inferior Masters, and five assistants; and of fourteen heralds of the army, seven professors of arts and sciences, together with a great number of physicians, surgeons, and apothecaries.

One of the most remarkable of Christophe's palaces was built at a place about twelve miles from Cape François, called "Sans Souci." It was planned and constructed under his immediate superintendence; and was destined for occasional retirement from the cares of the government, for a watching-place whence to observe whatever was going forward in the neighbourhood of the Cape, and for security in case of rebellion among his own subjects. It was situated on a lofty mountain, which commanded a view of the capital, and of the country around to the distance of several miles, and with its guard-houses and other buildings, its gardens and promenades, it occupied a greater part of the summit. In its form it resembled a square, having its grand entrance on one of its sides, leading to a spacious court within. The palace consisted of two stories, having galleries along the first floor, which looked, through glass casements, into the court below; and besides the grand salon, the audience-hall, the dining-room, and the library, it had numerous other apartments, occupied by different members of the royal family and household. All these rooms were spacious, lofty, and magnificently furnished; their floors were made of mahogany, the produce of the Island; and their splendid mirrors, superb paintings, and costly furniture, gave to the whole an appearance altogether princely.

Although the atmosphere of this mountain was comparatively cool, a stream of water was conveyed under the building, in various directions, and at length emptied itself into a large basin, prepared for its reception at one extremity of the palace. By these means, all the rooms were kept in a state of refreshing coolness, even during the hottest and most oppressive hours of the day.

Either from policy or from caprice, Christophe caused the windows of this palace to be disproportionately small, to be placed in the most irregular manner, and to be divided into parts as diminutive as they could be made. They were at the same time exceedingly numerous and had they been placed in a more regular order, the exterior would have borne no slight resemblance to an English manufactory.

The gardens behind the palace were laid out with considerable taste: they rose in squares one above another, having marble steps leading from the lowest to the highest, and were planted with an abundant variety of shrubs and flowers. That of the Queen, which stood on one side of the mountain, was kept in excellent order; and being consequently more productive than the rest, it presented the most gay and interesting appearance.

Christophe would frequently range from one part of the mountain to another, apparently in search of amusement, and on these occasions he was generally accompanied by a page carrying, in a large damask napkin, the telescope which he used in viewing the different parts of his domains. He also frequently entertained himself with music, of which he was passionately fond ; and the most popular martial airs, played by the whole band in the court of the palace, which was usually done towards evening, appeared to afford him the highest gratification. In short, notwithstanding the magnificence of the palace, there was an insupportable dullness and insipidity in the general scene, and than the sounds of musical instruments nothing could be more soothing or grateful.

The election of the nobility being one of the prerogatives of the Crown, Christophe proceeded to select persons on whose talents and integrity he might rely, and whom he thought entitled to rank as the nobles of the kingdom ; and immediately on his ascending the throne, he bestowed on these men the most pompous titles. Thus the Haytians had not only a King, who assumed all the titles, pomp, and prerogatives of royalties ; but also dukes, counts, barons, and knights, whom they were required to honour as the dignitaries of the kingdom. Negroes who, a few years before, were subjected to all the sufferings and degradation of slavery ; and mulattoes, whose former condition was but a step above that of their black brethren, now demanded to be addressed as their *Royal Highnesses*, their *Serene Highnesses*, their *Graces* and their *Excellencies* ; and required from those who entered their presence, that respect and deference which men of rank and influence are accustomed to demand from their inferiors.

In imitation of their sovereign, they decorated their habitations with every variety of ornament ; they procured the most splendid equipage of carriages, phaetons, and other vehicles ; and they supplied their attendants with the most expensive liveries of the most gorgeous colours. Their tables were said to be furnished with a profusion of viands, and of rare and costly wines; and their entertainments on fête days were hardly less splendid than those given by their royal master.

But while the nobility lived in great splendour, and received from their inferiors the respect due to their rank, they were subject to restraints imposed upon them by their sovereign, calculated to repress their vanity, and to create dissatisfaction. Their constant attendance at Court, and the etiquette they were required to observe, because foreign to their previous freedom and familiarity of manners, the majority of them found intolerably disagreeable and burdensome; and provided they could have retained a moderate portion of their income, many of them would have cheerfully abandoned their empty titles to be enabled to live in a manner more agreeable to their settled habits. They were, however, vain of their rank, and puffed up with the idea of their imaginary importance; and, though they generally behaved towards their inferiors with great familiarity, they sometimes treated them with the most unprovoked insolence: they therefore required to be kept under proper restraints, lest the increasing pride of some would render them ungovernable. But in imposing these restraints, Christophe did not act with his accustomed prudence; but rendered them more numerous and more rigorous than either the follies of the nobles, or his own safety, demanded. He acted with equal impolicy, not to say injustice, in inflicting punishments too frequently for minor offences; and in chastising them with undue severity for the most trifling neglect of duty, without regard to their rank or their services.

All the officers of the army, whatever their rank or character, were fond of dress to an extravagant degree. They were required to possess good clothing, and were furnished with the means of procuring it: but in the expense of their garments, and the ornaments with which they were decorated, they far exceeded the desire of their sovereign, and often rendered their appearance ridiculous. Their coats were so bedecked with gold lace, that it was difficult to determine of what material they were made: their shoulders were burdened with epaulets of an enormous size; their caps were adorned with feathers nearly equalling their own height: and these articles, together with their beautiful white small-clothes and elegant silk hose, rendered their appearance supremely fantastical.

The education of Christophe's daughters was another object of his solicitude, yet one which had been somewhat neglected. To supply this defect, he at length procured the assistance of two ladies from America, well qualified to direct their studies; under whose superintendence they made considerable progress, and with whose services both the King and the Queen expressed their entire satisfaction. The following particulars, communicated by one of the ladies, may be satisfactory and interesting.

"We embarked," this lady observes, "at Philadelphia, and in fifteen days reached Cape François. We landed much debilitated by the illness we had suffered during the passage. The next morning Madame Christophe sent for us, that we might repair to 'Sans Souci'; but, not having recovered from the effects of the voyage, we begged our visit might be deferred a few days.

"At the appointed time, an elegant London-built chariot, drawn by four greys, was sent to convey us to the palace. On reaching 'Sans Souci,' we alighted at Prince John's, the king's nephew. His wife, a stout, fat, well-looking mulatto, was awaiting our arrival; by whom we were ushered into a saloon, where we were immediately surrounded by a crowd of visitors. They stared at us as though their curiosity would never be satisfied; but theirs happened to be a stupid gaze of wonder and ignorance. Some of them had never seen white ladies before; and their repeated exclamations of "Gueté femme blanche la qu'elle belle!"[1] amused us exceedingly. After taking coffee, we retired *pour nous reposer un peu*.

[1] "Look at that white woman: how beautiful she is!"

"About 11 o'clock we were summoned to the palace, and conducted into the library, where the Comte de Limonade,[1] the Secretary for Foreign Affairs, was awaiting us. After handing us chairs, he remained some minutes in silence, and then made this sage remark—that 'We must be surprised to see him with a handkerchief about his head, as if he was ill'; and when we replied that we were not, well knowing it to be the custom in tropical climates, he as sagely wondered. In about a quarter of an hour, we heard a bustle in the adjoining passage—the door opened—and Christophe, preceded by six young negroes, as pages, and accompanied by some of his nobles, made his appearance. We rose and made a profound *salue*: he desired us to be seated; we knew better, and stood while he remained; not in the least intimidated by the appearance or manners of his sable majesty. He said little to us, but, turning to Baron de Dupuy, he enquired if our house at the Cape was in readiness;—and finding it was not so, he said, 'Oh, these ladies can come here and instruct my daughters'; and immediately left us to prepare them for our reception.

"We were now conducted to another part of the palace, and shown into a spacious saloon, furnished with great magnificence and taste. We were scarcely seated when the large folding doors by which we entered again opened, and Christophe, with the Queen, the Prince Royal, and the Princesses, appeared, dressed most handsomely, and with a degree of elegance which we had not expected. The Queen was exceedingly obliging and affable; she made kind enquiries respecting our passage and health; she expressed her hope that we should be perfectly happy as long as we should remain with them; and she assured us that she would be always ready to assist us—and her evident sincerity convinced us that she had a kind and affectionate heart. Her daughters were equally polite; and appeared quite pleased at the idea of our coming to reside in the palace.

[1] The Comte de Limonade and the Duc de Marmelade took their titles from places that had been so named by the French in derision.

On the whole we were much pleased and satisfied with the interview.

The breakfast hour approaching, we retired to another apartment, where we partook of an elegant *déjeuner* in company with the king's niece, and the officers of the household, black and yellow barons. It was impossible not to observe how voraciously they ate, and how rapidly the dishes disappeared. But they were very attentive to us, and the conversation, though on commonplace topics, we thought more interesting than could have been expected.

"It was five weeks before the necessary arrangements were made for our residence at the palace. The apartments with which we were at length furnished, were sufficiently large for our purpose; and as soon as we were comfortably settled, we commenced instructing our royal pupils. They studied English, French, composition, and drawing; and the hours we were engaged with them were from between 7 and 8 till 10, in the morning; and from 3 to 5, in the afternoon. The princesses differed much in their abilities and dispositions. The elder sometimes appeared to think the difficulty of acquiring knowledge greater than it was worth. She was disposed to learn, but often yielded to that listlessness so common among natives of tropical climates. The youngest was lively and amiable; she had great quickness of apprehension; but was rather averse to application, and careless of improvement. Yet the progress of both was considerable, and the Queen, and we believe the King also, felt perfectly satisfied with our endeavours.

"It is unnecessary to give many particulars of our subsequent residence; they would be devoid of interest to any but ourselves. A few months only had passed away, ere we felt our situation disagreeable in the extreme. We occasionally dined with the Queen; our pupils also sometimes stopped after the hours of instruction for conversation, or we accompanied them to the gardens; but we felt, in a great measure, excluded from society; for there was none with whom we could hold a free and friendly intercourse. If we used the carriage which was at our service we could ride only to a prescribed distance; and we were perpetually annoyed by the guard, if we ventured on a ramble, enquiring who we were, and whither we were going. The etiquette of the court was intolerably irksome; and the inquisitiveness of the officers whom we occasionally met, not to be endured. We had come from America; and the confinement, restraint, and ceremony we had been quite unaccustomed to, and could not suffer. The Queen's kindness and attentions, indeed, made up for many inconveniences; nor was there anything in her power which she would not have gladly done, to render our situation agreeable. Circumstances, however, continually occurring to render it unpleasant, we determined at length to resign our charge, and to quit the place. But though our stay was shorter than we originally intended, we can never recollect our residence in Hayti but with feelings of deep and lasting interest."

. . . .

While Christophe was celebrating the Queen's fête at one of his palaces named "Belle-vue," which was at a considerable distance from the Cape, he was seized with a fit of apoplexy, so alarming in its symptoms that it was at first feared it would be impossible for him to recover. After immediate and copious bleeding, however, his physician began to hope that his royal patient might ultimately revive, and at the end of a month it was thought necessary to remove him to his palace at Sans Souci, a change which was attended with considerable difficulty and danger.

About a week after, the troops stationed at St. Marc's, a town on the western coast, mutinied against their officers; and in a moment of rage, excited by the impolitic conduct of the latter, put two of their number to death, and compelled the remainder to escape for their lives. On intelligence of this event being communicated to Christophe—for he being now somewhat recovered it was deemed necessary to inform him of the matter—he appeared for a moment unusually agitated, as though unable to determine what directions to give on the occasion. But he at length dispatched a messenger to the Cape, with orders for the garrison at that place to march without delay to St. Marc's; and on their arrival there, to seize and put to death the ringleaders of the mutiny, and to confine the rest in prison till further orders should be given respecting them.

This whole circumstance could not have occurred at a moment more unfortunate for Christophe, and more favourable to the designs of the nobles. On the arrival of the messenger with these orders to the Cape, one of the more powerful barons, addressing his associates said, "Who has given him the right of condemning men to death? and why shall we go and cut the throats of our brethren? Let us rather go straight to Sans Souci, and cut off the fellow's head." "If you are disposed that way," answered the Duc de Marmelade, "I am ready to join you."

On the following morning, the whole garrison, accompanied by all the inhabitants of the town capable of bearing arms, marched to Haut-de-Cap, which lay on the road to the palace; and as the King's guard, whose opposition they expected, was a numerous and powerful body, they encamped on this spot, till additional troops from other parts of the Island should join them.

When news of this formidable revolt reached the ears of Christophe, so unexpected was it on his part, and so great was his agitation in consequence, that his usual firmness and resolution wholly forsook him. But he soon recovered from the momentary shock, and gave his orders with his accustomed calmness; he directed the entrances of his palace to be secured, the cannon to be arranged on different parts of the mountain, and his guard to stand in readiness to support him. Having made these arrangements, he summoned the officers of his guard; and addressing them individually, he called on them to defend him, the master of their fortunes, with the same zeal and bravery as they had formerly defended their rights. He then gave each of them handsome presents, and furnished them with a large sum of money to be distributed among the men; and he received from them, in return, their most solemn assurances to stand by him to the last.

But Christophe's race was run. His principal adherents had deserted him; men whom he considered indebted to him for their distinction, were now risen in arms against him; and last of all, his guards, in violation of their promised fidelity, joined the forces of the faction, and thus abandoned him to his fate. The moment he heard that they on whom alone he relied for support had also deserted his cause, he desired those in his presence to withdraw; and, fearing if he should fall into the hands of the factious leaders he would be devoted to an ignominious death, he seized one of the pistols with which he was always provided, and instantly shot himself through the head.

5. THE ENTRY OF LOUIS XVIII INTO PARIS

THE emergence of the Bourbon family, with their thousands of decayed and obsolescent supporters, into the full light of a nineteenth-century France, was at the same time one of the most poignant and the most absurd spectacles which that era affords. To extract from this scene its full flavour, it must be remembered that during their absence as much change had taken place as is usually effected during the course of several hundred years. From a feudal and out-of-date country, France had become a model of modern organisation, and the ideal that the young of every European country sought to attain.

During the twenty years that had elapsed, the Bourbons of France had been completely forgotten, and the possibility of their return had long been banished from the realm of practical politics. The new King was already an old man, and was now put on the throne more because of a sudden whim of King George IV than for any other reason. On the defeat of Napoleon, nobody had for a moment dreamed of a relapse to Bourbon monarchy; but someone had suggested it to the English King, and on a sudden impulse, and in remembrance of a past friendship, he insisted on it with all the urgency of a somewhat eccentric man.[1] Yet although it originated in this way, the Restoration met with general approval in England—which it can never be said to have done in France.

The strangeness of this scene was heightened by the

[1] King George IV, like all the Guelph family, had strong dynastic sympathies. It was said that, had he lived, he would never have allowed Charles X to have been driven out of France in 1830.

old-fashioned appearance of those who took part, their rich and out-of-date clothing, to which, after their long sojourn across the water, they could not help but import an unpopular English accent. It was as if the wood had been cut down that had for so long surrounded the Sleeping Beauty, to reveal her and her courtiers in all their antique and outlandish splendour.

First came the aged Prince de Condé, who with his son seemed hardly to notice the crowd in their amazement at the complete transformation of the city during their absence. In the next carriage sat the old King, and his resemblance to his executed brother added a note of almost superstitious horror to the proceedings; it was rather as if Charles I had made an unlooked-for entry into the London of Queen Victoria. But by far the most romantic figure in that procession, and the real object of the people's enthusiasm, was the plain, sullen-looking woman who sat by the King's side.

The Princess Marie Theresa Charlotte, Duchesse d'Angoulême, was then thirty-six years old. She had left Paris at the age of seventeen, when she was released after her three years' imprisonment in the Temple. Her sufferings had been terrible, and it is said that she owed her life only to Robespierre's secret plan to marry her. She was lucky to have escaped with her reason, for during the last year of her imprisonment she was kept almost entirely isolated. But her long confinement in the Temple, the tragic loss of her family, and subsequent enforced exile and poverty, had made her extremely shy and awkward, and had given her an appearance of being sullen. Moreover, forced to take life seriously as she was, she could find no time for frivolity, prayed much and dressed badly. Such qualities did not endear her to the French people, and in time the aversion she inspired reached such a pitch that it was said that all those who cheered her on her rare public appearances were paid to do so by the police. But this had not come about yet—it was not "Madame La Rancune," as they were to call her, but the daughter of the unhappy Marie Antoinette, the Orphan of the Temple, whom they saw driving by, and to whom they tried to show their remorse and affection. Lamartine, for all his pomposity, gives us a good account of the arrival of the royal niece and her uncle at the palace that day in May, 1814.

"The countenances of the King and the Duchesse d'Angoulême were overcast on approaching the Tuileries, where their residence had been prepared. The King had never seen the palace since the day that Louis XVI and the Queen had left it for Varennes—the eve of their captivity and long suffering; nor the Duchesse d'Angoulême, since the morning of the 10th of August, when she fled, holding her father's hand, on the noise of the assault which demolished the doors, and over the bodies of their brave defenders. The acclamations of the crowd, which seemed to attempt a reparation for her immolated family, mingled in her memory with the clamour of the great seditions which had formerly besieged her infancy in these same courts. When passing before the ancient palace of Saint Louis, the Conciergerie, she could not see, without shuddering, the air-holes and gratings of her mother's dungeon; and on alighting from her carriage, at the entrance of the Tuileries, she fainted in the arms of her servants. They bore her half dead to her apartments, where she shut herself up, for the remainder of the day, with God and the memory of her slaughtered family. Solitude and prayer were necessary to inure her to those grandeurs of which she had experienced the reverse, and to those triumphs in which she had a misgivings of a change."

We now append two other accounts of the procession. Both are written from the same angle. Alison, from whose *History of Europe* our first is taken, though not actually an eye-witness, arrived in Paris a week or two after the event.

"The unanimous transports which had greeted his [the King's] entry into London and passage through England

Dessiné aux séances que son A. R. a accordés, par Gounod ancien pens. de l'école de rome.

Gravé par C. Richomme ex pensionnaire de l'académie de france à rome.

MADAME

DUCHESSE D'ANGOULÊME

Dédié à sa Majesté Louis XVIII.

Roi de france et de Navarre.

Par son très respectueux et très fidèle sujet Gounod.

were no longer to be discerned. The feeling of loyalty was nearly extinct in the great mass of the people: the return of the royal family was associated with circumstances of deep national humiliation: the principal feeling in the multitude was curiosity to see the strangers. The King arrived at Compiègne on the 29th April and made his public entry by the gate of St. Denis on the 3rd May, in the midst of a prodigious concourse of spectators. The Duchesse d'Angoulême was seated by him: and the Old Guard of Napoleon formed his escort: the national guard of Paris kept the streets. The procession proceeded first to Notre-Dame, where the King and the royal family returned thanks for their restoration, and then advanced by the quays and the Pont Neuf to the Tuileries.

"From a delicate desire to save Louis the pain of seeing foreign uniforms, it was arranged that the streets should be lined by French soldiers, and the Old Guard were stationed between Notre-Dame and the Tuileries. Never was indignation more strongly marked than in their visages. Some, in pretence of saluting the cortège, bent their heads down and drew their bear-skins over their eyes so as to see nothing; others ground their teeth in the vehemence of their rage, or showed them like tigers; several shed tears of rage. When commanded to present arms, they did it with a vehemence which made the spectators start; it was like bringing down their bayonets to the charge.

"When the Duchesse d'Angoulême reached the foot of the principal stair of that palace which she had not seen since the 10th August, 1792, when, in company with Louis XVI and Marie Antoinette, she left it to take refuge from the insurgents in the National Assembly, her emotions were so overpowering that she fell down insensible at the King's feet. But these awful recollections produced little or no effect on the Parisians; and the principal observation made was, that the King's and Princess's dresses were cut in the London fashion, and that the Duchesse d'Angoulême was a perfect fright with her low English bonnet."[1]

From the Memoirs of the Comtesse de Boigne.

"We went to see the entry of the King from a house in the Rue Saint-Denis. The crowd was very great, and most of the windows were decorated with festoons, mottoes, *fleurs de lys*, and white flags. The absence of foreign uniforms was a restful sight. General Slacken, the Russian Governor of Paris, was the only officer to be seen in the city.

"The procession was escorted by the old Imperial Guard. It marched quickly, silent and gloomy, full of remembrances of the past. It stopped, by a look, our outburst of affection for those who were arriving. The shouts of "Long live the King!" died on our lips as it rode by. Here and there were heard shouts of "Long live the Guard! Long live the old Guard!" But it did not welcome these, and appeared to accept them in derision. As it passed by, the silence became general, and soon nothing could be heard but the monotonous tramp of the quick step striking our very hearts. The consternation increased, and the contagious sadness of these old warriors gave to the whole ceremony the appearance of the Emperor's funeral rather than that of the King's accession.

"Monsieur was on horseback, escorted by the marshals, the officers-general of the Empire, those of the King's household, and of the Line. The King was in an open carriage, with Madame at his side. In front were the Prince de Condé and his son, the Duc de Bourbon.

"Madame wore the feather toque and the dress with the silver thread that had been sent to her to Saint-Ouen, but she had managed to give a foreign touch to this

[1] At this period, the English fashion for bonnets was exceedingly low, and the French proportionally high; so that the contrast between the Duchesse d'Angoulême's haymaker's bonnet and the splendid coiffures and feathers with which the ladies were adorned at Paris was sufficiently striking.—*Original Note from Alison.*

Parisian costume. The King wore a plain blue coat with very large epaulettes, and the blue order and badge of the Saint-Esprit. He had a handsome face, which was expressionless when he meant to be gracious. He presented Madame to the people with an affected and theatrical gesture. She took no part in these demonstrations, but remained impassive and, in her way, was the counterpart of the Imperial Guard. Her red eyes, though, gave the impression that she was crying. Her silent sorrow was respected, and everyone sympathised with her in it. . . .

" Prince de Condé, already almost in his dotage, and his son did not seem to take any part in the proceedings. They only figured there as images in the ceremony. Monsieur alone appeared there to advantage. He had a frank, contented expression on his face, identified himself with the populace, bowed in a friendly and familiar way, like a man who finds himself at home and among his own people. The procession ended with another battalion of the Guard, which reproduced the impression of the first detachment.

" I must own that, as far as I was concerned, the morning had been very painful in every way. The people in the open carriage did not correspond to the hopes I had formulated. I was told that Madame, on arriving at Notre-Dame, sank down on her *prie-Dieu* in a way that was most graceful, noble, and touching. There was such resignation, and at the same time such gratitude, in this action that tears of sympathy had flowed from all eyes. I was also told that on arriving at the Tuileries she was as cold, awkward, and sullen as she had been beautiful and noble in the church.

" At that time, the Duchesse d'Angoulême was the only person of the royal family whom people remembered in France. . . . But everyone knew that Louis XVI, and the Queen and Madame Elisabeth had perished on the scaffold. For everyone Madame was the orphan of the Temple, and all the interest aroused by such frightful catastrophes was felt for her. The blood that had been shed baptised her as the country's child."

6. THE ALLIES IN PARIS

I

From Alison's[1] "*History of Europe.*"

THE world had never seen—probably the world will never again see—so marvellous a spectacle as the streets of Paris exhibited from the 31st March (1814), when the entry of the Allies took place, till the 16th June, when, upon their finally retiring, the service of the posts was restored to the national guard of the capital. In a state of the most perfect tranquillity, the capital of Napoleon was occupied by the troops of twenty different nations, whom the oppression of his government had roused to arms from the wall of China to the Pillars of Hercules. Beside the veterans of Napoleon's old Guard, who still retained, even in the moment of defeat, their martial and undaunted aspect, were to be seen the superb household troops of Russia and Prussia; the splendid cuirassiers of Austria shone in glittering steel; the iron veterans of Blücher still eyed the troops of France with jealousy, as if their enmity was unappeased even by the conquest of their enemies. The nomad tribes of Asia and the Ukraine strolled in wonder along every street; groups of Cossack bivouacs lay in the Champs-Élysées; the Bashkirs and Tartars gazed with undisguised avidity, but restrained hands, on the gorgeous display of jewellery and dresses which were arrayed in the shop-windows, to attract the notice of the numerous princes and potentates who thronged the metropolis. Every morning the noble columns of the Preobazinsky and Simonefsky Guards marched out of the barracks of the École Militaire, to

[1] Alison was in Paris at the time, and wrote this passage of his history from personal observation.

THE COSSACK BIVOUACS IN THE CHAMPS ÉLYSÉES

p. 62

exercise on the Champ de Mars; at noon, reviews of cavalry succeeded, and the earth shook under the thundering charge of the Russian cuirassiers. Often in the evening the Allied monarchs visited the opera, or some of the theatres; and the applause with which they were received resembled what might have been expected if Napoleon had returned in triumph from the capture of their capital. Early in June, Wellington, who had been appointed ambassador of England at the court of the Tuileries, arrived among them; he was received with enthusiasm; and the opera-house never shook with louder applause than when he first made his appearance there after the battle of Toulouse.

II

From the Autobiography of B. R. Haydon.

It might be said that when we arrived at Paris the ashes of Napoleon's last fire were hardly cool; the last candle by which he had read was hardly extinguished; the very book he had last read was to be seen turned down where he left it. From boyhood upward we had been accustomed to think of this man as a mysterious being—the Apollyon of the Revelation—the produce of a mighty revelation—the hero, the genius, the emperor who had fought his way from the school at Brienne till he snatched the crown from the hands of the Pope and put it on his own head; and now this wonderful Napoleon was dethroned, and we could be admitted to his palaces, to his bedroom, we could see the table he had leaned upon and inked, the chairs which he had sat upon and cut, the bell-ropes he had pulled, the servants who had served him.

It was delightful to discover that he who had annihilated armies, hurled down kings and reigned in the capitals of Europe, did like most of us when alone; that he sometimes fell asleep, sometimes got into a pet if a servant did not answer his bell at once, that now and then he slept longer than he ought, and now and then sat up later, that he poked the fire if it was going out, that he yawned when he was sleepy, and put his extinguisher on his candle when he no longer wanted it.

At that time (1814) every step in Paris excited mighty associations. Every church, every palace, every street, and every corner was remarkable for some slaughter, or struggle, or some wonder connected with the revolution and blood; yet everywhere a sense of despotism pressed on your mind. There was in everything a look of gilded slavery and bloody splendour, a tripping grace in the women, a ragged blackguardism in the men, and a polished fierceness in the soldiers, which distinguished Paris as a capital of a people who combine more inconsistent vices and virtues than any other people on the earth.

At this moment, too, there was with all this an air of mortified vanity and surprised exasperation which was natural. By the side of the Russian, Austrian, Prussian, and English officers, the remnant of Napoleon's army had a look of blasted glory, of withered pride and lurking revenge, which gave one a shudder of the sublime, and it was clear to anyone of the commonest sagacity that they must seize the first opportunity to regain their lost position.[1]

In the middle of the day the Rue St. Honoré was the most wonderful sight. Don Cossack chiefs, loosely clothed and moving as their horses moved, with all the bendings of their bodies visible at every motion; the half-clothed savage Cossack horseman, his belt stuck full of pistols and watches and hatches, crouched up on a little ragged-maned, dirty-looking, ill-bred, half-white, shaggy pony; the Russian Imperial guardsman pinched in at the waist like a wasp, striding along like a giant, with an air of victory that made every Frenchman curse within his teeth as he passed him; the English officer, with his boyish face and broad shoulders; the heavy Austrian; the natty Prussian; and now and then a Bashkir Tartar, in the ancient Phrygian cap, with bow and arrows and chain-armour, gazing about from his horse in the midst of

[1] This, Haydon tells us in a footnote, was written before Napoleon escaped from Elba.

black-eyed grisettes, Jews, Turks, and Christians from all countries in Europe and Asia. It was a pageant that kept one staring, musing and bewildered from morning till night.

The ignorance of the French people as to their own political position and that of other nations was most extraordinary to Wilkie[1] and me. A French gentleman asked me in whose possession San Domingo was, and when by my expression I showed my astonishment, he shrunk back into himself, a degraded, oppressed, and ignorant human creature. Napoleon should have seen his look. It might have gratified his contempt for his own species, but a great mind could never have felt pleasure in having kept men so brutishly vacant. And yet, after having these aspirations towards sympathy with the oppressed one moment, in an hour after you would feel inclined to kick the French, and say Napoleon knew how to treat them—a vain, silly, chattering, thoughtless, unprincipled, active, fiendish people.

[1] The painter, afterwards Sir David Wilkie.

7. CARABOO, PRINCESS OF JEVASU

From a pamphlet published in 1817.

"On Thursday evening the 3rd of April, 1817, a young Female entered a cottage in the village of Almondsbury and made signs that it was her wish to sleep under its roof; but not speaking a language which its inhabitants understood, it was thought right to refer to Mr. Worrall, a Magistrate for the county, for his advice. The female was in consequence brought up to Knole Mansion,[1] but to which removal she showed signs of reluctance. After some entreaty, she was prevailed upon to go in, and was presented to Mr. and Mrs. Worrall; who were unable to understand the language in which she addressed them; but intimated to her by signs, that they wished to ascertain whether or not she had any papers in her possession; upon which she took from her pocket a few half-pence with a bad sixpence, and implied that she had nothing else. She had a small bundle on her arm containing a very few necessaries, and a piece of soap pinned up in a bit of linen. Her dress consisted of a black stuff gown, with a muslin frill round the neck, and a black cotton shawl on her head, and a red and black shawl round her shoulders; both loosely and tastefully put on in imitation of the Asiatic costume."

It was arranged that the woman should sleep in the village inn, and Mrs. Worrall sent her maid and footman to escort her there and see that she was provided with a good meal and a comfortable bed.

"When shewn to the room in which she was to sleep, she appeared reluctant to go to bed, and pointed to the

[1] This house was in Gloucestershire, and should not be confused with the seat of the Sackvilles.

floor, but upon the landlady's little girl getting into the bed, and making her understand the comfort of it, she undressed, and after kneeling and appearing to say her prayers, she consented to lie on the bed."

Early next morning Mrs. Worrall came to the inn, and while she was there the clergyman of the parish arrived to pay a visit to her protégée. He brought with him pictures of the East, for he thought it possible that she might recognise some of the places.

" Upon looking them over, she gave the spectators to understand that she had some knowledge of the prints which were descriptive of China; but made the signs, that it was not a boat, but a ship, which had brought her to this country. Gaining very little information from this enquiry, Mrs. Worrall determined to take her back with her to Knole, and keep her under her roof till something satisfactory transpired concerning her; and on being invited she followed Mrs. Worrall, exhibiting symptoms of reluctance and apprehension. Upon her arrival at Knole, she was led to the housekeeper's room, where the servants were at breakfast; and observing some cross-buns on the table (it being Good Friday) she took one, and after looking earnestly at it she cut off the Cross and placed it in her bosom.

" Upon Mrs. Worrall's return from church, she summoned the young woman before her; and addressed her in the following soothing and compassionate language: 'My good young woman, I very much fear that you are imposing upon me, and that you understand and can answer me in my own language; if so, and distress has driven you to this expedient, make a friend of me; I am a female as yourself, and can feel for you, and will give you money and clothes, and will put you on your journey, without disclosing your conduct to anyone; but it must be on condition that you speak the truth. If you deceive me, I think it right to inform you that Mr. Worrall is a magistrate, and has the power of sending you to prison, committing you to hard labour, and passing you as a vagrant to your own parish.'

" During this address the countenance of the stranger evinced an ignorance of Mrs. Worrall's intentions, at the same time making it apparent that she did not comprehend what Mrs. Worrall had said to her; and she immediately addressed Mrs. Worrall in her unknown tongue. Mrs. Worrall then attempted to ascertain her name, by writing her own upon paper and placing it before her, and pronouncing it several times, and putting a pen in her hand, intimated her wish, that she would write her name; but this was declined, shaking her head, crying, 'Caraboo, Caraboo,' pointing to herself. At dinner she declined all animal food, and took nothing to drink but water, showing much disgust at meat, beer, cyder, etc."

Caraboo stayed at Knole until Monday, and then she was taken to a home for the destitute in Bristol. Her story became known and several people came to visit her, bringing with them foreigners in the hope of finding out her nationality. Among them was a Portuguese from Malay, who declared that he understood her language. She was a princess in her own country, he said, and had been decoyed by pirates from Jevasu, her island home in the East Indies, brought to England, and then abandoned. The language she spoke was not a pure dialect, but a mixture of languages used on the coast of Sumatra, and other islands in the East. Mrs. Worrall's suspicions were now allayed, and she took Caraboo back to Knole and treated her as an honoured guest.

" Upon giving her some calico, she made herself a dress in the style she had been accustomed to wear. It was very short in the petticoat, the sleeves uncommonly wide and long enough to reach the ground but only half-scored up, and confined at the wrists. She wore no stockings, but open sandals on the feet with wooden soles. She expressed much pleasure at the sight of a Chinese chain purse, which was shown to her, which she put on, first in the Chinese and afterwards in the Jevasu fashion; in both instances veiling her face. She sometimes twisted her hair and rolled it up on the top of her head, fastening it with a skewer. A vocabulary of words and the meanings to which she applied them were collected and she was always consistent and correct in using them in the same sense, meaning, or object. Mrs. Worrall's housekeeper, who slept with her, never heard at any interval any other language or tone of voice than that which she first assumed.

"During her stay she used to exercise herself with a bow and arrows, and made a stick answer to a sword on her right side, the bow and arrows slung on her left shoulder. She oftentimes carried a gong on her back, which she sounded in a very singular manner, and a tambourine in her hand, a sword by her side, and a bow and arrows slung as usual, her head dressed with flowers and feathers, and thus she made it appear she was prepared for war.

"Mrs. Worrall was one evening absent from Knole on the day of a wake in the parish, and on her return found her missing. The gardens were searched, and she was discovered sitting in a high tree, in which she explained herself to have climbed, because all the females in the house had gone into the village, and she feared contamination from the men.

"A jocose clerical gentleman, of Bath, tried to move her by flattery; he drew his chair close to her; looked steadily and smilingly in her face, and observed, 'You are the most beautiful creature I ever beheld. You are an angel.' Not a muscle of her face moved; no blush suffused her cheek; her countenance was motionless."

But Caraboo did not intend to spend the rest of her life at Knole, and one day in the beginning of June she left the house secretly and made her way to Bath.

Rumours of her arrival there reached her hostess, and within a week Mrs. Worrall had followed her, determined to reclaim her protégée.

" She found the Princess at the very pinnacle of her glory and ambition in the drawing-room of a lady of *haut ton*. Cervantes himself could not have expected the realisation of so fine a scene. What was the situation of Sancho Panza at the palace of the Duchess, in comparison with the Princess of Jevasu in the drawing-room of Mrs. —— ? The drawing-room was crowded with fashionable visitants, all eager to be introduced to the interesting Princess. There was one fair female kneeling before her, another taking her by the hand, another begging a kiss ! . . .

" Dr. Wilkinson of Bath was another of the *Cognoscenti* who was led likewise by the same love of the marvellous to try his skill at developing the character and nation of the unknown foreigner.

" ' Her mode of diet seems to be Hindoostanic,' wrote the Doctor to the *Bath Chronicle*, ' as she lives principally on vegetables, and is very partial to curry ; whatever she eats, she prepares herself. She is extremely neat in her attire ; is very cautious in her conduct with respect to gentlemen ; never allows them to take hold of her hand, and even if their clothes should casually come into contact with hers, she retires from them : when she takes leave of a gentleman, it is by the application of the right hand to the right side of the forehead, and, in like manner, on taking leave of a lady, it is with the left hand. She appears to be devout ; and on a certain day in the week is anxious to go to the top of the house and there to pay adoration to the sun from the rising to the setting. She carries about with her a cord, on which some knots are made, like the Chinese *abacus*, which afterwards gave rise to the sliding beads, the *suon puon*. She writes with great facility from left to right, as we are accustomed. She has made Mrs. Worrall understand that in her country neither pens or paper are used; but what is supposed to be a camel-hair pencil and a species of papyrus. All the assistance to be derived from a Polyglott Bible, Fry's Pantographia, or Dr. Hager's Elementary Characters of the Chinese, did not enable us to ascertain either the nature of her language, or the country to which she belongs; one or two characters bear some resemblance to the Chinese, particularly the Chinese *cho*, a reed. There are more characters which have some similitude to the Greek, particularly the ι, π, and ε; different publications have been shown to her in Greek, Malay, Chinese, Sanscrit, Arabic, and Persic, but with all she appears entirely unacquainted. Her letter has been shown to every person in Bristol and Bath versed in Oriental literature, but without success. A copy was sent to the India House, and submitted by the Chairman of that Company to the examination of Mr. Raffles, one of the best oriental scholars, yet he could not decipher it. The original letter was sent to Oxford, and the members of that university denied its being the character of any language; it has been by some conjectured as being an imperfect Javanese, others have supposed it the style of the Malay and Sumatra. From my own observation, although entirely unacquainted with any single character of her writing, I have deemed her more resembling a Circassian; her countenance, her complexion and her manners, favour such a supposition; and probably her appearance here may be connected with the Corsairs who have been hovering about our coast. The Supreme Being she styles *Alla Tallah*. All who have seen her are highly interested about her.'"

But Dr. Wilkinson, in giving Caraboo's affairs this publicity, got rather more than he bargained for. A lodging-house keeper was reading the story when the thought crossed her mind that in appearance and ways this stranger reminded her of a certain Mary Baker, who had lodged with her some months before, and who, in her habit of telling wildly improbable stories, had seemed to her almost out of her mind. Caraboo was confronted with this woman, and she instantly burst into tears and owned up to imposture. But she gave such an extraordinary account of her life that her second story could no more be believed than her first. This much was certain—that she was a servant-girl from Devonshire with a far from unblemished reputation. Her restless disposition had prevented her from ever staying long in any of her situations, and she had taken to roaming about the countryside until she conceived the idea of enlisting sympathy by pretending to be a foreigner. Mrs. Worrall generously forgave her, and afterwards helped her to emigrate to America. Nothing more was heard of her—except for a fantastic story of her meeting with Napoleon on St. Helena. It appeared on September 13th, 1817, in *Felix Farley's Bristol Journal*,[1] but we must admit that otherwise history is silent on this episode.

" Sir Hudson introduced her to Bonaparte under the name of Caraboo. She described herself as Princess of Caraboo, and related a tale of extraordinary interest, which seemed in a high degree to delight the captive chief. He embraced her with every demonstration of enthusiastic rapture, and besought Sir Hudson that she might be allowed an apartment in his house, declaring that she alone was an adequate solace in his captivity.

" Since the arrival of this lady, the countenance and figure of Bonaparte appear to be wholly altered. From being reserved and dejected, he has become gay and communicative. No more complaints are heard about the inconveniences at Longwood. He has intimated to Sir Hudson his determination to apply to the Pope for a dispensation to dissolve his marriage with Maria Louise, and to sanction his indissoluble union with the enchanting Caraboo."

[1] Quoted in Timbs's *Eccentrics*.

8. THE DISCOVERY OF PERPETUAL MOTION

An advertisement from the "Dublin Evening Post," August, 1817.

Perpetual Motion

Take notice, that I will exhibit, after six days' notice, for the sum of £300,000, that long-wished-for perpetual motion, now going in its rapid velocity, without the aid or assistance of man or beast, springs, weights, or balance, steam, wind or water, or any other visible assistance, and will continue in its rapid velocity as long as a body of any substance lasts.

Let the reader not doubt my undertaking, as I will undergo any penalty requested of me to exhibit an art which no second mortal can effect by study or ingenuity. Now, all gentlemen who study the merit and honour of their country, let them appeal to me, and I will, for the above sum, exhibit the art that will be an honour to Ireland until the expiration of time.

An art that had therefore defeated the great Sir Isaac Newton, after many years study, likewise the known world. This art I have effected at my first trial of it, on a small scale, with a few minutes' study and three hours' labour.

An art that no second mortal can effect, I now challenge the known world; I dare their study or ingenuity to execute what I have done. Should this undertaking be left unnoticed, I will sell its merits to another country.

9. THE CORONATION OF GEORGE IV

Henry Brougham to Mr. Creevey.

19th July, 1821.

This town is in a state of general lunacy, beginning most certainly with the Illustrious Person on the throne. George III was an ill-used man to be shut up for ten years. His son has slept none, I believe, since you left town; nor will, till it is over.[1]

To-day the Queen's being allowed to enter the Abbey is doubted. . . . But I still think it possible the Big Man may have gout and not be up to it.[1]

20th July.

The Ministers are still sitting squabbling; nor have they to this hour (5) made up their minds whether to stop her or not. My belief is they will let her pass, and also admit her at the Abbey if she persists. She is quite resolved to do so, and goes to sleep at Cambridge House for the purpose. But she is sure to blunder about the hour, and to give them excuses for turning her back by being late. . . . We (Brougham and Denman) thought at one time she meant to command our attendance, which we had resolved, of course, to refuse, but she did not venture.

From the account of the Coronation, Annual Register, 1821.

Soon after four o'clock, it was ascertained that her Majesty's coach was making ready, and the crowd, both in South Audley Street and in Hill Street, became very great. The wall opposite to her Majesty's house was covered with spectators, who announced to the crowd

[1] The Coronation.

below each successive step of preparation. "The horses are to"—"Everything is quite ready"—"The Queen has entered the coach"—were the gradual communications, and they were received with the loudest cheers.

Soon after five, the gate was thrown open, and a shout was raised, "The Queen! The Queen!" The Queen immediately appeared in her coach of state, drawn by six bays. Lady Hood and Lady Anne Hamilton sat opposite to her Majesty. Lord Hood followed in his own carriage. Her Majesty looked well; and acknowledged with great dignity and composure, the gratulations of the people on each side of her coach.

They made their way through the crowded streets, and arriving at last at the place where the tickets were received, Lord Hood demanded admission for the Queen.

The Door-keeper said that his instructions were to admit no persons without a peer's ticket.

Lord Hood: "Did you ever hear of a queen being asked for a ticket before? This is your Queen."

The Door-keeper said that his orders were general, and without any exceptions. He had never been in a similar situation before and could say nothing as to the propriety or impropriety of refusing her Majesty admission.

Lord Hood: "I present to you your Queen, do you refuse her admission?"

Her Majesty added that she was his Queen, and desired to be permitted to pass.

The Door-keeper repeated that his orders were peremptory—and said, however reluctant he might be, he could not suffer her Majesty to pass without a ticket.

Lord Hood: "I have a ticket."

Door-keeper: "Upon presenting it, I will permit you to pass."

Lood Hood then took from his pocket one ticket for the Abbey, for a Mr. Wellington, which he tendered to the Door-keeper.

The Door-keeper said that would admit but one individual.

Lord Hood then asked her Majesty, if she would enter alone.

Her Majesty hesitated—upon which

Lord Hood asked, whether there had not been some preparation made for her Majesty's reception.

The Door-keeper answered in the negative.

Lord Hood: "Then I am to understand you refuse your Queen admittance to Westminster Abbey?"

The Door-keeper said he was ready to admit her Majesty with a ticket, but not without.

After a short consultation with her Majesty, whether she would go into the Abbey alone, or not—her Majesty declined—and it was resolved that she should return to her carriage.

As she was quitting the spot, some persons in the doorway burst into a vulgar laugh of derision. Her Majesty looked at them contemptuously; and turning about, passed through a group of fashionable women who were going to the Abbey with tickets, but who did not take the slightest notice of her. She was followed by a crowd to the platform, some of whom were approving, and some disapproving of her conduct. On entering her carriage, there was considerable disapprobation, intermingled with cries of "Shame, shame," "Off, off"; while other parts of the populace repeated the cries of "The Queen, the Queen," with great enthusiasm.

The knowledge of her Majesty's presence drew forth many of the persons who had assembled to take part in the procession. The grotesqueness of their dresses, as they appeared on the leads of the committee rooms of the House of Commons, had a most singular appearance. Some of them joined in the cries of "Shame" against her Majesty.

10. SHELLEY'S DEATH AND THE BURNING OF HIS BODY

From an obituary notice which appeared in the "Gentleman's Magazine" in September, 1822.

"*July 8th.*—Supposed to have perished at sea in a storm, somewhere off Via Reggia, on the coast of Italy, between Leghorn and the Gulf of Spezia, Percy Bysshe Shelley, Esq. He went out sailing with his friend, Capt. Williams. He had been to Pisa and was returning to his country abode at Lerici. The boat has since been found capsized. . . .

"Mr. Shelley is unfortunately too well known for his infamous novels and poems. He openly professed himself an atheist. . . ."

The bodies were washed up, and, after being identified, were temporarily buried in the sand. In order to avoid trouble with the authorities over the Quarantine Laws, it was decided to reduce the bodies to ashes before conveying them to the place where they were to be buried. Trelawny describes in his *Recollections of the Last Days of Shelley and Byron* the burning of Shelley's body.

"Three white wands had been stuck in the sand to mark the poet's grave, but as they were at some distance from each other, we had to cut a trench thirty yards in length, in the line of the sticks, to ascertain the exact spot, and it was nearly an hour before we came upon the grave.

"In the meantime, Byron and Leigh Hunt arrived in the carriage, attended by soldiers, and the Health officer, as before.[1] The lonely and grand scenery that surrounded

[1] On the previous day, Williams's body had been burnt in the same way.

us so exactly harmonised with Shelley's genius, that I could imagine his spirit soaring over us. The sea, with the islands of Gorgona, Capraji, and Elba, was before us; old battlemented watch-towers stretched along the coast, backed by the marble-crested Apennines glistening in the sun, picturesque from their diversified outlines, and not a human dwelling was in sight. As I thought of the delight Shelley felt in such scenes of loneliness and grandeur whilst living, I felt we were no better than a herd of wolves or a pack of wild dogs, in tearing out his battered and naked body from the pure yellow sand that lay so lightly over it, to drag him back to the light of day; but the dead have no voice, nor had I power to check the sacrilege—the work went on silently in the deep and unresisting sand, not a word was spoken, for the Italians have a touch of sentiment, and their feelings are easily excited into sympathy. Even Byron was silent and thoughtful. We were startled and drawn together by a dull hollow sound that followed the blow of a mattock; the iron had struck a skull, and the body was soon uncovered. Lime had been strewn on it; this, or decomposition, had the effect of staining it of a dark and ghastly indigo colour. Byron asked me to preserve the skull for him; but remembering that he had formerly used one as a drinking-cup, I was determined Shelley's should not be so profaned. The limbs did not separate from the trunk, as in the case of Williams's body, so that the corpse was removed entire into the furnace. I had taken the precaution of having more and larger pieces of timber, in consequence of my experience of the day before of the difficulty of consuming a corpse in the open air with our apparatus. After the fire was well kindled we repeated the ceremony of the previous day; and more wine was poured over Shelley's dead body than he had consumed during his life. This with the oil and salt made the yellow flames glisten and quiver. The heat from the sun and fire was so intense that the atmosphere was tremulous and wavy. The corpse fell open and the heart was laid bare. The frontal bone of the skull, where it had been struck with the mattock, fell off; and, as the back of the head rested on the red-hot bottom bars of the furnace, the brains literally seethed, bubbled, and boiled as in a cauldron for a very long time.

"Byron could not face this scene, he withdrew to the beach and swam off to the *Bolivar*. Leigh Hunt remained in the carriage. The fire was so fierce as to produce a white heat on the iron, and to reduce its contents to grey ashes. The only portions that were not consumed were some fragments of bones, the jaw, and the skull, but what surprised us all, was that the heart remained entire. In snatching this relic from the fiery furnace, my hand was severely burnt; and had any one seen me do the act I should have been put into quarantine.

"After cooling the iron machine in the sea, I collected the human ashes and placed them in a box, which I took on board the *Bolivar*. Byron and Hunt retraced their steps to their home, and the officers and soldiers returned to their quarters. . . .

Byron's idle talk during the exhumation of Williams's remains, did not proceed from want of feeling, but from his anxiety to conceal what he felt from others. When confined to his bed and racked by spasms, which threatened his life, I have heard him talk in a much more unorthodox fashion, the instant he could muster breath to banter. He had been taught during his town-life, that any exhibition of sympathy or feeling was maudlin and unmanly, and that the appearance of daring and indifference, denoted blood and high breeding."

11. THE FEJEE MERMAID

From the " Gentleman's Magazine," July, 1822.

The Rev. Dr. Philip, Cape Town, writes :

" I have to-day seen a Mermaid, now exhibiting in this town. The head is almost the size of that of a baboon. It is thinly covered with black hair, hanging down, and not inclined to frizzle. The head is turned back, and the countenance has an expression of terror, which gives it the appearance of a caricature of the human face. The ears, nose, lips, chin, breasts, nipples, fingers, and nails, resemble those of a human figure. The appearance of the teeth afford sufficient evidence that it is full-grown. The canine teeth resemble those of a full grown dog ; all the others resemble those of a human subject. The length of the animal is three feet.

"The resemblance to the human species ceases immediately under the mammæ. On the line of separation, and directly under the breast, are two fins. From the point where the human figure ceases, which is about twelve inches below the vertex of the head, it resembles a large fish of the salmon species. It is covered with scales all over ; on the lower parts of the animal, the scales resemble those of a fish ; but on that part of the animal which resembles the human form, they are much less, and scarcely perceptible, except on a near inspection. The pectoral fins are very remarkable ; they are horizontal, and evidently formed as an apparatus to support the creature when in an erect posture, like that in which it has been sometimes represented combing its hair. The figure of the tail is exactly that which is given in the usual representation of the mermaid.

" It was caught somewhere on the north of China by a fisherman."

Later in the year, the mermaid was exhibited at a well-known coffee-house in Piccadilly, where for some weeks it attracted a crowd of over three hundred persons a day. Its ownership gave rise to litigation, and this is probably the only instance in English law when a judge has been called upon to decide the fate of a mermaid.

Twenty years afterwards, Barnum re-discovered it, lying forgotten in a Boston museum. By ingenious advertising, the "Fejee Mermaid," as he christened it, created an even greater excitement on its second public appearance than its first. Every afternoon, a distinguished London naturalist (looking very much like one of Barnum's showmen) gave learned lectures on mermaids. "But I lived two years on the Fiji Islands, and I never heard of any such thing as a mermaid," said a visitor to Barnum. "There's no accounting for some men's ignorance," was the reply.

But, alas, the belief in the existence of mermaids had waned, and the sceptical attached great importance to this curious creature's likeness to a monkey and a salmon. It had probably been manufactured, they said, by the Japanese fishermen from whom it had originally been bought.

12. THE COURT AT PARMA

From the " Gentleman's Magazine," 1822.

THE illustrious consort of Napoleon has been variously represented to the world. Like many great personages, she is but little known; little is known of her domestic habits; and her public actions neither want praise nor demand censure. The Principalities over which she rules are amongst the finest in Italy and her subjects generally contented. Her Prime Minister, Baron Glaive, is a man of ordinary talents; to whom everything is confided, and his duty is little more than being the steward over the estates of a large family.

About four years ago a rumour was current in this country, that an infant had made its appearance in the world at Parma under curious circumstances.[1] The tale died away, and is only revived from the circumstance of this illustrious lady having gone to the castle of Schoenbrunn with a splendid equipage and royal suite, amongst which is a young child apparently five or six years old; it is nursed and attended upon by persons of rank, and is daily seen by the Archduchess, who takes it in her carriage. It is said by some to be a natural daughter of Baron Glaive: this is very probable, but who is the mother becomes a question not easily solved. The Ex-Empress makes no secret of her affection for the infant; she nurses it, and is never better pleased than when it is with her.

[1] As a matter of fact, this child, who was born on May 1st, 1817, was the daughter of Marie Louise by Count Neipperg, whom, on Napoleon's death, she ultimately married.

FONTHILL ABBEY

(From Ritter's Delineation of Fonthill)

p. 83

13. FONTHILL ABBEY

From the " Gentleman's Magazine," 1844.

" On his return from Portugal, Mr. Beckford employed himself in rearing the magnificent but unsubstantial Gothic structure known as Fonthill Abbey. His buildings commenced by the erection of a tower on the summit of the highest hill upon the estate; it was to have the appearance of a convent, partly in ruins and partly perfect, but to contain a few rooms which might afford shelter for a day either of sunshine or of shower. From this germ arose, with continual alterations of plan, the far-famed Abbey of Fonthill. For many years no intention of converting the convent into a permanent residence was entertained; nor, indeed, did the impatience of Mr. Beckford admit of the necessarily slow progress of a work of such dimensions, when constructed of solid materials. Timber and cement were therefore the principal articles in its composition; and every expedient was used to complete the building within a given time, regardless of the consequence that might almost have been expected to ensue. At one period every cart and wagon in the district was pressed into the service, though all the agricultural labour of the country stood still. At another, even the royal works of St. George's Chapel, Windsor, were abandoned, that 460 men might be employed night and day on Fonthill Abbey. These men were made to relieve each other by regular watches; and, during the longest and darkest nights of winter, the astonished traveller might see the tower rising under their hands, the trowel and torch being associated for the purpose. Mr. Beckford was fond of watching the work thus expedited, the busy levy of masons, the high and giddy dancing of the lights, and the strange effects produced upon the architecture and woods below from one of the eminences in the walks. One immediate result of this injudicious haste was the destruction of the great tower, which was carried up to the extreme height of 300 feet (and furnished with pinnacles and weather vanes) without time being allowed to complete its fastenings to the base on which it was erected : a gust of wind acting suddenly upon a large flag attached to a scaffold-pole at its summit, carried it off its base altogether. The fall was tremendous and sublime, and the only regret expressed by Mr. Beckford was that he had not witnessed the catastrophe. He instantly gave orders for the erection of a new tower."

In 1800, Nelson and the Hamiltons were in England, and Beckford invited them to Fonthill for a short visit in December. He prepared to entertain them in a style that at once gratified his own taste for magnificence and was worthy, in his opinion, of the great Admiral, who was everywhere being fêted by his countrymen. The Abbey was still in the course of construction, and it occurred to him that he might use it to provide a novel entertainment for his guests. Accordingly he kept 500 masons working on it day and night, and, to prevent them from flagging, supplied them liberally with ale and spirits. (We can well imagine how his delight in watching them build by torch-light must have been intensified by their drunken antics.) These expedients were so effectual that, by the time his guests arrived on the 20th of December, his plans had been carried out to his complete satisfaction.

A large number of other distinguished persons had been invited to meet them, and the first three days passed pleasantly with music and conversation. But though Beckford's hospitality seemed to his guests sufficiently lavish, it was carefully moderated, so as not to lessen the effect of the banquet he intended to give in the Abbey as the climax to their visit. Cyrus Redding, Beckford's biographer, gives an account of that evening. Amongst the other guests, we are told that West, the President of the Academy, and Dr. Wolcot (Peter Pindar) were included.

"It was the hour of five when the noise of carriage-wheels at the door of the mansion met the ear. The company entered the vehicles, and took their places in the order previously arranged. Slowly wended the train of carriages towards the Abbey, as the dusk of evening gathered fast in the darkness. It occupied three-quarters of an hour, by the circuitous route taken, to pass from Fonthill House to the Abbey. The wall enclosing the Abbey woods was scarcely passed when the procession, under a Gothic arch, was supposed first to enter the abbot's domain. The road then lay winding through thick woods of pine and fir, illuminated by numberless lamps suspended in the trees, and flambeaux without number carried by the sides of the vehicles. The procession was escorted by the military, their band playing solemn airs and marches. The effect was greatly enhanced by the continuous roll of drums placed about on distant eminences, by the blaze of lights displayed here and there, sometimes moving, at others stationary; now gleaming from bright arms and armour, now darkness being permitted to enshroud all, to make the contrasts more striking, for in these Mr. Beckford delighted.

"The appearance, on the arrival of the company at the Abbey, hushed them all into silent admiration at the increased splendour of the lights, contrasted with the deep shadows falling on the walls, battlements, and turrets of the edifice. On the summit, over all, attached to a flag-staff, 50 feet long, waved the broad flag of a vice-admiral, in compliment to Nelson.

"The company was set down in a groined Gothic hall, between two lines of soldiers. They proceeded onwards to the great saloon, which was hung with very fine tapestry. Before the arched windows drooped long, full curtains of rich purple cloth. Ebony chairs, and tables studded or inlaid with ivory, composed the character of the furniture. The whole was strictly in monastic taste, and lit with wax in sconces of silver. In this parlour the dinner was laid out on a table which occupied its whole length of 53 feet. A superb repast was served up in a long single line of enormous silver dishes, wholly in the massy style and fashion of the ancient abbeys. Their contents were unmingled with any of the refinements of the modern culinary art. The sideboards and tables glittered with piles of plate, and a profusion of light blazed over all. A huge Christmas fire of fir and pine cones increased the novelty and splendour of the *coup d'œil.*

"When the dinner was over, the company mounted the stairs to some of the apartments above. The staircase was lighted by mysterious-looking figures, dressed in hooded gowns, holding large wax torches. The company entered the library, where, among other conspicuous objects, stood credences, or antique-looking buffets, exhibiting wrought plate, cups, vases, and ewers of solid gold. As the company entered the gallery, which was supported by a large gothic screen from the library, music struck the ear as from some invisible hand, suggesting a service of the old gothic times. There, after the old custom, a species of confectionery was presented in gold-wired baskets, with wine and spiceries, while chairs were arranged in the adjoining room to receive the company. When the company had returned to that room and taken seats, Lady Hamilton entered, attired in the character of Agrippina carrying in a golden urn the ashes of Germanicus. The actress showed on this occasion the benefit of the assiduous care Sir William Hamilton had taken to instruct her in Roman history and manners. Her actions were so correct and natural that she drew tears from some of the company.

"The party at 11 o'clock, left the Abbey, in order to return to supper at the Mansion House. On quitting the vast building, in which the lights were fading fast, the lamps and torches no longer visible to any considerable extent made it seem as if all that had been taking place, before passing the boundary wall, was the awakening from a dream, or the reversal of some magical spell which had enchanted all persons."

This hospitality, however, was entirely foreign to Beckford's usual mode of life, for he lived a strictly secluded life. A wall twelve feet high surrounded his estate, and, at the heavy double gates, servants were stationed with orders to exclude strangers. It was a rare mark of favour to be invited inside the entrance, and it is said that even George IV was denied a sight of the Abbey. Strange stories began to circulate of what went on there, but the truth is that Beckford lived absorbed in his books and his building, with only his doctor and one or two artists for company, and an Italian dwarf as his personal attendant. We are told that the sight of this hideous little creature opening the Abbey doors, thirty feet high, provided another of those contrasts that so delighted his master.

The end of Fonthill Abbey, in 1825, was as remarkable as anything else in its history, but by that time it no longer belonged to Beckford. His extravagance, together with the depreciation of his property in the West Indies, forced him to sell his estate, and it passed into the hands of an eccentric old miser called Farquhar. For some years Beckford had used the Abbey as a residence, and his successor followed his example. A description of the catastrophe appears in Timbs's *Modern Eccentrics*.

"The tower had given indications of insecurity for some time. Mr. Farquhar, however, who then resided in one angle of the building, and who was in a very infirm state of health, could not be brought to believe there was any danger. He was wheeled out in his chair on the front lawn about half an hour before the tower fell.

"From the lightness of the materials of which it was constructed, neither Mr. Farquhar, nor the servants who were in the kitchen preparing dinner, knew that it had fallen, though the immense collection of dust which rose into the atmosphere had assembled almost all the inhabitants of the village. Only one man saw the tower fall: it first sank perpendicularly and slowly, and then burst and spread over the roofs of the adjoining wings on either side. The cloud of dust was enormous, so as completely to darken the air for a considerable distance around for several minutes. It is almost incredible that neither Mr. Farquhar nor the servants in the kitchen should have heard the tower fall, or known that it had fallen, till they saw through the window the people of the village who had assembled to see the ruins. Mr. Farquhar, it is said, could scarcely be convinced that the tower was down, and when he was so he said he was glad of it, for that now the house was not too large for him to live in. Mr. Beckford, when told at Bath by his servant that the tower had fallen, merely observed that it had made an obeisance to Mr. Farquhar which it had never done to him."

14. TRELAWNY'S VISIT TO BYRON'S DEAD BODY

From "Trelawny's Recollections of the Last Days of Shelley and Byron."

With desponding thoughts I entered Missolonghi on the third day from my leaving Salona. Any spot on the surface of the earth, or in its bowels, that holds out a prospect of gain, you will find inhabited; a morass that will produce rice, the crust of a volcano in which the vine will grow; lagunes, in which fish abound, are temptations which overcome the terror of pestilence or death. So I was not surprised at seeing Missolonghi, situated as it is on the verge of the most dismal swamp I had ever seen. The marvel was that Byron, prone to fevers, should have been induced to land on this mudbank, and stick there for three months shut in by a circle of stagnant pools which might be called the belt of death. Although it was now the early spring, I found most of the strangers suffering from gastric fevers. It was the 24th or 25th of April when I arrived; Byron had died on the 19th. I waded through the streets, between wind and water, to the house he had lived in; it was detached, and on the margin of the shallow slimy sea-water. For three months this house had been besieged, day and night, like a bank that has a run upon it. Now that death had closed the door, it was as silent as a cemetery. No one was within the house but Fletcher, of which I was glad. As if he knew my wishes, he led me up a narrow stair into a small room, with nothing in it but a coffin standing on trestles. No word was spoken by either of us; he withdrew the black pall and the white shroud, and there lay the embalmed body of the Pilgrim—more beautiful in death than in life. The contraction of the muscles and skin had effaced every line that time or passion had ever traced on it; few marble busts could have matched its stainless white, the harmony of its proportions, and perfect finish; yet he had been dissatisfied with that body, and longed to cast its slough. How often I had heard him curse it! He was jealous of the genius of Shakespeare—that might well be—but where had he seen the face or form worthy to excite his envy? I asked Fletcher to bring me a glass of water. On his leaving the room, to confirm or remove my doubts as to the cause of his lameness, I uncovered the Pilgrim s feet, and was answered—the great mystery was solved. Both his feet were clubbed, and his legs withered to the knee—the form and features of an Apollo, with the feet and legs of a sylvan satyr. This was a curse, chaining a proud and soaring spirit like his to the dull earth. . . . In the drama of *The Deformed Transformed*, I knew that he had expressed all he could express of what a man of highly-wrought mind might feel when brooding over a deformity of body: but when he said

> *I have done the best which spirit may to make*
> *Its way with all deformity, dull deadly,*
> *Discouraging weight upon me,*

I thought it exaggerated as applied to himself; now I saw it was not so. His deformity was always uppermost in his thoughts, and influenced every act of his life, spurred him on to poetry, as that was one of the few paths to fame open to him—and as if to be revenged on Nature for sending him into the world "scarce half made up," he scoffed at her works and traditions with the pride of Lucifer; this morbid feeling ultimately goaded him on to his last Quixotic crusade in Greece. . . .

I was exclaiming, "Poor fellow, if your errors were greater than those of ordinary men, so were your temptations and provocations," when Fletcher returned with a bottle and glass, saying, "There is nothing but slimy salt water in this horrid place, so I have been half over the town to beg this bottle of porter," and, answering my ejaculation of "Poor fellow!" he said—

"You may well say so, sir, these savages are worse than any highwaymen; they have robbed my Lord of all his money and his life too."

Whilst saying this, Fletcher, without making any remark, drew the shroud and pall carefully over the feet of his master's corpse—he was very nervous and trembled as he did it; so strongly had his weak and superstitious nature been acted upon by the injunctions and threats of his master, that, alive or dead, no one was to see his feet, for if they did, he would haunt him.

15. THE *MARY RUSSELL*

On June 23rd, 1828, Captain Callendar, of the *Mary Stubbs*, sighted a vessel flying a signal of distress. They were 300 miles off the coast of Ireland. He hailed her three times without receiving a reply. As he came alongside, a man put his head out of the cabin porthole and called out: "For God's sake, come and help me. There is a mutiny on board."

Captain Callendar shouted back reassuringly, but the man was beside himself with terror. "For God's sake, hurry," he cried, "or I shall jump overboard." He was now on deck, and Callendar recognised him as a certain Captain Stewart of his acquaintance, a very good fellow, and a general favourite. Within a few weeks he had changed, almost beyond recognition. His eyes were sunken, and his face thin and haggard. Talking incoherently, he took Callendar down into the cabin, and showed him the corpses of seven men. They had been securely bound with stout cords by the arms and legs, and their heads battered in by some heavy, pointed instrument.

"I can trample over those like dead sheep," said Captain Stewart. "Was I not a valiant little fellow to kill so many men?" The man was mad, and, while bringing both ships safely back to Cork, Callendar kept him under close observation.

Fortunately there were a few survivors, for the first mate and one of the crew were discovered, trussed up like the others and severely wounded, but still alive. There were also four boys, the youngest of whom was only eleven, who emerged in a dazed and terrified condition. All but the child had been tied up, and only released by Stewart on the approach of the *Mary Stubbs*.

At the inquest, the survivors told the story of what had happened. No one on board appears to have had an inkling that the captain was subject to fits of insanity. On the outward voyage to Barbadoes, nothing unusual occurred; the captain had given satisfaction to everyone, and was on easy and even familiar terms with his crew. On the way home, his demeanour changed; he was restless, and seemed afraid to go to sleep. For forty-seven days and nights, he told Captain Callendar, he had not dared to close his eyes. He was convinced that a mutiny was brewing. To quiet his nerves (for they had an affection for the man), and to prove their innocence, the crew and passengers submitted to be bound. When they were helpless, he proceeded in cold blood to kill them one after another. The following appeared in the *Cork Advertiser* on June 28th, 1828, and is a summary of the mate's evidence:

"About a week after they left Barbadoes, the Captain called the mate and told him a singular dream he had, which was that they were both going to be killed by the crew. The mate told him that dreams were always false, but the Captain replied that it was God Almighty warned him in it. Some time after, the Captain heard Raynes [a passenger] speak to the crew in Irish, and he checked him for so doing. Raynes expressed his regret. The Captain then threw the log-rail and log-glasses overboard, and said that if he heard him do so any more he would throw the charts overboard.[1] On the 16th May, he told the mate not to mind writing the log any more. On Wednesday night, the mate was on watch, and came down three times to relight the binnacle lamp: the Captain remarked that his coming down so often was very odd, and asked if he went to the nail-locker for an iron bolt to murder him. The mate replied that he had not, and that the Captain might get up and search him. The Captain replied that he was afraid to do so, as he

[1] This, of course, was to prevent the crew from being able to navigate the ship in the event of their seizing control.

was sure that the mate intended to knock him down as soon as he came out of his state cabin.

"Two days later, the Captain called all hands on deck, and told the people to lash the mate's hands behind his back; the crew refused and walked away. Some time after, the second mate and two of the others came to the mate, and said he had better be lashed as the Captain was getting in such a rage. The mate was then lashed in the cabin, and put into the lazarette under the cabin floor. The mate got no food until the Sunday night following.

"On Saturday, the mate heard the Captain call Connell, a passenger, down to the cabin, and say to him that he would blow out his brains if he did not confess the truth. He then heard the Captain call the other men, one after the other, about 20 minutes elapsing between the calling of each man; he heard no struggling. During the night, the mate heard some of them say that the lashing was too tight, and others that it was too loose—all remained quiet.

"On Sunday, he heard the Captain say there was a ship in sight—she came within hail and bore away, and the Captain remarked that it was extremely odd that she should go away, seeing them lying to, and declared that the curse of God was on them all. After this, another ship hove in sight and went away, after which the Captain knelt down and got the prayer book, and swore that if they would leave the ship he would give them the long-boat; some were disposed to take it, and others were not. He then took the crow-bar, and killed one of the men with a blow of it. He then killed them all round, striking each a blow or two—the mate heard them crying and then afterwards moaning and groaning, which was terrible. While doing so, the Captain said, 'You ruffians, I'll kill you all.'

"He then came to the mate in the hole over the lazarette, and stuck the point of the crow-bar down at him, which went through the collar of the mate's shirt near his neck, and through the leg of his trousers; he afterwards struck him with the point of a harpoon, and cut his head and his ears. The mate had the appearance of being dead. The Captain put his hand on the back of the mate's neck, and found it quite cold. He nailed a bit of deal plank over the hold, and then had his supper, and a glass of grog, and went to bed.

"The mate heard him say to the boys that they would get a hundred guineas from Lloyd's, and that he would get £7,000 or £8,000 for their conduct in protecting the vessel. He repeatedly told the boys that if they flinched from him, he would blow out their brains. They were terrified by him."

The next morning the boys were rescued from the madman by the arrival of the *Mary Stubbs*.

Captain Stewart was tried for murder at the Cork Assizes, and found guilty but insane. He lived on for more than twenty years in a lunatic asylum in Dublin, devoting much of his time in prayer. "Though I am a Protestant," he used to say, "I cannot help sometimes praying for the souls of my poor men."

16. PRINCESS OLIVE OF CUMBERLAND

TO THE BRITISH PUBLIC

Dec. 1821.

The Princess Olive of Cumberland will be grateful for a sufficient loan by subscription, to enable her Highness to proceed in the recovery of her JUST RIGHTS, being, at this period, without funds for that purpose, or daily support!—not having received one guinea on the account of her royal birth, either from the government or any branch of the Royal Family! !

The Princess has been now nearly ten months a prisoner for debt!—and having experienced a severe illness, from a dislocated and broken leg in the last winter, her health is but indifferent at this time. Her appeal is to the patriotic and humane subjects of her late Royal Uncle, the King George the III; assured that, in this trying season, they will become her protectors and friends—which preserving kindness she will gratefully appreciate to the last moments of her existence!

OLIVE.

"*Gentleman's Magazine*," 1822.

"The first pretentions of this Lady were set forth in a petition to the House of Commons on the 14th of July, 1820. This petition stated, that the petitioner, Olivia Wilmot Serres, was the legitimate daughter of the late Duke of Cumberland, whose marriage with her mother had been solemnised in the year 1767, and that she became the offspring of that marriage in the year 1772. The marriage was kept secret; and the Duke afterwards married again; this second marriage did not, however, vitiate the first; and the Petitioner, in consequence of her Royal Birth, conceived herself to be entitled to certain property belonging to her deceased father. She further said, that she had in her possession a document with the late King's sign-manual, acknowledging her to be his brother's child; and she prayed the House to institute an enquiry into her claims."

A newspaper called the *British Luminary* took up her cause, and on December 16th, 1821, the following statement appeared:

"Dr. Wilmot in early life was a Fellow of Trinity College: he was a high-spirited, intelligent character, of great talent, and the friend and favourite of many of the young nobility then at Oxford. Stanislaus, afterwards King of Poland, was at that time studying at Oxford; and Dr. Wilmot became intimate with him. Stanislaus had a sister living with him (Princess Poniatouski), a very beautiful creature, and from the intimacy which subsisted between the Prince and the Doctor, he was frequently in company with the young princess; and a mutual attachment took place between them; but the princess was not rich, and they were at length privately married. Only a few confidential friends were acquainted with the transaction; for had it been generally known, the Doctor would have lost his fellowship and his other high pretensions.

"In due time the princess presented Dr. Wilmot with a daughter. Some family and political matters separated the parties for a while. He doated upon his lovely child, who was placed under the care of Mrs. Payne, the sister of the Doctor and the wife of Capt. Payne.

"All the time the Doctor could spare from his studies and different occupations, he devoted to his beloved and interesting child, who grew up the beautiful image of her royal mother, with a mind as superior as her person, and at the age of eighteen the Duke of Cumberland and the Earl of Warwick became her admirers: at length the Earl gave way to the Duke; and on the 4th of March, 1767, they were married by Dr. Wilmot at the house of his friend Lord Archer, in the presence of Lord Brook (afterwards Lord Warwick) and Mr. Addez, which was only known to a few persons about the court.

"The apparently happy Duke and his lovely bride lived in hopes that they should soon be allowed to make their marriage public; but in the year 1771, a transaction took place which proved a cruel death-blow to the young Duchess, for she never recovered the effect . . . ! ! !

"Young, amiable, and beautiful, and tenderly attached to the Duke, she took leave of him, and went to Warwick, in a state of misery not to be described. On Tuesday, April 3rd, 1772, she gave birth to the Princess Olive, at the house of Mrs. Wilmot, mother of Dr. Wilmot, in Jury Street, in the town of Warwick. The Earl of Warwick and Dr. Wilmot were both present, which fact is confirmed by their separate friends.

"The unfortunate Duchess was conveyed to France, in a state scarcely to be described, where she afterwards died of a broken heart."

The Princess Olive, referred to above, now came forward in 1820, in the person of Mrs. Serres, to claim £15,000, which she said was due to her from her royal father's estate.

Among the many who believed in the justice of her claim was Creevey, and we find in his diary an entry dated November 11th, 1820: "I have said nothing to you of my City feast. . . . My attention was directed to a much more splendid object—the Princess Olivia of Cumberland. No one can have any doubt of the royalty of *her* birth. She is the very image of our Royal family. Her person is upon the model of the Princess Elizabeth only at least three times her size. She wore the most brilliant rose-coloured satin gown you ever saw, with fancy shawls (more than one) flung in different forms over her shoulders, after the manner of the late Lady Hamilton. Then she had diamonds in profusion hung from every part of her head, but her nose, and the whole was covered with feathers that would have done credit to any hearse. It turned out that Princess Olivia of Cumberland had made her claim as Princess of the Blood to sit at the right hand of my Lord Mayor. The worthy magistrate, however, with great spirit resisted these pretentions, and after much altercation she was compelled to retreat to another table."

The Princess's claim naturally excited considerable attention, and the *Leeds Mercury* published the following :

"In the year 1772 [mark the time] there was born, in the borough of Warwick, a young lady, the daughter of Mr. Robert Wilmot, a house-painter, by Anna Maria, his wife. This infant was baptised at the parish church of St. Nicholas, in that borough, on the 15th of April, 1772, by the name of *Olive*. When of a proper age she was put to school, and displayed the first fruits of a very vivid imagination ; and such was her power of imagination, that if she had honestly employed her faculties in the production of a new series of Arabian tales, she might at this moment have been in the enjoyment of respect and competency. Subsequent to quitting school, she went to reside with her uncle, the Rev. Dr. Wilmot, who enjoyed the living of Barton-on-the-Heath. While in this situation, she appeared as a witness upon a very extraordinary trial for a burglary in her uncle's house, against two men, who were tried, convicted, and executed for that offence. Her story was most marvellous, and her own conduct, as she represented it, most heroic. After the death of the Doctor, a book was published, of which our heroine was the author, the object of which was to prove that her uncle was the real Junius. In the meantime she was married to a person of the name of Serres, we believe a foreigner by birth, and a dancing master or portrait-painter by profession. The rest of her history is oblivion ; possibly she became a Princess.

"The Lady of whom we speak was famed for dealing in documental evidence ; but, unfortunately for herself, the writers of all her documents always happen to die before their letters and certificates are produced. The Warwick family have long been the objects of her solicitude; and so much regard had she for their honour and reputation, that she made an offer to one of that family to withhold from the Public the letters, real or pretended, to another member of them, then deceased, for a valuable consideration....

"We have not another word to add upon the subject, except to enquire whether the Olive Wilmot, christened at Warwick as the daughter of Robert Wilmot in 1772, is the same Olive Wilmot who was christened in London, in 1772, as the daughter of the Duke of Cumberland? If not, there is here a most extraordinary coincidence of names, dates, and circumstances."

Her petition was disregarded, and the following year found her in prison for debt, whence she issued the appeal we have already quoted.

"We understand," said the *Gentleman's Magazine* in 1822, "that this heroic princess is still pursuing her claims. The boldness of her claims has produced an impression on the minds of many worthy individuals who may in consequence become the dupes of their own credulity.... But though Imposture may be suspected, it has not been proved, and we wish her a happy deliverance from all her difficulties."

But the Princess's appeal to the nation must have been answered to some extent, for we hear of her in the summer of 1822 driving about in her own carriage, her footmen wearing the royal liveries. In July, Sir Gerard Noel was induced by her supporters to move for an investigation of her claims in the House of Commons. But Sir Robert Peel, in a clear and convincing speech, disposed of her case, and seemed to set the matter at rest for ever. From this time the Princess was forced to give up her carriage and footmen, and she spent the rest of her life in poverty and obscurity.

After her death, however, her daughter, Mrs. Ryves,

taking the title of Princess Lavinia, took up her claim. Taking advantage of the Legitimacy Declaration Act of 1861, Mrs. Ryves brought her case into court. She first obtained a declaration of the validity of the marriage of her mother with her father. Having thus prepared the ground, she petitioned the court in 1866 to declare that the Duke of Cumberland and Olive Wilmot were legally married, and that Olive, afterwards Olive Serres, was their legitimate child. She produced innumerable documents, bequeathed her by her mother, signed by royalties and well-known people, to prove her royal descent. These the jury unanimously declared to be forgeries, and the case was dismissed.

"No less than eighty-three documents," said *The Times*, "were produced at the trial, and besides these there are about fifty more which have been referred to at different times. These, for the most part, consist of declarations and protestations of all the great personages introduced into the story, who would seem to have thought it the best means of keeping their secret by constantly committing it to little bits of paper. They are written, for the most part, on mere scraps, and the petitioner attempted to account for their size by alleging that they had been cut smaller by Lord Warwick, that they might be the easier kept. These documents are manifestly forgeries, whether we have regard to the hand-writing, to the supposed signatures which, the Attorney-General states, are sometimes not those which were commonly made use of by the personages intended, or to their contents, which are so egregiously absurd that none but a person more or less insane could have written them. The Lord Justice enumerated several of their absurdities; but it will be sufficient to mention that George III is represented as making away with the Duchy of Lancaster (in a gift to Mrs. Serres), which he had no power to do, and that this illegal act of royal prodigality is counter-signed by Pitt and Dunning. But one of the most suspicious points in these extraordinary documents is furnished by a certificate which, if genuine, would tend to invalidate the title of the present Royal Family to the Throne, and which, with the strange madness which marks the rest of the case, was evidently produced at first with a view of intimidation. At the back of one of the documents attesting the marriage of Olive Wilmot was a certificate affirming the marriage of George III in 1759 to a person named Hannah Lightfoot, and it was alleged that three children were the issue of this marriage, so that the children of the King by the Princess Charlotte were illegitimate. . . .

"In short, a wilder story, supported by more extravagant or more foolish forgeries, was never invented. Not the least curious part of the case is that if Mrs. Ryves had succeeded in making out that her mother was a Royal Princess she would have established at the same time her own illegitimacy. The alleged marriage of the Duke of Cumberland was celebrated before the Royal Marriage Act, and, consequently, if Mrs. Serres had been the Duke's daughter she would have been a Princess of the Blood Royal. But that act had been passed before her marriage with Mr. Serres, and would have rendered it invalid, so that her issue would have been illegitimate. As it is, Mrs. Ryves obtains a declaration of her legitimacy, but at the cost of her pretended royal descent."

17. BURKE AND HARE

AT No. 10 Surgeons' Square, Dr. Knox, the famous Edinburgh anatomist, held his demonstrations in front of large and enthusiastic classes. Taciturn, gloomy, and sour, he was intensely disliked by his colleagues, but, once inside the class-room, the brilliance of his lectures and the raciness of his stories made him the idol of his students. He certainly owed nothing of this popularity to his personal appearance, as his biographer and former pupil, Dr. Lonsdale, is obliged to admit. His head was bald and shiny, and the natural ugliness of his features was accentuated by the coarsening effect of the worst form of small-pox. " His involuntary twitchings were far from agreeable, especially those which affected his under-lip, the crossing of which from side to side produced a kind of smacking noise."[1] His only redeeming feature was his eye (he had but one), which, his admirer tells us, was " perfection itself." But what he lacked in physical charm he made up in sartorial elegance; he always appeared before his class immaculately dressed in the very height of fashion.

Dr. Knox, however, concerned himself little with what people were thinking of him, for he lived only for dissection, which in his opinion was by far the most valuable part of a medical training. The success of his demonstrations was largely due to the fact that his tables were more plentifully supplied than any of his rivals. He could not bear to see any of them empty, and thought nothing of the trouble or private expense he might incur in furnishing them with " subjects." He fired his students with the same enthusiasm, and in the vacation they would travel in search of bodies for the coming session.

[1] *The Life of Robert Knox*, by Henry Lonsdale.

But, like the rest of his profession, he was obliged to depend for his main supply on the "Resurrection-men"—those sinister beings who traded in dead bodies.

At night, when the lectures were over, they came to No. 10 with their wares. The porter, David Paterson, gave a brief glance at what they brought, asked them its age, sex, and condition, and paid them half their money in advance; he then stored the bodies in a cold, damp cellar. The next day, Dr. Knox, or one of his three assistants,[1] examined the body, and, if he was satisfied, would instruct the porter to pay the rest of what was owing. Out of this Paterson, no doubt, received a commission. They usually came during the night, for the bodies had all been obtained more or less surreptitiously. But however suspicious the circumstances might seem, Paterson had special instructions from Dr. Knox not to ask unnecessary questions, or to interfere in any way. The Resurrectionists were seldom known to him by their real names, and in order to escape recognition they were studiously nondescript in their dress and appearance.

Throughout the summer of 1828, Dr. Knox relied for his best subjects on two Irishmen, afterwards known to him by their names of William Burke and William Hare. Burke was an old patient of his, and, before he took to this trade, had often come to him for treatment. He was a sturdy, active little man, and could dance the Irish jig particularly well. He had a soft voice and a pleasant manner, but his eyes were hard and cruel. Hare was more heavily built, and in the contemporary drawing of him his pointed chin, high cheekbones, narrow, slanting eyes, and laughing grimace give him the look of a satyr. Both lived with a woman, each of whom had the most forbidding appearance. Helen M'Dougal, Burke's mistress, and "Mrs. Hare" were both of them gaunt and skinny, with every sign of degeneracy visible on their

[1] These three assistants afterwards became well known as Sir William Fergusson, T. W. Jones, and Alexander Miller.

drink-sodden faces. Burke afterwards gave an account of the way he and Hare came to enter the business.

It appears that in the winter of 1827 the Hares kept a tramps' lodging-house in the West Port, and one of their boarders died owing them £4. A day or two after his death, Hare proposed to Burke that they should sell his body to the doctors, but, as neither of them had ever been concerned in anything of the kind before, they did not know the procedure. They went to Surgeons' Square, where they saw a young man whom they took to be a student. They asked his advice, and he referred them to Dr. Knox. At No. 10 they were received by the doctor's assistants, who, hearing they had a body to dispose of, asked no questions, but told them to come back with it after dark. On their return they were cordially received, and given £7 10*s*. for the body. "Jones," said Burke, "said that they would be glad to see them again when they had any other body to dispose of."

Encouraged by this, they brought more and more bodies, until they outstripped all the professional Resurrectionists. They commanded top prices, for their bodies were in perfect condition, showed no trace of any natural disease, and had obviously never been interred. Dr. Knox personally complimented them on their "freshness," and, indeed, one of them was still warm when it arrived. This was the body of a young girl of more than ordinary beauty, which was immediately recognised by one of Dr. Knox's assistants as that of Mary Paterson, a well-known figure in the Edinburgh streets.

Next day, when she was laid on the table, her loveliness caused a sensation among the students, and Dr. Lonsdale describes how they crowded round her "to study a model worthy of Phidias and the best Greek art. Here was publicity beyond the professional walk; nay, more, a pupil of Knox's who had been in her company only a few nights previously stood aghast on observing the beautiful Laïs stretched in death, all ready for the scalpel of the anatomist. This student eagerly and sympathisingly sought for an explanation of her sudden death; Burke, on his next visit, was confronted with his questioner in the presence of two gentlemen, and declared that he bought the corpse from an old hag in the Cannongate, and that Paterson had killed herself when drunk. He offered to go and show them the house if they doubted him. His explanation was a possible one; it rested on the whisky tendency of all such women—and Paterson's body smelt of liquor when brought in—their reckless life and exposure, and their frequent abandonment when at death's door."[1] But she was not dissected for many weeks, for Dr. Knox, wishing to illustrate in his lectures the perfection of female development, kept her body preserved, appropriately enough, in whisky.

Nor was Mary to be the last of the town's characters to be found on Dr. Knox's tables. One day in October, "Daft Jamie," a poor idiot boy, was missing. That evening Burke and Hare brought to No. 10 a heavy tea-chest. It was not opened until the next morning, and then they saw the body of the unfortunate boy. Dr. Knox ridiculed the idea that it was Jamie, but, although he was the latest and the "freshest" arrival, ordered his immediate dissection; within an hour recognition ceased to be possible.

It was only a few weeks after this incident that the firm of Messrs. Burke & Hare suddenly went smash. The body of an old woman was discovered hidden in Burke's room in suspicious circumstances, and the two of them, with their wives, were arrested and accused of murder. From the evidence of the neighbours the story was this.

On Friday, October 31st, 1828, a little old woman came into the shop in the West Port where Burke was accustomed to have his morning drink, and begged for alms. Hearing her speak with a brogue, he claimed her as a compatriot, and asked her name and where she came from. Her name was Docherty, and he made the pleasing

[1] *The Life of Robert Knox*, by Henry Lonsdale.

discovery that she was a relation of his mother; and cordially invited her to come and have breakfast with him. Presently she was seen entering his house. M'Dougal welcomed her husband's relation, and they pressed her to spend the night with them. She accepted, and, to make room for her, their two lodgers, Mr. and Mrs. Gray, were sent to stay with the Hares. It was Hallowe'en, and they bought plenty of liquor in anticipation of a festive evening. Hare and his wife joined them, and soon they were all making merry, drinking and dancing. During the night a noise of quarrelling and cries of murder were heard; but the neighbours, knowing that they were all half drunk, and having heard similar uproars from that quarter before, paid no attention. There was quiet for a time—another outburst of noise—and then silence.

At midnight, Burke sent a message to David Paterson, Dr. Knox's porter, to say that he wished to see him at once. Paterson went round to the house, and Burke, pointing to some straw lying at the foot of the bed, whispered that he had something for the doctor which would be ready the next day.

When a neighbour came in after breakfast, she found Burke, M'Dougal, and two others, drinking. Burke was sitting on a chair at the foot of the bed and freely dispensing the whisky. When he had filled all their glasses, he threw some more upwards in the direction of the bed, giving as his reason that he wanted to empty the bottle in order to get it refilled. She commented on the noise in the night, and asked what had become of their visitor. There had been a dispute, she was told; "she had a fit of drink-like, but she was quiet enough now."

Meanwhile, Mrs. Gray had come in with her husband to look for some articles she had left under the straw at the foot of the bed where they were accustomed to sleep. She was smoking a pipe at the time, and, as she came near, Burke swore at her and told her to "keep out of there."

Mrs. Gray came in at intervals throughout the day, but the chair at the foot of the bed was always occupied, and she was never allowed to approach. At last, between five and six, she and her husband found the room empty. They lifted the straw, and there lay the naked corpse of the little old woman. They hastily packed up their belongings and fled from the room.

The police were told at once of their discovery, but by the time they arrived at the house the body was gone. Early on Sunday morning, Dr. Knox's dissecting-rooms were visited, and Paterson produced a box from the cellar, which had arrived the previous evening but had not yet been unpacked. It was opened, and the body of the beggar-woman was revealed.

Although their guilt was perfectly plain, it was difficult to prove, for direct evidence was wanting, and the most the doctors could say was that her death was "probably due to suffocation." All four prisoners strenuously declared their innocence, and it seemed likely that they would get off scot-free. In this dilemma, Hare and his wife were allowed to turn King's evidence, and on their testimony Burke was hanged.[1]

M'Dougal was more fortunate, for Mrs. Hare swore that neither she nor M'Dougal was present when the murder was committed. Burke and Hare, she said, began to fight, and, while they were struggling, she and M'Dougal retreated into the passage. When they returned, there was no sign of their visitor, and they asked no questions. On being asked whether she had not felt suspicious, she replied, "I had a supposition that she had been murdered; *I have seen such tricks before*." M'Dougal's charge was accordingly found "not proven," and she was the first of the three to be released.

Before his execution on January 28th, 1829, Burke

[1] After his execution, Burke was publicly dissected by Dr. Knox's chief rival, Professor Munro, who at the same time lectured on the murderer's brain to a large audience of students. The skeleton was placed, where it can still be seen, in the Anatomical Museum of the University of Edinburgh.

made full confession, and his revelations roused the public to frenzy. He described in a cold-blooded way how they killed their first victim, and how, finding their method so successful, they repeated it on all of the subsequent occasions.

"Early last spring, 1828, a woman from Gilmerton came to Hare's house as a nightly lodger—Hare keeping seven beds for lodgers: That she was a stranger, and she and Hare became merry, and drank together; and next morning she was very ill in consequence of what she had got, and she sent for more drink, and she and Hare drank together, and she became very sick and vomited; and at that time she had not risen from bed, and Hare then said that they would try and smother her in order to dispose of her body to the doctors: That she was lying on her back in the bed, and quite insensible from drink, and Hare clapped his hand on her mouth and nose, and the declarant laid himself across her body, in order to prevent her making any disturbance—and she never stirred; and they took her out of bed and undressed her, and put her into a chest; and they mentioned to Dr. Knox's young men that they had another subject, and Mr. Miller *sent a porter to meet them* in the evening at the back of the Castle; and declarant and Hare carried the chest till they met the porter, and they accompanied the porter with the chest to Dr. Knox's class-room, and Dr. Knox came in when they were there; the body was cold and still. *Dr. Knox approved of its being so fresh, but did not ask any questions*. . . .

". . . Declares, with the exception of the body of Docherty. . . . That there were no marks of violence on any of the subjects, and they were sufficiently cold to prevent any suspicion on the part of the Doctors; and, *at all events, they might be cold and still enough before the box was opened up*, and he and Hare always told some story of their having purchased the subjects from some relation or other person who had the means of disposing of them, about different parts of the town, and the statements which they made were such as to prevent the

Doctors having any suspicions; and *no suspicions were expressed by Dr. Knox or any of his assistants, and no questions asked tending to show that they had suspicions.*"[1] [2]

"They often said to one another that no person could find them out, no one being present at the murders but themselves, and that they might be as well hanged for a sheep as a lamb. They made it their business to look out for persons to decoy into their houses to murder them. Burke declares, when they kept the mouth and nose shut a very few minutes, they could make no resistance. . . . Burke declares that it was God's providence that put a stop to their murdering career, or he does not know how far they might have gone with it, even to attack people on the streets as they were so successful, and always met with a ready market: *that when they delivered a body they were always told to get more.*"[3]

Burke admitted as many as sixteen murders, though he owned that on such a trivial point his memory was unreliable. He thought that "Dr. Knox would be more likely to remember by the dates of paying him the money for them." There were many who believed, and who did not hesitate to say, that Dr. Knox knew far more about the murders than only their dates. But he kept a dignified silence, and how much he had seen with that one eye can only be a matter for conjecture.

[1] From Burke's official confession.

[2] "When the reader notices what is printed above in *italics*, he will see that the facility with which Burke and Hare got a purchaser for the body of Donald (the first of their transactions) and the desire to 'see them again when they had any other body to dispose of,' must have been great inducements to such miscreants to commence their career of murder."—*Original note.*

[3] From Burke's second confession, which appeared in the *Edinburgh Evening Courant*, February 7th, 1829.

LADY FLORA HASTINGS
(After a painting by E. Hawkins)

p. 111

18. LADY FLORA HASTINGS

From the Lady Flora Hastings, Lady of the Bedchamber to the Duchess of Kent, to Hamilton Fitzgerald, Esq.

Buckingham Palace,
March 8th, 1839.

My dear Uncle,—Knowing what a very good-natured place Brussels is, I have not a hope that you have not already heard a story with which I am told London is ringing; but you shall, at all events, have from my own pen the account of the diabolical conspiracy from which it has pleased God to preserve the Duchess of Kent and myself; for that it was intended to ruin the whole concern, though I was to be the first victim, I have no more doubt than *that a certain foreign lady, whose hatred to the Duchess is no secret, pulled the wires*, though it has not been brought home to her yet. I told you I was ill when I came to town, having been suffering for some weeks from bilious derangement, with its agreeable accompaniments, pain in the side and swelling of the stomach. I placed myself immediately under the care of Sir James Clark, who, being physician to the Duchess as well as to the Queen, was the natural person to consult. Unfortunately, he either did not pay much attention to my ailments, or did not quite understand them, for in spite of medicines the bile did not take its departure. However, by dint of walking and porter I gained a little strength, and, as I did so, the swelling subsided in a very remarkable degree. You may guess, therefore, my indignant surprise when, about a fortnight since, Sir James Clark came into my room and announced to me the conviction of the Ladies of the Palace that I must be privately married, or at least ought to be—a conviction into which I found him completely talked over. In answer to all his exhortations to "confession" "as the only means of saving my character:" I returned, as you may believe, an indignant but steady denial that there was anything to confess. Upon which he told me that nothing but my submitting to medical examination would ever satisfy them, and remove the stigma from my name. I found the subject had been brought before the Queen's notice, and all this had been discussed, and arranged, and *denounced* to me without *one* word having been said to my own mistress, one suspicion hinted, or her sanction obtained for their proposing such a thing to me. From me Sir James went to the Duchess, and announced his conviction that I was in the family way, and was followed by Lady Portman, who conveyed a message from her Majesty to her mother to say that the Queen would not permit me to appear till the examination had decided matters. Lady Portman (who with, you will grieve to hear, Lady Tavistock, are those whose names are mentioned as most active against me) took the opportunity of distinctly expressing her conviction of my guilt. My beloved mistress, who never for one moment *doubted* me, told them she knew me and my principles, and my family, too well to listen to such a charge. However, the edict was given. The next day, having obtained the Duchess's very reluctant consent, for she could not bear the idea of my being exposed to such a humiliation (but I felt it right to her, and to my family and myself, that a point-blank refutation should be instantly given to the lie), I submitted myself to the most rigid examination, and I have the satisfaction of possessing a certificate, signed by my accuser, Sir James Clark, and also by Sir Charles Clarke, stating, as strongly as language can state it, that "there are no grounds for believing pregnancy does exist, or ever has existed." I wrote to my brother who, though suffering from influenza, came up instantly.

It would be too long to detail all his proceedings, but nothing can be more manly, spirited, and judicious than his conduct. He exacted and obtained from Lord Melbourne a distinct disavowal of his participation in the plot, and would not leave town till he had obtained an audience of the Queen, at which, while disclaiming his belief of any wish on the part of her Majesty to injure me, he very plainly, but respectfully stated his opinion of those who had counselled her, and his resolution to find out the originator of the slander, and bring him or her to punishment. I am quite sure the Queen does not understand what they have betrayed her into. She has endeavoured to show her regret by her civility to me, and expressed it most handsomely with tears in her eyes. The Duchess was perfect. A mother could not have been kinder, and she took up the insult as a personal one, directed as it was at a person attached to her service, and devoted to her. She immediately dismissed Sir James Clark, and refused to see Lady Portman, and would neither re-appear, or suffer me to re-appear at the Queen's table for many days. She has crowned her goodness by a most beautiful letter she has written to poor mamma, whom the accounts, kept from her while there was a hope that matters might not become public, would reach to-day. I am told there is but one feeling as respects me—sympathy for the insult offered to one whose very name should be a protection to her, and that in many places the feeling is loudly expressed that public reparation should have been offered me by the dismissal of the slanderers. This does not, however, appear to be the view of the Ministers ; and as personally I wish for no revenge on those who have insulted me, I cannot say I much regret it, though I doubt whether they are quite judicious as respects the general feeling. And poor Clark who has been the women's tool, can hardly be sacrificed alone. The Duchess has stood by me gallantly, and I love her better than ever. She is the most generous-souled woman possible, and such a heart ! This business made her very ill. It shattered me, too, very much, and I am wretchedly thin ; but, under Dr. Chamber's good management, I am getting round, and hope soon to be well. Hastings says he has not done with the business, nor never will while there is anything left to sift.

Good-bye, my dear uncle. I blush to send you so revolting a tale, but I wished you to know the truth, the whole truth, and nothing but the truth—and you are welcome to tell it right and left.

Your affectionate niece,

FLORA ELIZ. HASTINGS.

Lady Flora's health continued to decline, and she died at Buckingham Palace on July 5th in the same year.

19. PRINCE LOUIS NAPOLEON'S LANDING AT BOULOGNE

The Annual Register, 1840.

An absurd attempt was made in the month of August by Prince Louis Napoleon Bonaparte, to bring about a revolution in that kingdom (France) in favour of himself and his family. He hired an English steamer called the *City of Edinburgh* in London, and embarking there on board with Count Montholon, General Voisin, and fifty-three other persons, besides a tame eagle (which was destined to act no unimportant part in the drama), on Thursday, the 6th of August, landed at Boulogne. They marched into the town about 5 o'clock in the morning, and traversed the streets shouting " Vive L'Empereur." The first attempt they made was at the guardhouse, where they summoned the troops to surrender or join with them. The only man who proved a traitor to his sovereign was a young Lieutenant of the 42nd, who tried to induce the soldiers to accompany the Prince. He, however, failed in the attempt, and as the national guard soon beat to arms and began to muster in force, Prince Louis retreated with his motley followers out of the town, towards the pillar on the height above Boulogne, called the Colonne de Napoleon, and there he planted a flag with a golden eagle at the top of the staff. Finding, however, that he was hard pressed with unequal odds, he retreated to the beach and was captured in attempting to escape to the steamer which lay in the harbour. His followers were also taken, but one unfortunate man was shot while struggling in the waves. When Prince Louis landed at Boulogne he immediately scattered printed papers, addressed to the French nation, in which he commenced by saying that the Bourbon dynasty had ceased to reign, and that he appointed M. Thiers, President of the Council, and Marshal Clausel, Minister of War. We must not forget to mention that the tame eagle on board the *Edinburgh* had been intended to create stage effect, by being let loose from the vessel and flying straight to the Colonne de Napoleon, where it was to alight, and thus be an omen of success to the revolution. For this purpose we believe the bird had been trained to take its food from Prince Louis Napoleon, but we certainly cannot explain how these mad visionaries hoped to make it play its part in the tragi-comedy they were acting.

20. THE EXTERMINATION OF THE GREAT AUK

A TRAVELLER to St. Kilda's in the 'eighties heard one of the inhabitants describe a remarkable incident in his life. Forty years before, said the old man, he and four others had caught and killed a witch. But from his account it became clear to the listener (and his impression has been subsequently confirmed by ornithologists) that they had captured not a supernatural being, but a creature almost as mythical—a great auk. The last of this species was seen on the island in 1821, and, until this episode came to light, it had been considered as extinct as the dodo or the dinosaur. The story, as repeated by the traveller, was as follows:

"They found the bird on a ledge of rock; they caught it asleep, tied its legs together, took it up to their bothy, kept it alive for three days, and then killed it with a stick, thinking it might be a witch. They threw the body behind the bothy and left it there.

"It was Malcolm M'Donald who actually laid hold of the bird, and held it by the neck with his two hands, till the others came up and tied its legs. It used to make a great noise, like that made by a gannet, but much louder, when shutting its mouth. It opened its mouth when anyone came near it. It nearly cut the rope with its bill. A storm arose, and that, together with the size of the bird and the noise it made, caused them to think it was a witch. It was killed on the 3rd day after it was caught, and M'Kinnon declares they were beating it for an hour with two large stones before it was dead: he was the most frightened of all the men, and advised the killing of it. The capture took place in July in or about 1840."[1]

[1] Quoted in *Fauna of the Outer Hebrides*, by Harvie-Brown and Buckley.

21. A SECRET TREATY

COUNT JOSEPH ORSI describes in his *Recollections* an interview which took place in London on December 3rd, 1845, between himself and the exiled Duke of Brunswick. Count Orsi was a Florentine merchant who acted as banker to the Bonaparte family, and for many years had been an intimate friend of Prince Louis Napoleon (afterwards Napoleon III). To him the Prince had entrusted the practical details of both the Strasbourg and Boulogne adventures. He was arrested with the Prince at Boulogne, and served a term of imprisonment at Ham in the same fortress, where at this date the Prince was still incarcerated.

"The outward appearance of Brunswick house is far from being attractive, and from the heavy gloomy aspect of the exterior building, one would fancy it more fit for a prison than for the residence of a gentleman.

"The Duke had made it still more unsightly. From the entrance gate to the house, which stood in the middle of a large courtyard, nothing struck your eyes that was cheerful or comfortable. Everything was stiff, dull, and as silent as a graveyard. Two large dogs chained to the wall were the vigilant guardians of the place. Twice had I to show the letter of audience before I could get in. I was at last ushered into a dark cold room, having a round table in the centre, and four chairs, two of which were armchairs by the fireside. A single candle was lit on the table, the walls were bare, and no vestige of comfort could be seen.

"Twenty minutes had already elapsed, when I saw a slight movement in a thick curtain hanging over the side door of the room. All of a sudden the head of a man covered with a huge black plush hood, which concealed all but the nose, peeped in through the curtains. The hood formed part of a long gown, also of black plush, which was fastened to the waist by a thick silk cord. It was the Duke of Brunswick. His hands were plunged in the two side pockets of his *robe de chambre*, grasping a revolver in each of them, as I learnt from himself a few days after my first interview.

"The Duke came right to the table, which stood between us as a sort of barrier. His eyes were flashing through the narrow opening of his hood, as if he imagined I was planning to commit a murder. We looked at each other for a few seconds, which seemed to me to be a long time; at last he broke out:

"'You asked for an audience; what is it you want?'

"'Your Highness will, I hope, allow me to say that the object for which I came here is such as to require some little time, and I shall consider it a favour if you will let me explain it while your Highness is seated.'

"By a movement of his hand he pointed to an armchair by the fireside. The Duke sat opposite to me.

"'I entreat your Highness to make some allowance for the agitated state of my mind, owing to the delicate and difficult mission entrusted to me; and if what I am going to say is unpalatable to you, I crave most earnestly your pardon for having so intruded upon your Highness. Remembering with pleasure the friendly relations which existed between your Highness and Prince Louis Napoleon during his stay in this country, and acting under the impression that political interests of the greatest magnitude might find a favourable issue in the combined efforts of your Highness and himself, the Prince, now a prisoner of Ham, has requested me to make an appeal to your Highness's generosity for a loan he requires to effect his escape from the prison.'

"Scarcely had I uttered the last words, than the Duke, pulling back his hood with both his hands by a frantic movement, showed his denuded head, and with a sort of indescribable yell, exclaimed:

" 'What! A loan? Did I understand you right? Say it again, say it again'

" I remained silent a few seconds. The Duke looked at me without uttering a word.

" 'It is quite natural that your Highness should feel surprise at an application which is one of no ordinary character, but no one better than yourself could see at a glance the political interests at stake, in refusing or complying with the request of the Prince for the loan of £6,000.'

" The Duke rose as pale as a ghost, and stretched his arm to lay hold of the bell-rope. Before he could ring, I rose and said:

" 'For God's sake, please, your Highness, listen to me. I have much to say that can alter your mind. I implore you to hear me for a few seconds.'

" The Duke flung the bell-rope against the wall, and in a stout, stern voice, said:

'I do not know which I have to admire the most—my own patience or your unheard-of impudence. A loan of £6,000 to Prince Napoleon, indeed! How likely that I should agree to it! *Your* Prince seems to be unaware that I am a staunch republican. I am the friend of Cavaignac, of Marrast, and of all the chief leaders of that party; I am the largest shareholder in the "National," which I supply with all the money it requires. Backed by the republican principles, I will and shall wage war against all monarchical powers, and Germany in particular. Your Prince's advent to France means nothing if it does not mean royalty or empire. I will not betray my new friends. I refuse the Prince the £6,000 you ask in his name.'

" This declaration of republican principles on the part of the Duke of Brunswick took me aback. I did not expect that. I had never heard of his being now mixed up with the 'National' party. . . . I saw it was all over. There was a moment of dead silence on both sides. We were face to face for a few seconds. At last I took my hat and walked to the door, which I opened and held by the knob.

" 'I hope your Highness will forgive my intruding upon you as I have done. In giving me the mission of appealing to you for the means of recovering his liberty, Prince Louis Napoleon meant something more than putting himself under any pecuniary obligation towards you as a friend. His views were broader, and, under existing circumstances, were more conducive to the political welfare of both. In accepting this mission, and on your granting me this audience, for which I shall ever be grateful, I felt sure of having at last met with the only man capable, by his lofty position, to understand the advantages to be derived by linking his future political prospects to those of a man whose popularity was then at the highest point. I had imagined that your Highness was aware of the true state of public opinion in France as regards the name of Napoleon. Had I been allowed to converse freely with your Highness, I would have brought home to you the irresistible conviction that the prisoner of Ham was destined to mark the milestone at which the old world will finish and the new will begin. I own that my disappointment is extreme. May your Highness not think me too presumptuous in predicting that in less than two years you will regret the refusal made to the demand of the Prince.'

"I bowed and was retiring, when the Duke said: '*Restez, je vous prie.* I never believed in prophecies, and still less do I believe in the one referring to the prisoner of Ham. In fact, I have as great a reluctance in believing in prophecies as I have in doing anything of importance on any day bearing in its number the figure 7. Had you asked me for an audience on the 7th, or the 17th, or the 27th, I would have taken no notice of it. However, your prophesying to me the future advent to power of the Prince in such glowing colours has awakened my curiosity. I should like to see whether your prophecy will turn out true. Mind,

I make no engagement by speaking thus: but as you seem to know the state of public opinion in France better than I do, I may be induced to do something for the Prince if you can show me in a tangible and comprehensive way that the advent of the Prince to the supreme power in France is simply *a question of time*.'

"It took me one hour and a half to lay before the Duke the real state of French politics. He never interrupted me. At last he got up, and after walking across the room backwards and forwards for some time, like a man who awakens from a dream, he said: 'Write to the Prince that I put £6,000 at his disposal on the following terms:

"'(1) That the Prince shall accept three bills for £2,000 each, payable in five years at five per cent.

"'(2) That £800 out of the £6,000 shall be taken by him in shares of the "National" and at par.

"'(3) That an offensive and defensive alliance shall be entered into between him and me, by which the Prince, in the event of his coming to be elected king, president, or emperor, will engage to assist me in my views on Germany, I undertaking to do the same on his behalf in the event of my advent to power in Germany before he succeeds in France.

"'(4) That you shall start immediately for Ham with Mr. George Thomas Smith, in order to ascertain the state of affairs and carry out the programme in its entirety.'

"I agreed, in the name of the Prince, to the terms proposed by his Highness. Two days afterwards I started for Paris, where I met Mr. Smith, who had left London the day before.

"I had great difficulties to overcome before I could obtain permission to see the Prince. Having been a prisoner myself for five years, I was suspected in high quarters. After fifteen days of solicitation, I received the necessary leave to see the Prince with Mr. Smith; but as no one was allowed to see the Prince except in the presence of the Governor, I was obliged to make it appear that Mr. Smith was the purchaser of valuable pictures belonging to the Prince. The interview referred only to this transaction. The bills to be accepted by the Prince were given to him while we were shaking hands. They were returned to me, with the treaty[1] written on satin, in the afternoon, on taking leave of the Prince. . . .

"Mr. Smith and I arrived in London two days later, and the money having been paid to Messrs. Baring Brothers to the account of the Prince, the transaction was completed."

As little is remembered now of the eccentric Duke of Brunswick, it is necessary to give a brief account of his

[1] The text of the treaty was as follows:

"We, C.F.A.G. Duke of Brunswick, and we, Prince Louis Napoleon Bonaparte, hereby settle and agree as follows:

"ARTICLE I—We promise and make oath, on our honour and the gospel, to assist one another; We, Charles Duke of Brunswick, to be reinstated on the throne of the Duchy of Brunswick, to effect, if possible, the unity of Germany, and to grant her a constitution adapted to her temperament, requirements, and progress of the times; and we, Louis Napoleon Bonaparte, to restore France to her own right of sovereignty, of which she was deprived in 1830 and to enable her to pronounce in full liberty upon the form of Government she prefers to adopt.

"ARTICLE II—He who first attains the supreme power, under whatever title it may be, undertakes to settle the other with arms and money, and to authorise and facilitate the enlistment of such a number of volunteers as are considered sufficient for the execution of his project.

"ARTICLE III—Pending our exile we engage to help one another on every occasion, with a view to regain possession of our political rights wrested from us, and should one of us succeed in returning to his own country, the other shall uphold the cause of his ally by every possible means.

"ARTICLE IV—We engage never to promise, to enter into, or sign any renunciation or abdication injurious to our political or civil rights, but to console and help one another like brothers in every circumstance of our lives.

"ARTICLE V—Should we think proper hereafter, and when in full enjoyment of our liberty, to modify the present treaty as may be prompted by our respective positions, or by our common interest, we hereby engage to revise by mutual accord any clauses in this compact which might be found deficit from the circumstance under which they were framed.

"Approved, in the presence of

"COUNT JOSEPH ORSI and
"G. T. SMITH."

career. He took refuge in London in 1830, when his subjects, exasperated by his erratic rule, rose against him and burnt his palace to ashes. He was coldly received by the Royal Family, and this is hardly to be wondered at, for ever since he came of age, in 1827, he had persistently heaped abuse on his uncle and guardian, George IV.[1] Nor did he make himself more agreeable to William IV, and when the Duke's private estates in Brunswick were taken out of his control by the King and the Duke's brother and successor, William, on the ground of his insanity, his rage with the King knew no bounds. Thomas Duncombe, a Radical M.P., took up his cause and twice presented petitions to the House of Commons. He found, however, that the Duke was a difficult person to help, for at the very moment when he was trying to propitiate Parliament the Duke would issue a bombastic proclamation with sentences in it like this : "With regard to those swindling traitors who wield the arbitrary power of robbers at Brunswick they are fully aware that the scaffold and the headsman await their doomed heads, and that their estates, enriched through our spoil, will be confiscated to answer for their larcenies."

In spite of the failure of these petitions, Duncombe continued to act as the Duke's self-appointed political adviser, and it was his confidential secretary, G. T. Smith, who witnessed the treaty and went over to Ham to interview the Prince in the Duke's interests.

The truth was that, though the Duke's behaviour was unquestionably odd, he was far better fitted to manage his own affairs than most of us, for by judicious investments, chiefly in precious stones, of which he was an expert judge, he increased his capital until he was worth nearly a million. He showed considerable acumen, incidentally, in the terms of his loan to the Prince, for the shares he managed to "palm off" on him were quite worthless.

[1] George IV had married Princess Caroline of Brunswick, the Duke's aunt. For this reason and also because he was King of the neighbouring state, Hanover, he was chosen to act as Regent during the Duke's minority.

Napoleon discovered this very shortly, to his disgust, and as soon as he came into power made it a pretext to repudiate the treaty.

Napoleon's biographers have thrown doubt on the existence of this treaty, since no trace of it was ever found among the Imperial papers. They admit, however, that soon after this date there were undoubted indications of a heavy expenditure by him of money mysteriously obtained. The text of the treaty also appears in the *Life and Correspondence of Thomas Slingsby Duncombe*, and it is difficult to see what motive both his biographer and Count Orsi could have for concocting the story.

22. GENERAL TOM THUMB'S FIRST TRIP TO EUROPE

From a pamphlet printed by T. Brettell (1846).

THAT trite but expressive saying, " He must be seen to be believed," holds good in General Tom Thumb's case,[1] for the imagination cannot conceive the possibility of such extreme littleness ; and we find it difficult with the best artistic aids to picture him on the mental retina—a perfect MINIATURE MAN, only 25 *inches high*, perfect and elegant in his proportions, and weighing only *fifteen pounds* !

When standing on the floor, or parading the room, which he does, dressed in a style of Bond Street elegance, and with all the grace, dignity, and ease of a finished gentleman, his head scarcely reaches to the knees of a person of ordinary stature, and is about on a level with the seats of the chairs, sofas and ottomans of the drawing-room.

Unlike many other dwarfs, the General is exquisitely proportioned, his head being not large, but of the proper symmetry, and beautifully developed, and his hands and feet the prettiest ever seen. His boots are perfect Wellingtons made of the softest kid, by the most fashionable artists ; his clothes are the production of the most distinguished tailors, and his gloves are of necessity furnished to order, for nothing so small and fairy-like were ever before manufactured. His canes, of which he has several, are from ten to twelve inches long, and his hats, for the various occasions, are of themselves curiosities.

Soon after he entered London, he was honoured by the command of Royalty to appear at the Palace and received

[1] His real name was Charles S. Stratton.

from Queen Victoria and Prince Albert, not only tributes of wonder and admiration, but the most substantial tokens of their royal favour. This visit he several times repeated, until he was styled the "pet of the Palace." At the Princess's Theatre, he drew immense crowds, and portraits of him were the chief attractions in all the pictorial papers of the time. Through Scotland and Ireland he went, winning golden opinions from all men—aye, and women too; and then the Little General visited Paris in February 1845, and his little Equipage appeared at Longchamps in the great procession at the Champs Élysées. The General was soon summoned to the Tuileries, where he went several times, and was loaded with presents. He engaged the elegant *Salle des Concerts*, Rue Vivienne, and his levées for four successive months were crowded with the beauty and fashion of France. After his Evening Levée he appeared for seventy nights in a most interesting play, called "Petit Poucet," written expressly for the little General, and in which he showed great talent, and received the highest encomiums of the public and press.

We copy the following articles from the *Journal des Débats* in order to afford our readers an adequate idea of the flattering reception the General met with at the Court of France:—

"*Sunday evening, May 23rd*, 1845.

"General Tom Thumb accompanied by his guide, Mr. Barnum, has had the high honour of being received at the palace of the Tuileries, by their Majesties the King and Queen of the French, who condescendingly personally addressed the General several questions respecting his birth, parentage and career.

"After an interview which lasted upwards of an hour, during which the General went through various performances, much to the delight of the Royal Family, and especially to the young Princes, the General withdrew, amidst many plaudits, and laden with precious presents.

"The King presented this courteous and fantastic little man with a splendid pin, set in brilliants, but it has the inconvenience of being out of proportion to his height and size. It might answer for his sword. However the General expressed his desire to place it in his cravat, which he did; having previously unfastened the one which he received from Fanny Ellsler. This was no infidelity of Tom Thumb's, but merely an act of courtesy and deference toward the King. For we are assured that of all the honours bestowed upon him, none seemed to give him more real pleasure than those bestowed by the pretty dancer.

"It is said that one day, pursued to the utmost in a public place by the curiosity of the Americans, he perceived far off Fanny Ellsler wearing her muff. Tom now made sure of a retreat, for he ran to her, jumped into her arms, thrust himself into the warm folds of her ermine, and thus escaped his pursuers.

"Tom Thumb is, in fact, of extraordinary lightness and nimbleness, even as a dwarf. In the King's presence he executed an original dance, which was neither the polka, nor the mazurka, nor indeed anything known. This dance was evidently invented for the General, and no one will ever venture to try it after him. The same may be said of another exercise which, with marked pleasure, he performs. We mean his personations of the Grecian Statues, or his embodiment, by attitudes of his frame and limbs, of scenes familiar in Ancient History. Thus, raised on a round table, he successively reproduces—'David's combat with Goliath,' 'The Fighting Gladiator,' 'Sampson Carrying off the Gates of Gaza' and 'Hercules Struggling with the Nemeaan Lion.' We believe he was asked to personify the 'Apollo Belvedere' and the 'Venus de Medici,' and doubtless he would have done so, had he not been prevented by a kind consideration for his health and strength, already tried by his long performance. We prefer seeing Tom Thumb when he appears in the character of a gentleman; he takes out his watch and tells you the hour, or offers you a pinch of snuff, or some pastilles, or a cigar, each of which are of uniformity with his size. He is still better when he sits in a golden chair, crossing his legs and looking at you with a knowing and almost mocking air. It is thus that he is amusing ; he is never more inimitable than when he imitates nothing—when he is himself. His originality can cost him but little effort ; there is scarcely anything to do ; let him but show himself, for no one resembles him.

Tom Thumb terminated his *soirée* at the Tuileries by a very brilliant exhibition of himself in his Highland Costume. His bonnet, which he wears in beautiful style, is surmounted by a plume, which, it is understood was presented him by the Queen of England. He handles his claymore with dexterity, and kills his enemy at the first cut. The brilliant plaid folds advantageously on his shoulders ; below his waist you perceive two vigorous legs with pretty little feet attached thereto. This costume is the General's triumph. We will not mention a celebrated uniform[1] which he wore in London, and which was amazingly successful with our over-sea neighbours. The General Tom Thumb had too much good taste to take this costume to the Tuileries. We hope, then, as he possesses such fine feelings, that while he sojourns in Paris, he will leave it at the bottom of his portmanteau."

[1] Costume of Napoleon.

23. THE ESCAPE FROM HAM

For six years Prince Louis Napoleon (afterwards Napoleon III) had been incarcerated in the fortress at Ham, a little town some miles to the north of Paris. Until lately he had endured his imprisonment with patience, and had passed the time, almost contentedly, in writing books. But, although he lived in comparative comfort, the surrounding country was low-lying and malarial, and his health now began to fail. When news reached him in May, 1846, that his father, the ex-King of Holland, was critically ill in Florence, the loss of his liberty became unendurable to him. He applied for permission to visit his father, but it was granted on conditions he would not accept. At the same time, Louis Philippe, realising that the death of King Louis, by which the Prince would become the heir to the Imperial throne, might awake in him fresh aspirations, guarded the prisoner more closely than ever. The Prince decided to escape, and his plan, which was entirely successful, was extraordinary only in its simplicity. He merely walked out of the fortress alone in full daylight.

An enquiry followed, and evidence was given which partially solves the mystery of why he was not recognised. It appears that, in order to degrade the Prince in their eyes, the soldiers were forbidden to salute him, and consequently in their embarrassment they used to avoid looking in his direction ; thus many of them were unfamiliar with his appearance.

A few days after he regained his freedom he wrote a letter describing how he effected his escape.

To the Editor of the " Progrès du Pas-de-Calais."

My dear M. Dégeorge,—The desire of once more seeing my father in this world has prompted me to undertake an enterprise the boldest which I have attempted, and for which more resolution and courage were necessary than for those of Strasbourg and Boulogne, for I had determined not to endure the ridicule which is the lot of persons arrested under a disguise, and a failure would have been insupportable. But listen to the details of my escape.

The fortress, as you know, was guarded by 400 men, who furnished a daily guard of 60 soldiers planted as sentinels within and without the castle. In addition, the gate of the prison was kept by three gaolers, two of them always on duty. It was, therefore, necessary first to pass them, next to traverse the whole interior court, in front of the commandant's windows ; having arrived at the gate, it was necessary to pass the wicket, kept by a soldier *de planton*, and a serjeant, a turnkey, a sentinel, and least of all a post of 30 men.

Being desirous of avoiding all understandings with the garrison, it was of course necessary to assume a disguise, and as considerable repairs were being made in the chambers which I used, it was easy to adopt a workman's dress. My good and faithful Charles Thélin[1] procured my blouse and sabots ; I cut off my moustache and took a plank upon my shoulder.

At half past six o'clock on Monday morning[2] I saw the workmen enter. As soon as they came to their work Charles took them into a chamber to drink, in order to remove them out of my way. I was also determined to call one of the keepers upstairs whilst Dr. Conneau conversed with the others. Scarcely, however, was I out of my room when I was accosted by a workman, who took me for one of his companions. At the bottom of the stairs I found myself face to face with the keeper. Luckily I screened myself with the plank which I carried, and I reached the court, always contriving to keep the plank towards the sentinels and those whom I met.

As I passed in front of the first sentinel I let my pipe fall ; I stopped, however, to pick up the fragments. I next met the officer of the guard, but he was reading a letter and did not notice me. The soldiers at the wicket

[1] The Prince's valet. [2] May 25, 1846.

seemed surprised at my figure; the drummer especially looked at me several times. In the meantime, however, the *planton* of the guard opened the gate, and I found myself outside the fortress. Then I met two workmen who were approaching me, and who looked at me with attention. I put the plank on the side towards them; they appeared, however, so curious that I thought I should not be able to escape them, when I heard them say: "Ah, it is Berthon."

Once beyond the walls, I walked rapidly towards the road to St. Quentin. Shortly after, Charles, who the evening before had engaged a cabriolet for himself, joined me, and we arrived at St. Quentin. I crossed the town on foot, after having got rid of my blouse. Charles having procured a post-chaise under pretence of a drive to Cambray, we arrived without hindrance at Valenciennes, from whence I took the railroad. I was provided with a Belgian passport, which was never asked for.

During this time Conneau, always so devoted to me, remained in prison, and made believe I was ill, in order to give me time to gain the frontier. I trust he will not be maltreated; this, as you may well suppose, would be a great grief to me. . . .

Adieu, my dear M. Dégeorge; although free, I am very unhappy. Receive the assurance of my warm friendship, and, if you can, endeavour to be useful to my dear Conneau.

NAPOLEON LOUIS.

On Tuesday the Prince was back in his old haunts in London, and that evening electrified Lady Blessington's guests by his re-appearance at her dinner-table.

"On the first day of Louis Napoleon's arrival in London after the escape from Ham," wrote one of them,[1] "I was one of a party of five—Lady Blessington, D'Orsay, Marguerite Power, his sister Ellen, and myself—who sat down with him to dinner at Gore House. . . . After

[1] John Forster in his *Life of Walter Savage Landor*.

dinner he described his way of escape by passing through the fortress-gates in a labourer's blouse and sabots, with a heavy plank on his shoulder, flinging off the plank into the ditch by the wall of the chateau, and afterwards, shod as he was, running nearly two miles to where a little cart waited to take him within reach of the coast : all of it was told in his usual un-French way, without warmth or excitement. Before or since I have never seen his face as it was then, for he had shaved his moustaches as part of his disguise, and his lower and least pleasing features were completely exposed under the straggling stubble of hair beginning to show itself."

24. LOLA MONTEZ

ONE day in October, 1846, an exquisitely dressed woman in black, with a veil thrown over her head and a fan in her hand, sauntered down the Brennerstrasse in Munich. A little girl stopped to gaze at her with open eyes, and then ran home breathlessly to tell her father that she had seen a lady as beautiful as a fairy. "That," he observed grimly, "must have been the Spanish dancer, Lola Montez."[1] After five years of Continental triumphs, she had arrived in Munich to make her first appearance at the Court Theatre.

As an adventuress she was notorious throughout Europe—her very name had a glamour—and the wildest rumours about her found a hearing. She was an international spy, with agents in every country; most, if not all, of the European princes had been at her feet; she had horsewhipped at least a dozen men, and was continually in trouble with the police; her birthplace was stated to be in Spain, Scotland, India, and Turkey; her mother was a Spanish gypsy, a Scotch washerwoman, and a Cuban half-caste; Lord Byron was her father. No one in Munich was likely to know that, when she made her first appearance in London, during a momentary silence a voice was heard to remark in surprise: "Why, there's Betty James!" For the truth is that she was born at Limerick of English parents in 1818, eloped at the age of fifteen, and, after a brief married life, started a stage career. Her début in London was only a moderate success, owing, it is said, to the enmity of Lord Ranelagh, whose pride she had deeply offended. Lola never danced again in England, but on the Continent she swept all before her.

[1] *Unter den vier ersten Königen Bayerns*, by Luise von Kobell.

LOLA MONTEZ

(From an engraving after a picture by Jules Laure)

p. 134

"Lola possesses 26 of the 27 points on which a Spanish writer insists as essential to feminine beauty," wrote a sober dramatic critic in Warsaw, "and the real connoisseurs among my readers will agree with me when I confess that blue eyes and black hair appear to me more ravishing than black eyes and black hair. The points enumerated by the Spanish writer are: three white—the skin, the teeth, the hands; three black—the eyes, the eyelashes, the eyebrows; three red—the lips, the cheek, the nails; three long—the body, the hair, the hands; three short—the ears, the teeth, the legs; three broad—the bosom, the forehead, the space between the eyebrows; three full—the lips, the arms, the calves; three small—the waist, the hands, the feet; three thin—the fingers, the hair, the lips. All these perfections are Lola's, except as regards the colour of her eyes, which I, for one, would not wish to change. Lola's silky hair, rivalling the gloss of the raven's wing, falls in luxuriant folds down her back; on the slender, delicate neck, whose whiteness shames the swan's down, rests the beautiful head. How, too, shall I describe Lola's bosom, if words fail me to describe the dazzling whiteness of her teeth? Lola's little feet hold the just balance between the feet of the Chinese and French ladies. Her fine, shapely calves are the lowest rungs of a Jacob's ladder leading to Heaven. She reminds one of the Venus of Knidos carved by Praxiteles in the 104th Olympiad."[1]

And on and on he raved, but so engrossed was he in drawing up the inventory of her charms that he never noticed that she could not dance.

For it must be confessed that as a dancer Lola was less than mediocre, and, fully conscious of this, she would boldly attract attention by throwing something at (and hitting) the most important member of the audience. After that, her beauty did the rest. "Lola Montez was an enchantress," wrote a Frenchman. "There was about her something provoking and voluptuous which drew you.

[1] These and subsequent extracts from newspapers, etc., are quoted in *Lola Montez*, by Edmund D'Auvergne.

Her skin was white, her wavy hair like the tendrils of the woodbine, her eyes tameless and wild, her mouth like a budding pomegranate. Add to that a dashing figure, charming feet and perfect grace. Unluckily, as a dancer, she had no talent."

Whether she had Spanish blood in her veins or not, she certainly had the appearance and temperament of a Southerner, and her bright blue eyes were the sole indication of her Saxon birth. Her temper was as quick and uncontrolled as her personal courage was high, and when she considered herself insulted she would seize the first weapon that came to hand and strike the offender.

Although her exploits must have been exaggerated, she undoubtedly had an amazing career. In Dresden she met Liszt, then as much adored by women as Lola was by men, and they lived together for a while ; in Poland, the Viceroy fell in love with her, and, after almost bringing about a revolution, she was banished from the country ; in St. Petersburg and Berlin, she was received at Court, and loaded with presents. As a dancer Lola was not so successful in Paris, but as the mistress of a popular Republican leader she associated with most of the brilliant writers and politicians of her time. From her lover she absorbed liberal ideals, and as a result of her friendship with the Dumas, *père et fils*, Méry, and de Musset, her mental powers developed rapidly. After her protector was killed in a duel, of which she was not, strange to say, the direct cause, she left Paris to wander among German watering-places, until at Baden she met Henry LXXII of Reuss. This prince, who ruled over a few square miles with all the pomp and state of an Emperor, graciously extended to the dancer an invitation to visit his dominions. She went, but her stay was cut short by a most unfortunate occurrence. She was seen walking over his flower-beds, and he instantly ordered her out of the country. She packed up and went the same day, but not before she had forced him to pay her a large sum for expenses. From there she journeyed to Munich.

At first Lola was refused permission to appear, for the

artistic reputation of the Court Theatre stood high in Europe, and her talents were slight, but, forcing herself into the presence of the King, she induced him to give his consent. She made her first appearance on October 10th, 1846.

"Lola Montez took the centre of the stage," wrote a member of the audience, "clothed not in the usual tights and short skirts of the ballet girl, but in a Spanish costume of silk and lace, with here and there a glittering diamond. Fire seemed to shoot from her wonderful blue eyes, and she bowed like one of the Graces before the King, who occupied the royal box. Then she danced after the fashion of her country, swaying on her hips, and changing from one posture to another, each excelling the former in beauty.

"While she danced she riveted the attention of all the spectators, their gaze followed the sinuous swayings of her body, in their expression now of glowing passion, now of lightsome playfulness. Not till she ceased her rhythmic movements was the spell broken."

The King very soon discovered that he would like to learn Spanish, and sent for Lola to teach him. How much he profited by her lessons will never be known, for the fact was that she knew even less about Spanish than about dancing. But all this was of little consequence, for on the 14th of October she appeared on the stage for the second and last time in Munich. The next day, the King, officially introducing her at Court, said: "Gentlemen, I present to you my best friend."

Ludwig I of Bavaria, then an elderly man, had all his life been peculiarly susceptible to feminine charm, and he fell an easy victim to Lola's fascinations. Apart from his admiration of her beauty, he was interested and stimulated by the bold political opinions which she had imbibed in Paris and now laid fearlessly before him. He had ascended the throne with liberal sympathies, but Munich was the stronghold of the Jesuits and Ultramontanes, and by the time Lola came to Bavaria he was completely under their thumb. He readily fell in with her views, and, seizing the first opportunity, he dismissed the ministry that had been in power for the last ten years and chose a more liberal Premier. In after years Lola wrote a highly picturesque, if somewhat inaccurate, account of her life, and in it she describes the conditions she found on her arrival.

"When Lola Montez arrived in Bavaria the nobility had such power that a tradesman could not possibly collect a debt from one by law, as they could only be tried by their peers. To remedy this enormity, Lola Montez had obtained the pledges of the king that he would introduce the Code Napoleon, and she was having it copied and put in due form when the revolution broke out and drove her from power. The blow that she had dealt at the swollen heads of the nobility was severe only in choosing ministers from the ranks of the people, but this introduction of the Code Napoleon was looked upon as the finishing blow. The priests used to preach that there was no longer a Virgin Mary in Munich, but that Venus had taken her place. At first they tried to win her to their side. A nobleman was found who would immolate himself in marriage with her; then Austrian gold was tried—old Metternich would give her a million if she would quit Bavaria—all, all was offered to no purpose. Then came threats and plots for her destruction. She was twice shot at, and once poisoned; and it was only the accident of too large a dose that saved her."

Within a few weeks of her arrival, Lola Montez was virtually the ruler of the kingdom. An English journalist, then living at Munich, published an article about her in *Fraser's Magazine* for January, 1848.

"The house of Lola Montez at Munich presents an elegant contrast to the large, cold, lumbering mansions, which are the greatest defects in the general architecture of the city. It is a *bijou*, built under her own eye, by her own architect, and is quite unique in its simplicity and lightness. The interior surpasses everything, even in Munich, where decorative paintings and internal fittings have been carried almost to perfection. The smallness of the house precludes much splendour. Its place is supplied by French elegance, Munich art, and English comfort. The walls of the chief room are exquisitely painted by the best artists from the paintings found in Herculaneum and Pompeii, but selected with great taste by Lola Montez. A small winter room, adjoining the larger one, is fitted up, quite in the English style, with papered walls, sofas, easy-chairs, all of elegant shape. A chimney, with a first-rate grate of English manufacture, and rich, thick carpets and rugs, complete the illusion. The walls are hung with pictures, among them a Raphael. There are also some of the best works of modern German painters; a good portrait of the King; and a very bad one of the mistress of the mansion. The rest of the establishment bespeaks equally the exquisite taste of the fair owner. Books, not of a frivolous kind, borrowed from the royal library, lie about, and help to show what are the habits of this modern Amazon.

"The morning, before and after breakfast, is devoted to what we must call semi-public business. The innumerable letters she receives and affairs she has to arrange, keep herself and her secretary constantly employed during some hours. At breakfast she holds a sort of *levée* of persons of all sorts—ministers *in esse* or *in posse*, professors, artists, English strangers, and foreigners from all parts of the world. As is usual with women of an active mind, she is a great talker, but although an egotist, understands the art of conversation sufficiently never to be wearisome. Her manners are distinguished, she is a graceful yet hospitable hostess, and she understands the art of dressing to perfection.

"As a political character, she holds an important position in Bavaria, besides having agents and correspondents in various Courts of Europe. The King generally visits her in the morning from 11 to 12, or one o'clock; sometimes she is summoned to the palace to consult with him, or with the ministers, on state affairs. On foreign politics she seems to have very clear ideas; and her novel and powerful method of expressing them has a great charm for the King, who has himself a comprehensive mind. On the internal politics of Bavaria she has the good sense not to rely upon her own judgment, but to consult those whose studies and occupations qualify them to afford information. For the rest, she is treated by the political men of the country as a substantive power. Whatever indiscretions she may, in other respects, commit, she always keeps state secrets, and can, therefore, be consulted with perfect safety in cases where her original habits of thought render her of invaluable service. Without intrenching too far upon a delicate subject, it may be added that she is not regarded with contempt or detestation by either the male or the female members of the royal family. She is regarded by them rather as a political personage than as a king's favourite. Her income, including a recent addition from the King, is 70,000 florins, or little more than £5,000."

Lola's reign, however, was soon to come to an end. She had not been in Munich many months before she weakened her position as a liberal by accepting the titles of Countess Landsfeldt and Baroness Rosenthal, and an estate with feudal rights over numerous tenants. Using this as a weapon, the Jesuits attacked her through the clerical Press, and the foreigner's power was increasingly resented. In February, 1848, a hostile demonstration was organised by a number of students, and the King, at Lola's wish, closed the university. A more serious insurrection resulted, and the immediate expulsion of the King's favourite was peremptorily demanded. Ludwig unwillingly acquiesced, and in the same month Lola fled from the country. Six weeks later Ludwig was forced to abdicate.

After this Lola took once more to roaming about the world, sometimes as a dancer, but more often as an actress in dramas describing her experiences in Bavaria.

She never moved in such exalted circles again, and gradually began to slide down the social scale. In '51 we hear of her in America, holding receptions at which the privilege of shaking the hand that had been held by so many royal princes was to be had for the fee of one dollar. Eight years later she was back in London, lecturing at St. James's Hall, and the public who had come there the previous week to gaze at Mr. Barnum's exhibitions of freaks, now crowded to see the famous adventuress, and hear her speak on "Beauty," "Gallantry," and "The Comic Aspects of Love"—subjects on which she was surely well qualified to speak. But instead of a beautiful tigress they saw a woman, no longer young, simply dressed in black, with a modest and intellectual expression. Her face was pale and thin, and her eyes, though still lustrous, shone only with a spiritual fire. She spoke quietly and earnestly, with an undefined foreign accent, and, in short, the entertainment proved dull in the extreme.

"The lecture might have been a newspaper article," said the *Era*, of April 10th, 1859, "the first chapter of a book of travels, the speech of a long-winded American ambassador at a Mansion House dinner . . . a more inoffensive entertainment could hardly be imagined; and when the six sections into which the lady had divided her discourse were exhausted, and her final bow elicited a renewal of the applause that had accompanied her entrance, the impression on the departing visitors must have been that of having spent an hour in company with a well-informed lady who had gone to America, had seen much to admire there and, coming back, had had over the tea-table the talk of the evening to herself."

At this time Lola's hours of leisure were spent in reading religious books of an Evangelistic tendency, and she gave herself up, we are told, to solemn thought. She became obsessed with the idea that she was dying of tuberculosis, and calmly and hopefully prepared herself for death. The last two years of her life were passed in

America, studying the Scriptures and visiting the inmates of the Magdalen Asylum, near New York. After her death from a sudden stroke, the Rev. Dr. F. L. Hawks, D.D., of the Protestant Episcopal Church, published an account of her life in the form of a tract, under the title of *The Story of a Penitent*, prefaced by the text, " Is not this a brand plucked out of the fire ? " In it he relates how he used frequently to visit Eliza G.[1] (as she is called throughout the little book) in her last days—always, he adds, in the presence of her nurse—and read to her the story of Christ's forgiveness to the Magdalen in the House of Simon. Never in his long experience as a minister had he seen a more humble penitent. He quotes from what she called her spiritual diary :

" How many, many years of my life have been sacrificed to Satan, and my own love of sin ! What have I not been guilty of, either in thought or deed, during these years of misery and wretchedness ?

" Oh, I dare not think of the past ! What have I not been ? I lived only for my passions ; and what is there of good even in the best natural human being ? What would I not give to have my terrible and fearful experience given as an awful warning to such natures as mine ! And yet when people generally, even my mother, turned their backs upon me and knew me not, Jesus knocked at my heart's door. . . . What has the world ever given to me ? And I have known *all* that the world has to give—*all*—nothing but shadows, leaving a wound on the heart hard to heal—a dark discontent."

[1] Her name was Marie Dolores Eliza Rosanna Gilbert, *née* James.

25. THE MURDER OF THE DUCHESSE DE PRASLIN

For the last eighteen months of Louis Philippe's reign, it was apparent to all clear-sighted Frenchmen that a revolution was approaching. The King's government was utterly corrupt, and, after that long series of exposures in the spring of 1847, no one, however high his rank or office, was wholly free from suspicion. But the greatest scandal was yet to come: in August, 1847, all classes of society were horrified to learn that one of the first peers in the land was involved in a most brutal murder.

The Duc de Praslin was the representative of the ancient and noble house of Choiseul-Praslin, and had been raised to the peerage by the King in 1845. The Duchess and he had been married for seventeen years, and to all appearances lived happily together.

They arrived late on August 18th at their house in Paris, and, being tired after a long journey, went to bed almost immediately. The servants followed their example.

In the early hours of the morning, a bell rang violently in the Duchess's room. The servant, whose duty it was to attend her, dressed hurriedly and ran to see what was wrong. The door was locked, and the sound of stifled groans reached him as he tried to force it open. Finding it too strong for him, he ran downstairs and up again by a staircase that led into a passage connecting the Duke's suite of rooms with those of the Duchess. He noticed that the door leading to the Duke's room was standing open. The other door was unlocked, and as he entered the room there was just enough light for him to see that some of the furniture had been overthrown. The groans had ceased, and in considerable alarm he opened the shutters and pulled back the curtains. There on the ground lay the Duchess with many gaping wounds, any one of which would have been fatal. A portion of the bell-rope was still clutched in her fingers, and strands of her hair lay strewn about the carpet. The man called aloud for help, and soon his fellow-servants came running from their rooms.

Presently the Duke emerged from his room, clad in his dressing-gown, and asked them the reason for all the noise. On being shown the body of the Duchess, he only said quietly, "Poor woman, who is the monster who has assassinated her?"

When the police arrived an hour or so later, they noticed a thin trickle of blood leading to the Duke's apartments. Hesitatingly and respectfully they asked him if he could account for it. He answered rather surprisingly that he had known of the Duchess's death before being summoned by the cries of his servant. Hearing her cry out, he went to help her, but found it was too late and returned to his room covered with blood. There they found several murderous weapons, and in a corner a pile of blood-stained clothes.

The police felt it their duty to examine the Duke's body, and to his disgust he was obliged to strip in front of them. He was covered with scratches, and his arm was almost bitten through. He made no reply to their questions, and, indeed, seemed not to hear them. Then he pleaded a sudden indisposition and retired.

They had no authority to arrest him, for he could only be tried by his peers, but the house was surrounded and no one was on any pretext allowed to leave it. The King hesitated long before he signed a warrant for the Duke's arrest, for France was on the eve of revolution, and to accuse a peer of murder was, to say the least, injudicious. On August 24th, 1847, however, the Duke was brought before the Chancellor of the Peers in the Palace of Luxembourg. He continued to complain of illness, and refused to answer any questions.

"You know," said the Chancellor, "the terrible crime

of which you are accused. You know what strong reasons we have to suspect you. I strongly advise you to throw off the apathy you see fit to assume, and tell us whether you are guilty or not."

"The question is a difficult one," the Duke answered wearily. "I have not the strength to reply. It would need such long explanations."

The Chancellor once more urged him to tell them the truth. "You need not enter into details. Yes or no would be enough."

The Duke heaved a deep sigh. "It would need great strength of mind to say yes or no. Such strength I have not got." He turned very pale, and they realised at last that his illness was genuine. He was, in fact, on the point of collapse, and a suspicion crossed the Chancellor's mind. He asked the Duke if he had taken poison. This time he replied by nodding, and half an hour later he was dead.

A packet of letters in the Duchess's writing, found partially burnt in the Duke's room, told the story of an unhappy married life. The Duchess was passionately devoted to her husband, and realised that her love was no longer returned. She mingled bitter reproaches with humble entreaties to him to forgive her for irritating him by her outbursts of grief and rage.

"The last four months," she wrote, "have taught me that I was wrong to try and force your confidence. I recognise how infinitely superior is your character and nature to mine; I only ask most humbly to go on sharing your life."

She looked round for some cause for jealousy, and found it in the Duke's interest in their daughters' governess. Although no one can say what might have happened had matters been left to themselves, it is certain that nothing existed between them then beyond a somewhat injudicious friendship. Mlle. Deluzy was an exceptionally intelligent young woman, and the Duke found her conversation more stimulating than that of his nerve-racked wife. The

Duchess tortured herself with jealousy and suspicion, and eventually succeeded in getting the governess out of the house. A scrap of paper among the Duchess's private papers bore in the Duke's handwriting this significant sentence: "By your act you have spoilt my life."

After her departure, Mlle. Deluzy kept up a correspondence with the Duke and her former pupils, who, as soon as they arrived in Paris on the evening of the tragedy, all three left the Duchess for an hour while they paid her a hurried visit at her hotel. This was as much as could be pieced together, and it hardly explains how the Duke, who had never before laid violent hands on his wife, came to make such a brutal assault on her that night.

A strange story was told by her friends which renders the affair still more mysterious. They remembered that a year before the Duchess had described to them a peculiar nightmare.

"Waking up suddenly," she said, "I seemed to see advancing towards me—the Devil! He was dressed in bright red from head to foot. He crept nearer and nearer, and I gave a loud scream. Then I heard a click—and he vanished into the wall."

Now, a short passage joined the rooms of the Duke and the Duchess in their home in the country, and there, after the tragedy, a fancy dress worn by the Duke as a young man was found in a cupboard. It represented Mephistopheles, and was bright red in colour. In the pocket lay a sharp pointed dagger.

26. THE SEA SERPENT SEEN BY H.M.S. *DÆDALUS*

THERE was hardly a year in the nineteenth century in which the Great Sea Serpent was not sighted in some part of the world. In 1848 it was seen off the coast of West Africa by the Captain and crew of one of His Majesty's ships, and almost simultaneously came the report that it had been seen a few miles south of this point by the crew of the *Daphne*. The descriptions of the monster agree in most essentials.

The following appeared in *The Times* for October 10th, 1848.

Plymouth, October 7th.

"When the *Dædalus* frigate, Captain M'Quhae, which arrived on the 4th inst., was on her passage home from the East Indies between the Cape of Good Hope and St. Helena, her Captain, and most of her officers and crew, at 4 o'clock one afternoon, saw a Sea Serpent. Its head appeared to be about 4 ft. out of the water, and there was about 60 ft. of its body in a straight line on the surface. It is calculated that there must have been under water a length of 30 or 40 ft. more, by which it propelled itself at the rate of 15 miles an hour. The diameter of the exposed part of the body was about 16 inches, and when it extended its jaws, which were full of large jagged teeth, they seemed sufficiently capacious to admit of a tall man standing upright between them."

The next morning Captain M'Quhae wrote to the Admiralty.

Her Majesty's Ship Dædalus, Hamoaze.

October 11th.

SIR,—In reply to your letter of this day's date, I have the honour to acquaint you, that at 5 o'clock p.m. on the

6th of August last, in latitude 24° 44′ S., and longitude 9° 22′ E., something very unusual was seen by Mr. Sartoris, midshipman, rapidly appoaching the ship from before the beam. The circumstance was immediately reported by him to the officer of the watch, Lieutenant Edgar Drummond, with whom and Mr. William Barrett, the Master, I was at the time walking the quarter-deck. The ship's company were at supper.

On our attention being called to the object, it was discovered to be an enormous Sea-Serpent with head and shoulders kept about 4 ft. constantly above the surface of the sea; and, as nearly as we could approximate by comparing it with the length of what our maintopsail-yard would show in water, there was at the very least 60 ft. of the animal *à fleur d'eau*, no portion of which was, to our perception, used in propelling it through the water, either by vertical or horizontal undulation. It passed rapidly, but so close under our lee quarter that had it been a man of my acquaintance I should have easily recognised his features with the naked eye; and it did not, either in approaching the ship or after it had passed our wake, deviate in the slightest degree from its course to the S.W., which it held on at the pace of from 12 to 15 miles per hour, apparently on some determined purpose.

The diameter of the Serpent was about 15 or 16 inches behind the head, which was, without any doubt, that of a snake; and it was never, during the twenty minutes that it continued in sight of our glasses, once below the surface of the water—its colour a dark brown, with yellowish-white about the throat. It had no fins, but something like the mane of a horse, or rather a bunch of sea-weed, washed about its back. It was seen by the quartermaster, the boatswain's mate, and the man at the wheel, in addition to myself and officers above mentioned.

I have, etc.,

PETER M'QUHAE,

Captain.

27. THE PRISONER IN THE TEMPLE

On June 8th, 1795, a child died in the Tower of the old Paris-Palace, or Temple, prison, and whether he was or was not the Dauphin, the ten-year-old son of Louis XVI, is a question that has been puzzling people ever since.

When his gaoler, Simon the Cobbler, left the Temple on January 19th, 1794, the Dauphin, despite his eighteen months' captivity, was in good health and spirits. Up to this point there is authentic information about his life in prison, but then follows a period of almost unbroken silence, until seventeen months later, when a deformed child, riddled with disease, died and was buried in his name. During this time only one person saw him who could have identified him, and that man died within a few weeks of his visit after a two days' illness.

The public, who had been told nothing of the child's failing health, received the news of his death first with surprise and then with suspicion : it was known that plots had been afoot to rescue the heir to the throne, and, indeed, for many months rumours had persisted that the escape had already been effected. Was this boy who had died really the Dauphin, or was he some sick child put there in his place, and, if so, when, and by whom, had this been done, and where was the prince himself? These were the problems that were continually being discussed in France during the nineteenth century, whenever one of the thirty or more claimants to the title of Louis XVII made his appearance.[1]

The Dauphin was taken away from his mother in July,

[1] M. Lenotre takes an interesting point of view in his book, *The Dauphin*. In his opinion every one of the claimants was an impostor, and yet he remains convinced that the prince escaped from the Temple on the day of Simon's departure.

1793, and placed under the care of Simon, who was instructed "to turn the boy into a democrat, to inculcate in him the principles of the Revolution, to teach him the ways of the common people." Simon was once depicted as little less than a monster taking a fiendish pleasure in torturing his little prisoner, but recent writers, while not denying that he drank heavily and was occasionally brutal, show him to have been, in his rough way, genuinely attached to the child. At all events, there is ample evidence that while in his charge the prince was well fed and decently clothed, and kept clean and tidy by Mme. Simon. His health was fairly good, and during some slight indispositions he was attended by competent doctors. His sister and aunt, who were confined to the third floor of the Temple, often heard his shouts of noisy laughter, so that it is clear that his spirit was not broken by his treatment. On January 19th, 1794, Simon left the Temple, but before he went he took the precaution of obtaining a certificate signed by four men, one of whom was a doctor and another a lawyer, to say that his charge, "Charles Capet," was in good health.

Until the day Simon left, the evidence that exists makes it impossible to believe that the child in the Temple was any other than the son of Louis XVI, but now the first doubt creeps in. One historian has sought to prove that Simon murdered the boy before he left, but, though this satisfactorily explains the silence that follows, it does not fit in with modern estimates of Simon's character. Others have suggested that the child was rescued at the time of his departure, either with or without his aid, and that a dumb child was put into his place. A passage which occurs in the memoirs of the prince's sister, afterwards the Duchesse d'Angoulême, is thought to give some support to this theory. "On the 19th January they (she and her aunt) heard a great noise in the Dauphin's room which made them conjecture that he was going out of the Temple, and they were convinced of it when, looking out through a key-hole, they saw luggage being taken away. The following day they heard the door open and steps in the room, and, still convinced that he had gone, they thought some important person had been put in the room below." After that day they never heard the child's voice again.

For the next six months little or nothing is known of the Dauphin, but those who think that he died in prison seventeen months later make the most of the scanty reports of his ill-treatment during this period. Tradition has it that he was "walled in," that no living person entered his room and that his food was passed in by means of some mechanical contrivance. But why, if this were so, did his sister not hear any cries of protest from him during the first few days of this treatment?

In July, 1794, the Terror came to an end, and the first thing that Barras did was to come and visit the royal prisoners. Besides the prince, his sister was now the only survivor, for their aunt had followed Louis XVI to the scaffold. The princess was well, and her only real cause for complaint was that she was not allowed to see her brother. Barras, accordingly, gave orders that the children were to be re-united. He found the prince ill and neglected, and he appointed a young Creole, Christophe Laurent, to act as his guardian and see that his conditions were improved. In spite of his orders, however, the children were not allowed to meet, and no doctor was called in to see the prince, who was more closely secluded than ever. Indeed, the guards began to murmur, and complain that they had no means of knowing whether they were keeping watch over "stones or anything." Laurent managed to pacify them, but continued to forbid anyone to go near the prince. This behaviour of Laurent is puzzling, for the princess in her memoirs has nothing but praise for his kindness to her, and it is curious that he should refuse to gratify her greatest wish, especially as by doing so he was disobeying the most explicit orders.

Various theories have been put forward to explain his conduct. One is that he was the first to discover that the real prince had escaped, and that another child had been substituted, and, on reporting it to the Government, he was ordered to keep it secret. Another is that when he arrived the prince had not yet escaped, but Laurent, acting under Barras's secret orders, hid him in a remote corner of the Temple, and a dumb child was then smuggled in by the Government to impersonate him. Finally, those who think that the little boy who died was in fact the Dauphin himself think it probable that, when it was discovered to what a terrible state six months' solitary confinement had reduced him, every effort was made to keep it from being known.

Laurent could not, however, keep the child secluded for ever, and on December 19th three members of the Committee for General Security visited the Temple. One of them, M. Harmand, wrote a description of the prisoner. "The young prince had the appearance of one with rachitis and a defect of formation; the legs and thighs were long and thin, the arms the same, the bust very short, the shoulders high and constricted, the head long and beautifully well kept, of a light auburn." Could this be the healthy, well-proportioned little boy who had entered the prison only a little over two years before, and eleven months ago had been still in good health? But the most remarkable feature of this interview was that the child *did not speak*. In reply to all their questions and entreaties he merely looked at them with a blank expression on his face. "His features did not change for a single moment; there was not the least apparent emotion, nor the least astonishment in his eyes, as though we had not been there." But was it that the child would not speak, or was it that he could not? It is from this account of Harmand's that the idea of the substitution of a deaf-mute originated.

In March, 1795, Laurent left the Temple, and two months later his successor reported to the Committee that the child's health was unsatisfactory. Desault, the leading physician in Paris, was called in. He visited his patient a number of times, but did not apparently take a serious view of his illness, for he only ordered him some simple remedies and issued no alarming report. At the end of the month both he and his assistant, Choppart, died suddenly from typhoid fever—or so it was said at the time—but Desault's widow, his niece, and his pupils afterwards gave it as their opinion that they had been poisoned. Many reasons have been suggested for their murder (if indeed it was), but it is enough to point out that Desault must have attended the prince before his imprisonment, and if a substitution had taken place he would immediately have realised that his patient was a stranger to him. Six days elapsed before fresh medical aid was called in for the prisoner, and, to account for the fact that the child is known to have spoken after this date, it has been suggested that during this period the dumb child was taken away and another child in a dying condition was substituted.

On June 5th two doctors were appointed, neither of whom could possibly ever have seen the Dauphin. The child was now much worse, and he died on June 8th. Besides the two gaolers, Gourlet, the turnkey, was the only one who knew of his death that day, and, to prevent the news leaking out, they kept him under lock and key, and continued to prepare the child's food and medicine as usual, so as to give the impression that he was still alive. The following day a post-mortem was held, and four doctors, including Pelletan and Dumargin, who had been attending the child, signed a report which was couched in curiously ambiguous words.

"*We found on the bed the corpse of a dead child who appeared to us to be about ten years old*, *which the commissioners told us was that of the deceased Louis Capet*, *and two of us recognised as the child whom they had been attending for several days*."

The boy, they stated, died of a scrofulous affection of long standing. In after-years, Pelletan said that he could not attribute his death to ill-treatment and moral suffering, but to a scrofulous disorder and to a hereditary disease from which it is known that Louis XVI's son did not and could not have suffered. Yet he must have been convinced of the child's identity at the time, for at the post-mortem he took the trouble to abstract the heart, and then to preserve it in spirits of wine. When the monarchy was restored he offered this relic both to Louis XVIII and the Duchesse d'Angoulême, and that they both refused to accept it seems to some people a proof that they did not consider the corpse from which it had been taken that of the Dauphin.

After the post-mortem, the two gaolers took the most remarkable precautions to have the corpse identified; they proceeded "to surround themselves," wrote Guerin, the Commissioner for the day, "still further with a greater number of witnesses to the identity of the individual who was to be buried, invited the two civil commissioners of the section of the Temple, and the whole staff of the guard on duty, to take part in this verification, and those of them who recognised the son of Louis Capet to declare it and attest it by their signatures." This certainly reads as though the corpse had been identified by persons who had seen the child when he entered the prison three years before, but in reply to this it would probably be urged that after a post-mortem examination recognition could be only a formality. And why, since he had obviously died from natural causes, was there a post-mortem at all? To disfigure the corpse, answer those who think that the prince had escaped. To dispel any suspicion of poison, say the others.

After the examination, the death of the Dauphin was announced, and on the next day, June 10th, he was buried in an unmarked grave in the cemetery of Ste. Marguerite.

In 1846, what was believed to be the Dauphin's coffin was dug up and opened, and doctors were called in to examine the bones. They were not unanimous. One held that, although the bones were those of the child Harmand had seen and described, and also belonged to the body on which Pelletan and his colleagues had performed a post-mortem, they were those of a boy between 15 and 18 years old. The other doctor considered that the bones in the coffin did not belong to one subject but to two—some to a boy of 15 or 16 and others to that of a very young child. In other words, if it was the right coffin, it had never contained the Dauphin's remains.

In 1814 the monarchy was restored, and it is certain that, whatever attitude Louis XVIII and the Duchesse d'Angoulême had taken up with regard to the fate of the prince, they would have been suspected of knowing more than they pretended. The King's policy was apparently to try and forget that his nephew had ever existed, and those who wished to curry favour at Court were careful never to mention his name. Immediately after his accession, he gave orders that the bodies of Louis XVI and Marie Antoinette should be dug up and reburied with ceremony, but he took no steps to rebury the body of their little son. Later on, a *chapelle expiatoire* was erected to the memory of Louis XVI, Marie Antoinette, and Mme. Elizabeth, the King's sister, but the Dauphin's name was not included. The Duchess's behaviour was curiously vacillating : sometimes she would ignore the existence of those who claimed to be her brother, and at other times she would secretly make enquiries into their claims. General de la Roche-Jaquelin declared that on her deathbed she confessed to him that she had always known that her brother had escaped, but, unfortunately, the General had no means of proving his statement.

Of all the stories told by the claimants, the most picturesque was that of the man known as Baron de Richemont.[1] One day, he said, when Simon was out a cardboard horse was brought into the Temple on the pretext of amusing the little prince. In its belly was concealed a boy of the same age who had been rendered insensible with opium. Mme. Simon was in the plot, and she took out the strange boy and substituted the prince. She then insisted on having the animal removed from the Temple on the grounds that her husband would be sure to object to it. Once outside, the boy was transferred to a similar

[1] His detractors say that he "lifted" the story from a historical romance called "*La Cimetière de la Madeleine*," which was published in 1798.

but larger animal, which was covered with a real horse's skin, and was so lifelike that it was almost impossible to tell it from a real one. When night fell it was harnessed to a cart and two live horses were placed in front. The legs of the sham horse were flexible, and the driver by pulling some strings was able to create the illusion of three trotting horses. The inside of the horse was padded, and under the tail was a large air-hole, and so, in comparative comfort, Richemont made his escape from Paris. He was partially supported in his story by the evidence of Mme. Simon, who, before she died in 1816, confessed that the Dauphin had escaped with her knowledge and help. Incredible as it may appear, his story was widely believed, and, although he was convicted of conspiracy in 1833, he emerged from prison after serving his sentence to spend the rest of his days in luxury on the strength of his pretensions.

At the time of Richemont's trial another claimant attracted attention. This was the man known as Charles Naundorff, whose story was accepted by many eminent men. It is said that Joly, a minister of the Crown under Louis XVI, who was actually with the royal family on the day when they were taken to the Tuileries, publicly stated that he recognised him as the Dauphin. In spite of this, however, Naundorff was arrested and banished. After his death his descendants took up the claim, and in 1851 an attempt was made to get the French courts to acknowledge him, but without success. Two other unsuccessful attempts were made—in 1874, and again for the last time in 1911.

His story was that he was taken from his room by Laurent, who was acting under secret orders from Barras, and hidden in a disused garret on the top storey of the Temple while a lay-figure was placed in the bed. The disappearance of the prince was discovered the same evening, and in order to conceal the truth a deaf mute was procured to impersonate the prince.

In spite of all precautions, however, rumours of the prince's escape got about. The Government decided that the dumb child must die, and they mixed some poison in his food. To avert suspicion, and to make a show of their fine feelings, they called in Desault to attend him. Desault soon discovered the truth, and persuaded his friend, Choppart, to prepare an antidote. This came to the ears of the Government, with the result that both Choppart and Desault were put out of the way. Despairing of ridding themselves of the deaf mute with safety, they smuggled him away, and procured instead a rickety child in such a condition that his speedy death was a certainty. It was this boy who died on June 8th, and his burial gave the claimant's friends the opportunity to smuggle him safely out of the Tower.

This is the story that has gained so much credence that books are still being written in support of Naundorff's claim.[1] In the most recent of these[2] the author traces out, by means of photographs, the likenesses between Naundorff and his descendants to the Bourbons. There certainly are some surprising resemblances—perhaps the most striking being that of two of the claimant's present-day descendants to the King of Spain. But the Bourbon features appeared unexpectedly in many European families, and there may be an explanation other than that put forward in this book.

Equally amazing stories were told by the other twenty-eight claimants, and, incidentally, we are entitled to a glow of patriotic pride for the imaginative powers of Augustus Meves, a British subject. He told an astonishing tale, but, unfortunately, became so confused by questions of identity that, on meeting Naundorff, he mistook him for himself, and was shortly afterwards certified as insane. As to the American claimant, Eleazar Williams, his story merits separate treatment.

[1] Had his claim succeeded an interesting situation would have arisen, for in that case Louis XVII would have succeeded Louis XVIII.

[2] *Louis XVII : ses deux suppressions*, by Henry Foulon de Vaulx.

28. WAS ELEAZAR WILLIAMS LOUIS XVII ?

From the journal of the Rev. Eleazar Williams, a missionary to the Indians at Green Bay, Wisconsin, U.S.A.

October 16th, Saturday (1841) *Mackinac.*

THE steamer arrived here at 2 o'clock, p.m. My son is somewhat indisposed, and on that account I am more willing to remain here until the Green Bay boat comes.

I have had a pleasant interview with the Rev. Mr. Coit, of the Congregationalist Church. Mr. C. has spent his time much among the Chippeway Indians. In his labours of love he has been successful. I trust many souls have been converted under his ministry.

Mackinac. October 17th, Sunday evening.

I performed the service this morning—all the gentlemen of the garrison, the soldiers and the citizens of the place were in attendance. My subject was upon Apostasy, which gave great offence to Mr. ——. I find he has been excommunicated for his apostasy. Truth will have its own weight upon the guilty conscience.

Two soldiers called and asked for Prayer-books. I was only able to give them one, which was accompanied with some tracts.

My son is much better—still complains of pain in the head. May God give him grace to be submissive to his Divine Will.

On Lake Michigan, October 18th, Monday.

The regular steamer for Green Bay arrived in the port of Mackinac to-day, at twelve o'clock. His Royal Highness, the Prince de Joinville,[1] and his suite, went immediately to visit the Arch Rock. In the meantime I had an interview, with Captain Shook, of the steamer, who

[1] The Prince de Joinville was the third son of Louis Philippe.

THE REV. ELEAZAR WILLIAMS.

From a Portrait by the Chevalier Fagnani

p. 158

said that the Prince had made enquiries of him, two or three times since leaving Buffalo, about Mr. Williams, the missionary to the Indians at Green Bay, and that as he knew no other gentleman in that capacity excepting myself, I must be the person, the object of his enquiry. I replied, "That cannot be, Captain. He must mean another person, as I have no acquaintance with the Prince."

"I shall now inform the Prince," said the Captain, "that there is a gentleman on board, of the same name as that of his enquiry, who is a missionary to the Indians at Green Bay." Upon this the Captain left me, and in about half an hour, he returned, and was followed by a gentleman, to whom I was introduced as the Prince de Joinville. I was struck at the manner of his salutation. He appeared to be surprised and amazed, as he grasped my hand in both of his, which was accompanied by strong and cheering gratulations of his having had an opportunity to meet me, and that upon the surface of one of the inland seas in the Western World. "Amazing sight!" he continued, "it is what I have wished to see for this long time. I trust I shall not be intruding too much on your feelings and patience, were I to ask some questions in relation to your past and present life among the Indians. We, the Europeans, to satisfy curiosity are sometimes too inquisitive." His eyes were intently fixed upon me—eyeing my person from the crown of my head to the soles of my feet.

The Prince in his cursory remarks upon the first adventures of the French in these western wilds was interesting. He spoke also with regret of the loss of Canada to France. He would attribute this to the want of energy and foresight in the ministry.

October 19th, Tuesday.

This morning the Prince resumed his observations upon the French revolution. The awful catastrophe that fell upon France, the desolation of the Royal Family, and the destruction of the king, he strongly asserted originated from the American Revolution, and that the people in the

United States can never be too grateful to the unfortunate Louis XVI for his powerful interposition in their behalf. "It is very evident," said he, "they do not duly appreciate the aid he afforded them in the day of distress. . . . The ingratitude of the American people towards the king's memory is one of the darkest stains upon the stars and stripes of the American flag of independence."

This afternoon the Prince expressed his wish to take my son with him to France for an education. In connection with this he was informed that we had an infant who had not yet received baptism. He readily consented to stand as a godfather, and would give the name of his mother to the child. But alas! on my first landing I received the melancholy intelligence that the lovely babe was in her grave—buried the preceding Sunday, service performed by the Rev. Mr. Porter of the Congregationist Church. When the news was communicated to the Prince, he appeared to sympathise with me and remarked, "Descendant of a suffering race, may you be supported in this affliction."

About ten o'clock, the Prince was pleased to enter into his remarks more particularly, upon the family of the unfortunate king, which were, at first with me, somewhat curious and interesting; but as he proceeded in his narration, my feelings were greatly excited, as it filled my inward soul with poignant grief and sorrow, which were inexpressible. The intelligence was not only new but awful in its nature. To learn, for the first time, that I am connected by consanguinity with those whose history I had read with so much interest; and for whose sufferings in prison, and the manner of their deaths I had moistened my cheeks with sympathetic tears. Is it so? Is it true, that I am among the number, who are thus destined to such degradation—from a mighty power to a hopeless prisoner of state—from a palace to a prison and dungeon—to be exiled from one of the finest empires in Europe, and to be a wanderer in the wilds of America—from the society of the most polite and accomplished courtiers, to be associated with the ignorant and degraded Indians?

Oh my God, am I thus destined! "Thy Will be done." To be informed that I had rights in Europe, and one of these was to be the first over a mighty kingdom; and this right is demanded of me, to surrender an ample and splendid establishment. The intelligence was so unexpected, my mind was paralysed for a moment, it was overwhelming to my feelings. There was a tremor in my whole system, accompanied with a cold perspiration. The Prince saw my agitation, and left the room, with an excuse, for 10 or 15 minutes.

A splendid parchment was spread before me for signature, to be affixed with the stamp and seal of Louis XVI. After consideration of several hours, weighing the subject with much and cool deliberation, it was respectfully refused. In those awful and momentous moments, it was happy that my mind was carried to the similar proposition and offers made to Louis XVIII by Napoleon in 1802. Being impelled from a sense of duty to sustain the honour of kings for centuries, the same answer was given, "Though I am in poverty, sorrow and exile, I shall not sacrifice my honour."

Gracious God! What scene am I passing through this night! Is it in reality or dream? My refusal to the demand made to me, I am sure can be no earthly good to me, but I save my honour, and it may be for the benefit of the generations yet unborn. It is the will of heaven. I am in a state of obscurity. So shall I remain while in this pilgrimage state. I will endeavour, with all humility, to serve the King of heaven, and to advance His holy cause among the ignorant and benighted people, which has been my delight.

. . . .

Twelve years after the date of these entries, an article appeared in *Putnam's Magazine* by the Rev. John H. Hanson, in which he informed his readers that, in his opinion, the Rev. Eleazar Williams was no other than Louis XVII. He reminded them of the story of the Dauphin, and how in December, 1794, a decree was passed in the Convention "That the committee of government should devise the means of sending the son of Louis out of the territories of the Republic."

Two years before the publication of this article, Mr. Hanson had happened to see in the newspaper a paragraph stating that facts had recently come to light which made it probable that the lost prince had been found in the person of the Rev. Mr. Eleazar Williams. His curiosity was excited, but no one could tell him what those facts were. One day, while travelling by train on his way to New York, he saw a stout old gentleman talking to some Indians in their own language, and after watching him for some time he began to think that this must be Mr. Williams of whom he had read. Some enquiries of the guard confirmed his suspicion, and he seized the first opportunity of introducing himself as a brother clergyman. They got into talk, and Mr. Hanson led the conversation to the subject of his identity. He began by asking Mr. Williams whether he remembered anything of his childhood.

"I know nothing of my infancy," said Mr. Williams. "Everything that occurred to me is blotted out, entirely erased, irrecoverably gone. My mind is a blank, until 13 or 14 years of age." But he had, he admitted later, a few vague impressions and images which he found it impossible to put into words. It appeared that when a gentleman of distinction, on his recent return from Europe, in an interview with Mr. Williams, threw some lithographs and engravings upon the table, at the sight of one of them, and without seeing the name, Williams was greatly excited, and cried out, "My God! I know that face. It has haunted me through life." On examination it proved to be the portrait of Simon the jailor.

"My reputed mother," continued Mr. Williams, "is still living at a very advanced age. . . . I ought, as soon as the Prince told me the secret of my birth, to have returned to the East and seen her. But I unfortunately neglected to do so for some time, and when I did go, I found that the Romish Priests had been tampering with her, and that her mouth was hermetically sealed. And all my efforts to extract anything from her were unavailing. Her immovable Indian obstinacy has hitherto been proof against every effort I could make. . . . But we have had the Baptismal Register at Caughnawaga examined, and the priest was made to certify to it, and though the names of all the rest of her children are recorded there, together with the dates of their birth and baptism, mine does not occur there. And the births of the children follow so closely upon each other at regular intervals, of two years between each, that it does not seem naturally possible I could have been her child, unless I was twin to some other child, whose birth and baptism are recorded while mine are not.

"And then comes evidence of a different description. A French gentleman died in New Orleans, in 1848, named Belanger, who confessed on his deathbed that he was the person who brought the Dauphin to this country, and placed him among the Indians in the Northern part of the state of New York.

"The next link in the evidence is yet more singular. A French gentleman hearing my story, brought a printed account of the captivity of the Dauphin, and read me a note in which it was stated, that Simon the jailor having become incensed with the Prince for some childish offence, took a towel, which was hanging on a nail, and in snatching it hastily drew out the nail with it, and inflicted two blows upon his face, one over the left eye, and the other on the right side of the nose. 'And now,' said he, 'let me look at your face.' When he did so, and saw the scars on the spots indicated in the memoirs he exclaimed, '*Mon Dieu*—what proof do I want more?'

"But that is not all. In the same memoirs, it is said that the Dauphin died of scrofula, and that the disease was on his knees. My knees are eaten up with scrofula, and there are no other scrofulous marks on my body. Such are the main points of evidence on which my claim rests, and you may judge of their strength—and further I can only refer you to the alleged resemblance between me and Louis XVII and the Bourbon family in general. I remember a gentleman putting his hand over the name attached to a picture of Louis XVII and asked a friend whose portrait it was. 'That of Mr. Williams' was the reply."

"I now proceeded," wrote Mr. Hanson, "to scrutinize more closely the form, features and general appearance of Mr. Williams and to re-examine the scars on his face. He is an intelligent, noble-looking old man, with no trace, however slight, of the Indian about him except what may be fairly accounted for by his long residence among Indians. Being far more familiar with their language than with English, which latter he speaks correctly and even eloquently as far as style is concerned, but pronounces imperfectly, his manner of talking reminds you of an Indian, and he has a habit of shrugging his shoulders and gesticulating like one; but he has the port and presence of a European gentleman of a high rank; and a nameless something which I never saw but in persons accustomed to command. . . . I should never have taken him for an Indian. . . .

"I asked him if he could account for the conduct of the Prince of Joinville in disclosing so important a secret as that of his royal birth, and requesting him to give up rights previously unknown to him, and which without information derived from the Prince he would have no means of ascertaining. He replied in substance that it might indeed seem strange. The only satisfactory explanation which he would suggest was that although he was personally ignorant of his origin, yet there were those both in Europe and this country who were acquainted with it, and that Louis Philippe, being at that time anxious to fortify his family in power by every possible means, contracting alliances with other royal lines of Europe, knew that in him existed an obstacle which might possibly prevent the accomplishment of all his designs, and had therefore perhaps delegated his son to reveal the fact to him so as to escape the consequences of its coming to light some other way.

"My interview with Mr. Williams soon had the effect of bringing unexpected evidence to light. In the year 1818, there was a social party at the house of Dr. Hosack, in New York. Of those present Dr. Francis alone survives. In the course of conversation, the subject of the Dauphin was introduced, and the enquiry was started as to his fate. At length, the French Minister, Genet, distinctly said, 'Gentlemen, the Dauphin of France is *not dead*, but was *brought to America*.' The conversation on this interesting subject was continued for some time, and Genet informed the company, among other things, that he believed that the Dauphin was in western New York, and that Le Ray de Chaumont knew all about it.

"From everything which I can ascertain of Le Ray, he was the very man to be mixed up in an affair of this kind, and there is every probability that on his return to France he communicated with Louis Philippe, and this may have led to the mission of the Prince de Joinville. . . .

"With regard to documents Mr. Williams has been unaccountably careless. A short time since he received a letter *purporting* to be from the private Secretary of Louis Napoleon, making enquiries in a respectful manner concerning the events of his life, and also similar communications from several French Bishops and a Cardinal, but for reasons best known to himself he returned no answer. These letters, together with one from Louis Philippe, were accidentally burned a few weeks since whilst lying on his table, but I have now lying before me a note from the Consul General of France, dated New York, April 16th, 1844, which accompanied the letter from the King of the French, some pencil memoranda of the Prince of Joinville, and two letters, one from his Aide-de-Camp, dated 'Frigate, *La Belle Poule*, à New York, 21 Oct're, 1841,' and the other from his private secretary, dated 'Tuileries, October 14th, 1843.' These are on different subjects, such as historical enquiries, and gifts of books for the Indians—but the conclusion of the first letter, which was written shortly after the interview at Green

Bay, is somewhat remarkable, both on account of its diplomatic style, natural if Mr. Williams's story be true, but otherwise out of character, and also for its invitation, for it amounts to that, to Mr. Williams to visit France.

" 'Si jamais vous venez visiter notre France, voulez-vous souvenir que S.A.R. vous recevrai avec plaisir.

" 'Recevez, Monsieur, toutes les assurances de ma considération la plus distinguée.

" 'LIEUT. DE VAISSEAU V. TOUCHAIZ.' "

" I do not trouble my mind much about the matter," said Mr. Williams to Mr. Hanson towards the end of their interview—by this time they were on board a steamer on Lake Champlain—" otherwise I might easily render myself unhappy by repining at the Will of God. But I submit myself entirely to His Will. My story is on the winds of Heaven, and will work its way without me. They have got it in France. Copies of my daguerreotype have been sent to eminent men there. God in His providence must have some mysterious ends to answer, or He never would have brought me so low from such a height. He has cast my lot among this poor Indian people, and I have ministered and will minister to them, if it pleases Him, until death. I do not want a crown. I am convinced of my royal descent; and so are my family. . . . You have been talking," he concluded, smiling, " with a king to-night. Come, let us go downstairs."

29. THE HOOF-MARKS IN THE SNOW [1]

"*The Times*," *February 16th*, 1855.

CONSIDERABLE sensation has been evoked in the towns of Topsham, Lympstone, Exmouth, Teignmouth, and Dawlish, in the south of Devon, in consequence of the discovery of a vast number of foot-tracks of a most strange and mysterious description. The superstitious go so far as to believe that they are the marks of Satan himself; and that great excitement has been produced among all classes may be judged from the fact that the subject has been descanted on from the pulpit.

It appears that on Thursday night last there was a very heavy fall of snow in the neighbourhood of Exeter and the south of Devon. On the following morning, the inhabitants of the above towns were surprised at discovering the tracks of some strange and mysterious animal, endowed with the power of ubiquity, as the foot-prints were to be seen in all kinds of inaccessible places —on the tops of houses and narrow walls, in gardens and courtyards enclosed by high walls and palings, as well as in open fields. There was hardly a garden in Lympstone where the foot-prints were not observed.

The track appeared more like that of a biped than a quadruped, and the steps were generally eight inches in advance of each other. The impressions of the feet closely resembled that of a donkey's shoe, and measured from an inch and a half to (in some instances) two and a half inches across. Here and there it appeared as if cloven, but in the generality of the steps the shoe was continuous, and, from the snow in the centre remaining

[1] This episode is fully discussed in R. T. Gould's fascinating book, *Oddities*.

entire, merely showing the outer crest of the foot, it must have been convex.[1]

The creature seems to have approached the doors of several houses and then to have retreated, but no one has been able to discover the standing or resting point of this mysterious visitor. On Sunday last the Rev. Mr. Musgrave alluded to the subject in his sermon, and suggested the possibility of the foot-prints being those of a kangaroo; but this could scarcely have been the case, as they were found on both sides of the estuary of the Exe.

At present it remains a mystery, and many superstitious people in the above towns are actually afraid to go outside their doors after night.

"*Illustrated London News*," 24*th February*, 1855.

. . . The marks which appeared on the snow (which lay very thinly on the ground at the time) and which were seen on the Friday morning, to all appearance were the perfect impression of a donkey's hoof—the length 4 inches by 2¾ inches; but, instead of progressing as that animal would have done (or as any other animal would have done), feet right and left, it appeared that foot followed foot, in a *single line*; the distance from each tread in each parish being exactly the same size and the steps the same length.

This mysterious visitor generally only passed *once* down or across each garden or courtyard, and did so in nearly all the houses in many parts of the several towns above mentioned, as also in the farms scattered about; this regular track passing in some instances over the roofs of houses, and hayricks, and very high walls (one 14 feet), without displacing the snow on either side or altering the distance between the feet, and passing on as if the wall had not been any impediment. The gardens with high fences or walls, and gates locked, were equally visited as those open and unprotected.

Now when we consider the distance that must have

[1] Read concave.

been gone over to have left these marks—I may say in almost every garden, on door-steps, through the extensive woods of Luscombe, upon commons, in enclosures and farms—the actual progress must have exceeded a hundred miles. It is very easy for people to laugh at these appearances and account for them in an idle way At present no satisfactory solution has been given. No known animal could have traversed this extent of country in one night, besides having to cross an estuary of the sea two miles broad. Neither does any known animal walk in a line of *single* footsteps, not even man.

Birds could not have left these marks, as no bird's foot leaves the impression of a hoof, or, even were there a bird capable of doing so, could it proceed in the direct manner above stated—nor would birds, even had they donkeys' feet, confine themselves to one direct line, but hop here and there ; but the nature of the mark at once sets aside its being the track of a bird.

The effect of the atmosphere upon these marks is given by many as a solution ; but how could it be possible for the atmosphere to affect one impression and not another ? On the morning that the above were observed the snow bore the fresh marks of cats, dogs, rabbits, birds, and men clearly defined. Why, then, should a continuous track, far more clearly defined—so clearly even, that the raising in the centre of the frog of each foot could be plainly seen—why then should this particular mark be the only one which was affected by the atmosphere, and all the others left as they were ?

30. DID MADELEINE SMITH POISON HER LOVER?

At 9 o'clock on a Sunday evening a young clerk in Glasgow announced to his landlady that he was going out and would probably be home late. In the early hours of the morning she heard a knock, and, on opening the door, she saw him standing there looking exceedingly ill. He complained of severe abdominal pains and said he had been violently sick. She sent for the doctor, and they did all that was possible, but he died at 9 o'clock the same morning.

Pierre Emile L'Angelier was a native of Jersey, and had worked for many years in Paris. He was now in the employ of Messrs. Huggins & Co., of Glasgow, who paid him the modest salary of ten shillings a week. He was a dapper little man, with a great belief in himself as a lady-killer. His friends used to listen indulgently to him whilst he complacently related his successes, yet whenever his advances were rejected he immediately threatened to blow out his brains. But now it was understood that he was engaged to be married, and a picture of his "intended" occupied a prominent position in his room.

Until recently he had apparently enjoyed robust health, but twice in the previous month he had experienced attacks of internal pain and vomiting. The doctor who attended him on the morning of his death declined to sign a death certificate; a post-mortem was held, and he was found to have died from the effects of a large dose of arsenic. The police searched the rooms, and the discovery of a bundle of letters resulted in the arrest of a Miss Madeleine Smith. She was put on her trial, and her outstanding beauty, combined with the most perfect composure, made an excellent impression on the Court. At the end of nine days a verdict was given of "not proven." The defence urged that he committed suicide, as he had frequently in the past threatened to do, but among the dead man's effects a diary was found, and it was lucky for the accused that this could not be admitted in evidence. The most interesting entries are as follows:

Thursday, 19*th Feb.*—Saw Mimi a few moments. Was very ill during the night.

Friday, 20*th Feb.*—Passed two pleasant hours with Mimi in the drawing room.

Saturday, 21*st Feb.*—Did not feel well.

Sunday, 22*nd Feb.*—Saw Mimi in drawing-room. Promised me French Bible. Taken very ill.

These entries coincide with the dates of his first two illnesses.

Madeleine Smith was a good-looking girl of 21, who lived with her parents in Glasgow. Her father was a prosperous architect, and they moved in intensely respectable circles. She was intelligent and over-emotional, and her vitality found no outlet in her life of parties and picnics.

L'Angelier saw her in the street in the spring of 1855 and fell in love with her, but so hopelessly ineligible was he that he could not even hope for an introduction. He found some way of speaking to her which came to the ears of her father, who sternly forbade her to have anything to do with him. The young man confided his troubles to a sentimental maiden lady, somewhat above him in station, and she began to arrange meetings for the couple at her house. The curly-headed young foreigner seemed to Madeleine the romantic hero of her dreams. They began to correspond secretly, and by the winter she was letting him into her house after the family had gone to bed. Madeleine was passionately in love with him, and was willing to elope, and risk her father's displeasure, but L'Angelier intended somehow to get his consent. It is possible that married life on ten shillings a week did not altogether appeal to him.

The Smiths always spent the summer months at their country house on the Clyde. There L'Angelier followed her in the summer of 1856, and they used to meet in the garden after dark.

MY OWN, MY BELOVED EMILE,—The thought of seeing you so soon makes me feel happy and glad. Well, beloved, you shall come to the gate (you know it) and wait until I come. I do not think there is any risk. Well, Tuesday 6th May. The Gate, half-past ten. You understand.

MIMI.

At last, despairing of ever gaining her father's consent, L'Angelier agreed to elope with her in September. Madeleine was willing, and even anxious, to face poverty with him.

" I shall be quite ready by September. . . . How I look forward to our happy union. . . . I shall leave all. Sacrifice friends, relations, family, and everything for your sake."

For some months Madeleine had written to him as her husband, signing her letters with his name, and she now became his mistress. Her love for him was at its height.

BELOVED, DEARLY BELOVED HUSBAND, SWEET EMILE,—How I long to call you mine, never more to leave you. What must occur ere that takes place, God only knows. I often fear some cloud may yet fall on our path and mar our happiness for a long time. I shall never cause you unhappiness again. . . . No, I am now a wife, a wife in every sense of the word, and it is my duty to conduct myself as such. Your income would be quite enough—don't for a moment fancy I want you to better your income for me—no, dearest, I am quite content with the sum you mention. If you only saw me now—I am all alone in my little bedroom—you would never mention your home as being humble.

Adieu sweet love, my own pet husband, my own true Emile. I am thine for ever, thy wife, thy devoted, thy own true,

MIMI L'ANGELIER.

Good night. God bless you. A kiss, pet love.

They exchanged the most passionate letters, and when her letters were made public, Madeleine's entire lack of reticence appalled the whole of Great Britain. But no sooner was her passion gratified than her affection began quickly to cool. She found an excuse for not marrying him in September.

"You know I did feel disappointed," she wrote, "at our marriage not taking place in September. But as it could not, why, then I just made up my mind to be content, and trust that it may be ere long."

The meetings went on, although they were not quite so frequent, and her letters were as passionate as ever.

August 14th.

"All by myself. So I shall write to you, dear husband. Your visit of last night is over. I longed for it. How fast it passed. . . . No one heard you. . . . Next night it will be a different window; that one is much too small."

But though she continued to write as affectionately as ever, she began to find excuses not to see him. The fact was that another and more suitable admirer had appeared on the scene, and Madeleine felt she would like to be comfortably settled in a home of her own. His name was William Minnoch, a middle-aged man of comfortable means. She mentioned him in a letter about this time.

"How must I thank you for your kind, dear letter. Accept a fond embrace and dear kisses and assurances that I do love you as much as ever and have never regretted what has occurred. . . . I cannot see you ere you go, for which I am sorry. You forget my little sister is in my bedroom and I could not go out by the window or leave the house and she there. It is only when Papa is away I can see you, for then Janet sleeps with Mama. You see I cannot see you. . . . I did tell you at one time that I did not like William Minnoch, but he was so pleasant that he quite raised himself in my estimation."

Madeleine was secretive by nature, and the only one who knew of her meetings with L'Angelier was a maid-servant, Christine Haggart, who helped her to see and correspond with her lover. She usually referred to her by her initials.

September 29th.

"I did not write you on Saturday as C. H. was not at home, so I could not get it posted. I hope, love, you are home, and well. . . . I do not think I can see you this week. But I think next Monday night as Papa and Mama are to be in Edinburgh but my only thought is Janet—what am I to do with her? I shall have to wait till she is asleep, which may be near 11 o'c. But you may be sure I shall do it as soon as I can. . . . I do love you very much. What cold weather we have had. Mr. Minnoch has been here since Friday—he is most agreeable—I think—and Papa being so fond of him I am sure he shall ask him in often.

Love again to you, sweet love.

Adieu, ever yours,

MIMI.

These naïve references to Minnoch did not fail to arouse L'Angelier's jealousy, although Madeleine assured him that it was unjustified.

October 8th.

"Our meeting was peculiar. Emile, you are not reasonable. I would to God we were not to be near to Mr. M. You shall hear all stories and believe them. You will say I am indifferent because I shall not be able to see you much. I forgot to tell you last night that I shall not be able of an evening to let you in—my room is next to B. and on the same floor as the front door. I shall never be able to spend the happy hours we did last winter. Our letters I do not see how I am to do. . . . Yes, you must think me cool—but it is my nature. . . . I shall never forget last night. There is a sentence still in my ear you said about God stricking (*sic*) you dead if ever you meet me again. Since my childhood that is a sentence I have shuddered to hear expressed."

December 14th.

MY VERY DEAREST EMILE,—Your note of Friday pained me much. . . . The tone of your letter was so different from the last; it has made me feel, I assure you, most unhappy. . . .

My Emile, I love you, and you only. It was Minnoch that I was at the concert with. You see I would not hide that from you. Emile, he is Papa's friend, and I know he will have him at the house. But need you mind that when I have told you I have no regard for him.

But Madeleine was perfectly aware that Minnoch was not coming to the house to see her father, and on January 28th she accepted his proposal of marriage. She tried to alienate L'Angelier's affections by showing her indifference for him, while he became more and more angry and suspicious. At last Madeleine resolved to break off her engagement with him by quarrelling with him openly.

February, 1857.

I felt truly astonished to have my last letter returned to me. But it will be the last you shall have an opportunity of returning to me. As you are not pleased with the letters I send you, then our correspondence shall be at an end, and as there is coolness on both sides our engagement had better be broken. This may astonish you, but you have more than once returned me my letters, and my mind was made up that I should not stand the same thing again. Altogether I think owing to coolness and indifference (nothing else) that we had better for the future consider ourselves as strangers. I trust to your honour as a gentleman that you will not reveal anything that may have passed between us. I shall feel obliged by your bringing me my letters and likenesses on Thursday evening at 7—be at the Area Gate, and C. H. will [take] the parcel from you. On Thursday night I shall send you all your letters, likenesses, etc. I trust you may yet be happy, and get one more worthy of you than I. On Thursday at 7 o'cl.

I am, etc.

M.

Apparently she had no answer to this letter.

9th February.

I attribute it to your having cold that I had no answer to my last note. On Thursday evening you were, I suppose, afraid of the night air. I fear your cold is not better. I again appoint Thursday night same place, Street Gate, 7 o'c.

M.

But L'Angelier did not mean to let her go so easily. He threatened to show her letters to her father. Madeleine was aghast, and then became panic-stricken.

February 10*th*, *Monday evening.*

Emile, I have just had your note. Emile, for the love you once had for me do nothing till I see you—for God's sake do not send my letters to Papa. . . . It will be an open rupture. I will leave the house. I will die. Emile, do nothing till I see you. One word to-morrow at my window to tell me or I shall go mad. . . . Oh, dear Emile, be not so harsh to me. . . . 10 o'c. to-morrow night, one line, for the love of God.

Tuesday morning.

I am ill. God knows what I have suffered. My punishment is more than I can bear. Do nothing till I see you, for the love of heaven, do nothing. I am mad. I am ill.

According to one of the servants, just about this time Madeleine sent him to the chemist to get her a small phial of prussic acid. She told him she wanted it for whitening her hands. The chemist refused to supply it without a doctor's prescription, and when the servant repeated this to Madeleine, she replied: " Oh, very well, never mind."

On the 12th a reconciliation took place, and the ardent meetings and letters began again. All this time Minnoch had no idea that Madeleine was not contentedly engaged in preparations for her coming marriage with him. She wrote to L'Angelier on the 11th, and again on the 14th.

My dear Emile,—I was glad to see you looking so well yesterday. I hope to see you very soon. Write me for next Thursday and then I shall tell you when I can see you. I want the first time we meet, that you will bring me all my cool letters back—the last four I have written—and I will give you others in their place.

Bring them all to me. . .

Yours with love and affection,

M.

On Tuesday, the 17th of February, L'Angelier told Miss Perry, the elderly lady who had helped the couple to meet two years before, that he was going to see Madeleine on Thursday. Thursday was the 19th, and the same night he had an attack of pain and sickness. He had recovered by the next day, but felt very weak. On Saturday, the 21st, Madeleine went herself to a chemist and bought a small quantity of arsenic, which she afterwards said was to improve her complexion. The following evening she saw L'Angelier, and he had another attack the same night. After this she wrote:

"I am so sorry to hear you are ill. I hope to God you will soon be better—take care of yourself—do not go to the office this week—just stay at home till Monday. . . . I have not felt very well this last two days—sick and headache. Everyone is complaining; it must be something in the air. I cannot see you Friday, but I think Sunday Papa will be away and I might see you, I think, but I shall let you know. . . . You did look bad Sunday night and Monday morning. I think you got sick with walking home so late—and the long want of food, so the next time we meet I shall make you eat a loaf of bread before you go out. I am longing to meet you again, sweet love. . . ."

But for all the trouble she took to make her letters sound affectionate, L'Angelier was not deceived, and began to reproach and cross-question her again.

From L'Angelier to Madeleine. March 5th.

Your cold indifference and reserved notes, so short, without a particle of love in them, and the manner you *evaded* answering the question I put to you in my last, with the reports I hear, fully convinces me, Mimi, that there is foundation in your marriage with another; besides, the way you put off our union till September without a just reason is very suspicious.

Answer me this, Mimi—who gave you the trinket you showed me? Is it true it was Mr. Minnoch? And is it true that you are, directly or indirectly engaged to Mr. Minnoch or to anyone else but me? This question I must know.

Madeleine received this letter late the same evening, and early next morning she went into a chemist's shop in

Sauchiehall Street. She asked for arsenic, and said it was to kill rats. The shopman suggested phosphorus instead, but Madeleine said that she had tried that and had found it unsuccessful. A friend who was with her that morning heard her ask the shopman something about what would be a dose, and his reply was that such a quantity as she named would kill a great many people. Madeleine turned to her friend and remarked that she only wanted it for rats. At the trial, Christine Haggart, the maidservant, said that at the Smiths' house there were no rats.

About this time L'Angelier dined with some friends, and told them of his recent illnesses. He said he had taken some coffee and cocoa, which he thought had not agreed with him. They seemed to have poisoned him, he said. To his friend, Miss Perry, speaking of Madeleine, he remarked: "I cannot think why I was so unwell after getting that coffee and chocolate from her." And again: "It is perfect fascination my attachment to that girl. If she were to poison me I would forgive her."

On the 12th of March, Madeleine fixed her wedding for a date in June. Minnoch said at the trial that he had no doubt in his mind that the wedding would take place.

The next day she was writing to L'Angelier:

DEAREST AND BELOVED,—I hope you are well. . . . I think we shall be home on Tuesday, so I shall let you know, my own beloved sweet pet, when we shall have a dear sweet interview.

On the 17th, Minnoch received this prim little letter from his fiancée.

MY DEAREST WILLIAM,—It is but fair, after your kindness to me that I should write you a note. The day I part from friends I always feel sad. But to part from one I love—as I do you—makes me feel truly sad and dull. Our walk to Dunblane I shall ever remember with pleasure. That walk fixed a day on which we are to begin a new life—a life which I hope may be of happiness and long duration to both of us. My aim through life shall be to please and study you. Dear William, I must conclude as Mama is ready to go to Stirling. I do not go with the same pleasure as I had the last time. Accept my warmest affection, kindest love, and ever believe me to be yours with affection.

MADELEINE.

On March 18th, Madeleine bought her third packet of arsenic. Three days later, she wrote to L'Angelier:

Why my beloved did you not come to me. Oh, beloved, are you ill? Come to me, sweet one. I waited and waited for you, but you came not. I shall wait again tomorrow night same hour and arrangement. Do come sweet love, my own dear love and sweetheart.

Your own, ever true fond

MIMI.

L'Angelier left home the next night at 9 o'clock, and at twenty minutes past was seen sauntering in the direction of Madeleine's house. Where he spent the rest of the night no one could tell, but he died from arsenic poisoning the next morning.

. . . .

When Madeleine returned home after the trial she wrote a letter to Miss Aiken, the matron of the prison.

DEAR MISS AIKEN,—You shall be glad to hear that I am well—in fact I am quite well, and my spirits not in the least down. I left Edinburgh and went to Slateford, and got home to Rowaleyn during the night. But, alas, I found Mama in a bad state of health. But I trust in a short time all will be well with her. The others are all well. The feeling in the west is not so good towards me as you kind Edinburgh people showed me. I rather think it shall be necessary for me to leave Scotland for a few months, but Mama is so unwell we do not like to fix anything at present. If ever you see Mr. C. Combe tell him that the panel was not at all pleased with the verdict. I was delighted with the loud cheer the court gave. I did not feel in the least put about when the jury were out considering whether they should send me home or keep me. I think I must have had several hundred letters, all from gentlemen, some offering me consolation, and some their hearths and homes. My *friend* I know nothing of. I have not seen him. I hear he has been ill, which I do not much care. I hope you will give me a note. Thank Mrs. Bell and Agnes in my name for all their kindness and attention to me. I should like you to send me my Bible and watch to 124, St. Vincent Street, Glasgow, to J. Smith. The country is looking most lovely. As soon as I know my arrangements I shall let you know where I am to be sent to. With kind love to yourself and Mr. Smith, ever believe me,

Yours sincerely,

MADELEINE SMITH.

31. D. D. HOME, THE MEDIUM

"Home's history," says the *Dictionary of National Biography*, "presents a curious and as yet unsolved problem." For there were literally dozens of witnesses in all grades of society who have left us their testimony to his extraordinary feats. He was seen to rise from the ground and float in the air; he elongated himself several inches while they watched a space grow between his trousers and waistcoat; bells floated round the room, ringing as they went, and accordions played without being touched; hands were felt, but not seen, and believers could carry red-hot coals on their heads without being harmed. To do these things, elaborate machinery must surely have been necessary, yet he accomplished them, apparently without preparation, in palaces and private houses all over Europe, and, in spite of the scepticism and even hostility of many of his sitters, he was never discovered in any fraud. Nor could money have been a motive for deception, as he gave his services free.

As a young man he became an ardent convert to Catholicism, and even thought for a time of entering a monastery. (It is curious to reflect that had he done so he would almost certainly now be known as St. Daniel, a worker of miracles.) On visiting Rome at that time, Pope Pius IX granted him an audience, and is said to have taken a personal interest in his spiritual welfare. The Chief of the Inquisition, on the other hand, seems to have regarded his performances with some misgivings, and, in a letter to *The Times*, Home gives the text of a statement he forced him to sign.

"I, Daniel Dunglas Home, hereby solemnly declare and avow that I have not sold my soul to the Devil, nor

H. W. Pickersgill pinx.

D. D. HOME

(By kind permission of the London Spiritualist Alliance)

p. 182

have I on any occasion been cognisant of holding communication with the Evil One.

"Rome, *March* 18*th*, 1856."

These suspicions were shared by the Roman police, and in 1864—by then Home had forfeited the protection of the Church—he was summarily expelled from Rome as a sorcerer.

Among the many European Courts he visited, Home was made especially welcome at the Tuileries. There, during a sitting, to the great joy of the Empress Eugénie, his hand wrote what purported to be a message from Napoleon I, and concluded by tracing the unmistakable signature of the Emperor. The Empress Eugénie, we read, raised the paper reverently to her lips.

The impartial historian cannot pass over one unfortunate episode in his career. In 1866, a quarrel with a wealthy old lady lost him many supporters. Mrs. Lyon was one of his most enthusiastic disciples, and had been persuaded by the spirit of her late husband (speaking through Home) to hand over to him the sum of £60,000. She now regretted this generosity, and, bringing an action against Home, forced him to return the money. Nothing very definite was proved against him, but somehow his reputation has never wholly recovered from the slur the affair cast over it.

In London society, Home's personal charm attracted even those who were dubious of his spiritual powers. He was tall and fair, with slender, sensitive hands, and he carried himself with a dignity that was probably inherited from his reputed grandfather, the 10th Earl of Home. He is said to have read poetry with spirit, and with strangers he preferred to discuss any subject but those mysterious powers for which he had become so celebrated.

Perhaps the most startling of his achievements was that which took place in 1868, when he floated out of one window of a third-floor room and in again at another. There were three witnesses to this feat, and each has left us his testimony. The first is that of Lord Adare, afterwards the Earl of Dunraven, and appears in his book, *Experiences in Spiritualism with D. D. Home.*

"Wynne and I went over to Ashley House after dinner. There we found Home and the Master of Lindsay. Home proposed a sitting. We accordingly sat round a table in the small room. There was no light in the room, but the light from the window was sufficient to enable us to distinguish each other, and to see different articles of furniture. Home went into a trance.

"Lindsay suddenly said: 'Oh, good heavens! I know what he is going to do; it is too fearful.'

"Adare: 'What is it?'

"Lindsay: 'I cannot tell you; it is too horrible—a spirit says that I must tell you. He is coming out of the window of the other room, and coming in at this window.'

"We heard Home go into the next room, heard the window thrown up, and presently Home appeared standing upright outside our window. He opened the window and walked in quite coolly. 'Oh,' he said, 'you were good this time'; referring to our having sat still and not wished to prevent him. 'Adare, shut the window in the next room.'

"I got up, shut the window, and in coming back remarked that the window was not raised a foot, and that I could not think how he had managed to squeeze through. He arose and said, 'Come and see.' I went with him: he told me to open the window as it was before. I did so: he told me to stand a little distance off; he then went through the open space, head first, quite rapidly, his body being nearly horizontal and apparently rigid. He came in again, feet foremost; and we returned to the other room. It was so dark I could not see clearly how he was supported outside. He did not appear to grasp, or rest upon the balustrade but rather to be swung out and in. Outside each window is a small balcony or ledge, 19 inches deep, bounded by stone balustrades, 18 inches high. The balustrades of the two windows are 7 ft. 4 in.

apart, measuring from the nearest point. A string course 4 inches wide runs between the windows at the level of the bottom of the balustrade; another, 3 inches wide, at the level of the top. Between the window at which Home went out and that at which he came in the wall recedes 6 inches. The rooms are on the third floor.

"I asked Lindsay how the spirit had spoken to him. He could scarcely explain; but said it did not sound like an audible human voice, but rather as if the tones were whispered or impressed inside his ear. When Home awoke, he was much agitated; he said he felt as if he had gone through some fearful peril, and that he had a most horrible desire to throw himself out of the window. He remained in a very nervous condition for a short time, then gradually became quiet."

Then here is Lord Lindsay's account of the incident:

"We heard the window in the next room being lifted up and almost immediately afterwards we saw Home floating in the air outside our window.

"The moon was shining full in the room; my back was to the light, and I saw the shadow on the wall of the window-sill and Home's feet about 6 inches above it. He remained in this position for a few seconds, then raised the window and glided into the room feet foremost, and sat down.

"Lord Adare then went into the next room to look at the window from which he had been carried. It was raised about 18 inches and he expressed his wonder how Mr. Home had been taken through so narrow an aperture.

"Home said (still in trance), 'I will show you'; and then, with his back to the window, he leaned back and was shot out of the aperture head first with the body rigid, and then returned quite quietly.

"The window is about 70 feet from the ground. I very much doubt whether any skilful rope-dancer would like to attempt a feat of this description where the only means of crossing would be a perilous leap."

The third witness, Captain Wynne, did not publish any account at the time but he wrote a letter, some years after, to Home to contradict the rumours of his scepticism. It is quoted in Mrs. Home's life of her husband:

"Your letter has just come before me. I remember that Dr. Carpenter wrote some nonsense about that trip of yours along the side of the house in Ashley Place. I wrote to the *Medium* to say that I was present and a witness. Now, I don't think that anyone who knows me would for a moment say that I was a victim to hallucination or any other humbug of the kind. The fact of your having gone out of the window and in at the other I can swear to; but what is the use of trying to convince men who won't believe—not even if they see it."

Of Home's elongation there are many accounts, but we quote only the one given by J. Hawkins Simpson, an electrical engineer and inventor, in a letter to the *Journal* of the S.P.R. in July, 1889.

"On one occasion in good light, and in the centre of the room, I tested his elongation and contraction *repeated several times* in rapid succession; Lord Crawford helping me. I placed Mr. Home—in trance—facing me, his heels on the floor and his toes on my insteps, and a large music book stretched over our two heads. Whilst I observed his face, Lord Crawford carefully handled muscles and legs, and observed the waistcoat rise two or three inches above the trousers tops and fall again. We then changed places. The changes Mr. Home's *face* underwent, first larger, then smaller, then normal size, were extraordinary. First his face seemed gradually to be enlarged at all points; then it gradually became smaller in features, and deeply wrinkled and puckered."

In a long article on Home in the *Cornhill Magazine* for August, 1860, Robert Bell gives a good description of the playing of an accordion by unseen agency—one of the most familiar features of the sittings. At that time Thackeray was the Editor, and he was severely criticised for allowing the article to appear. "It's all very well for you," he is said to have replied, "who have never seen any spiritual manifestations, to talk as you do, but had you seen what I have witnessed, you would hold a different opinion."

"Those who had keen eyes," wrote Robert Bell, "declared that they saw the accordion in motion. Concentrating my attention on the spot where I supposed it to be, I perceived a dark mass rise awkwardly above the edge of the table, and then go down, the instrument emitting a single sound produced by its being struck against the table as it went over. It descended to the floor in silence, and a quarter of an hour afterwards, we heard the accordion beginning to play where it lay on the ground.

"We listened with suspended breath. The air was wild, and full of strange transitions, with a wail of the most pathetic sweetness running through it. The execution was no less remarkable for its delicacy than its power. When the notes swelled in some of the bold passages, the sound rolled through the room with an astounding reverberation; and then, gently subsiding, sank into a strain of divine tenderness. It continued diminishing and diminishing, and stretching far away into distance and darkness, until the attenuated thread of sound became so exquisite that it was impossible at last to fix the moment when it ceased."

Ghostly hands and movements of objects without visible human contact are described in this letter from Count Tolstoy (a cousin of the writer) to his wife, June 17th, 1860.

"It is two o'clock in the morning; I have just left Home; this séance has been *overwhelming*. First there occurred all the manifestations you have witnessed; then, on the light being reduced, every article of furniture in the room took to moving of its own accord. A table placed itself on another table; a sofa moved into the middle of the room; a bell rose in the air and went all round the apartment, ringing as it floated.

"Finally, the remaining lights were put out, and we sat almost in darkness; there was only a faint light that came through the window from a gas-lamp outside. The piano played with no one near it; a bracelet unclasped itself from the arm of Mrs. Milner Gibson and fell on the table, where it lay surrounded by a luminous appearance. Home was raised from the ground; and I clasped his feet while he floated in the air above our heads. Hands touched my knees and laid themselves in my hands; and when I sought to retain one *it dissolved in my grasp*. A cold wind passed round the circle very distinctly, and perfumes were wafted to us."

What was known as the "fire test" is described by Mrs. S. C. Hall, the novelist, in a letter to Lord Dunraven, July 5th, 1869.

"We were seated round the table as usual in the small drawing-room. I think there was one lamp burning over the table, but a very large fire was blazing away in the large room—I know there was a great deal of light. After the lapse of nearly an hour, Mr. Home went into a trance. He got up; walked about the room in his usual manner; went to the fireplace; half knelt on the fender stool; took up the poker and poked the fire, which was like a red-hot furnace, so as to increase the heat; held his hands over the fire for some time, and finally drew out of the fire, with his hand, a huge lump of live burning coal, so large that he held it in *both* hands, as he came from the fireplace in the large room into the small room, where, seated round the table, we were all watching his movements. I saw Mr. Home, after standing for about half a minute at the back of Mr. Hall's chair, deliberately place the lump of burning coal on his head! Some one said, 'Is it not hot?' Mr. Hall answered, 'Warm, but not hot! Mr. Home smiled and seemed quite pleased; and then proceeded to draw up Mr. Hall's white hair over the red coal. The white hair had the appearance of silver threads, over the red coal. After four or five minutes Mr. Home, taking the coal off Mr. Hall's head, said (in the peculiar low voice in which, when in a trance, he always speaks) addressing Mrs. Y——, "Will you have it?" She drew back; and I heard him murmur, "Little faith—little faith." Two or three attempted to touch it, but it burnt their fingers. I said, 'Daniel, bring it to me; I don't fear to take it.' It was not red all over, as when Mr. Home put it on Mr. Hall's head, but it was still red in parts. Mr. Hall came and knelt by my side and placed it in my left hand, where it remained more than a minute. I felt it, as my husband said, warm; yet when I stooped down to examine the coal, my face felt the heat so much that I was obliged to withdraw it. When Mr. Hall brushed his hair at night he found a quantity of cinder dust."

32. THE ROAD HILL MURDER

Mr. and Mrs. Kent were on the point of getting up in the morning when they heard from the nurse that their little boy of four was missing from his cot. He was not in the house, and nothing had been seen of him that morning. In answer to their questions, the housemaid reported that, on first coming downstairs, she had found one of the drawing-room windows open, and this led to the idea that he might have been stolen. Mr. Kent set out immediately in his trap for Trowbridge, the nearest town, to ask the police to send out men to scour the neighbourhood. On his way he was overtaken by a messenger from home, who told him that his little son had been found murdered in an outhouse a few yards from the house. He showed the deepest grief.

Before the family retired to bed on that Friday, the windows were fastened, and every door securely bolted. There were no signs in the morning to indicate that the house had been broken into and no footsteps were visible outside the open windows; the dog had not barked, though on the approach of a stranger he usually roused at least one of the family. As soon as the Kents and their maids had recovered a little from the shock of the discovery, they drew the obvious inference—that the murderer must have been inside the house on the night of the crime. They began to eye each other with suspicion, and, on the next night, the only member of the household who was willing to sleep alone locked his bedroom door.

Twelve persons had slept in Road Hill House on the night of June 29th, 1860. On the first floor were Mr. and Mrs. Kent, who, with their five-year-old daughter, occupied one large room, and the murdered boy and his two-year-old sister, who slept with their nurse in a smaller room. On the next floor four children of Mr. Kent's by a previous marriage occupied three of the four rooms. The two eldest Miss Kents, aged 29 and 28, shared one, and Constance and William, aged 16 and 15, each slept alone. The two maids shared the remaining room.

Shortly after the body was discovered, Mr. Foley, the superintendent of the Trowbridge police, arrived to take charge of the case. He began by questioning the nurse. Elizabeth Gough was a nice-looking girl of 22, with an excellent reference from her previous employer, and had been with the Kents just on nine months. Her story was that she put the children to bed as usual at 8 o'clock on Friday evening, and went to bed herself shortly afterwards, leaving the door ajar. Mrs. Kent came in about three hours later, kissed the children good-night, and shut the door behind her. The nurse knew nothing until she woke at five the next morning, and then her eyes fell on the younger child, who had tossed off her bedclothes in her sleep. As the nurse knelt up on her bed to cover up the child, she noticed that the other cot was empty, and that the bedroom door was open. The little boy had not been very well, and thinking, she said, that he had been carried into the other room by his mother, she felt no uneasiness and went back to sleep. At six o'clock she got up and knocked twice on Mrs. Kent's door without receiving any answer. She then washed and dressed the little girl, and at 7.15 rapped once more on Mrs. Kent's door. This time the door was opened by her mistress, who seemed surprised at the nurse's request for the child, and said that she had not seen him since she kissed him good-night in the nursery.

The bedclothes of the boy's cot, which should have consisted of a blanket, a sheet, and a counterpane, had been tidily re-arranged, with the sheet turned back over the counterpane. It was impossible to tell from their appearance in the morning that they were not all there, but Mrs. Kent, on being questioned afterwards by Mr. Foley, remembered that the nurse had told her that the blanket was gone. "I am glad to hear that," Mrs. Kent recalled saying, "it will keep the poor little fellow warm." The nurse, however, now declared to Mr. Foley that she had known nothing of the loss until an hour later, when the boy was found dead, wrapped in the missing blanket. His head was almost severed from his body, and he had another savage wound in his chest. From the relatively small amount of blood, these wounds, in the opinion of the doctor who examined the body, must have been inflicted after death. The child, he thought, had been suffocated by the pressure of something soft on his mouth, and stabbed afterwards with great force by a sharp-pointed instrument. The boy had been dead for at least five hours. Near the body was a triangular piece of flannel soaked with blood, which was described by the police as a chest-protector of a kind sometimes worn by women. No one in the house acknowledged it as theirs, and the laundrywoman subsequently denied ever having washed it for any member of the household. It was held to the nurse's chest, and seemed to fit her exactly.

Mrs. Kent was too much upset to be closely examined that day, but she showed, in spite of her grief, considerable resentment towards the nurse for not giving the alarm when she first missed the child. She assured Mr. Foley that she never took the child into her room during the night, and, moreover, as she was very shortly to have another baby, the nurse must have known that she could not have carried such a heavy child. She had been awake most of the early part of the night, and for that reason slept all the more heavily towards morning. In this way she accounted for the fact that she had not heard the nurse's first knocks. But, sleepless as she said she had been, the child had been taken out of the next room, and neither she nor anyone else in the house had apparently heard a sound.

As soon as Foley had heard the whole story he set

to work to search the house. Mr. Kent readily gave him permission to look where he pleased. The knives were all in their place, but, unfortunately, had already been cleaned[1]; the nightgowns, worn that night, were examined in vain for traces of blood; nothing in any of the bedrooms afforded the slightest clue. One remarkable discovery, however, was made by the police, and this they kept to themselves. A bloodstained shift was found in the scullery boiler furnace.

On Saturday night, unknown to them all except Mr. and Mrs. Kent, Foley stationed two policemen in the kitchen, giving as his reason to Mr. Kent that he thought it possible that the nurse had an accomplice, and that she might let him in during the night. He really wanted to see if anyone would come downstairs to destroy the garment hidden in the scullery. Mr. Kent did not go to bed at all that night, but sat by himself in the library. During the night, one of the policemen got up to open the kitchen door. He found it had been locked from the outside. They made sufficient noise to attract Mr. Kent's attention, who, on opening the door, admitted having locked it. He explained that had he not done so the suspicions of the household would have been aroused, and the presence of the policemen discovered. In the early hours of the morning the men left the house, none the wiser for their night in the kitchen.

On July 10th, Elizabeth Gough was taken into custody, but nothing could be proved against her, and she was shortly afterwards released. By now Scotland Yard felt it was time to step in, and on July 15th Inspector Whicher came down from London to take over the case from Foley, who, it was generally felt, had grossly mismanaged the case. Five days after his arrival he arrested Constance Kent.

Constance was Mr. Kent's third daughter by his first wife, and she had recently returned from boarding-school.

[1] It is curious to read that the boy who cleaned the knives was dismissed and sent away from the house that morning before being cross-questioned by the police. No reason for his dismissal was ever made public.

She was tall and stout for her age, and her small, deep-set eyes gave her an unprepossessing appearance. It was hinted that there was ill-feeling between the first and second families of Mr. Kent, but no one could say definitely that they had heard either Constance or any of the others express any particular dislike of the dead child. The only proof of Constance's unhappiness at home was that three years before she had run away disguised as a boy with her brother William, and had been brought back much against her will. Her disposition was known to be a difficult one, and this was generally accounted for by the fact that the first Mrs. Kent had been out of her mind during her pregnancy. No traces of insanity, however, were ever detected in Constance.

As soon as Whicher arrived, he proceeded to make another and more careful examination of all the clothes belonging to the family and their servants. Now Constance could only produce two of her three nightdresses—the third she said had been lost at the wash the week of the murder. This seemed to Whicher highly significant, and he continued to ask questions until he drew from various sources the following facts. While the housemaid was getting ready the laundry on the Monday after the murder, Constance appeared, and after a brief conversation asked the girl to get her a glass of water. When she returned Constance drank the water, and then went back to her room. The basket was fetched as usual by the laundry-woman, but on reaching home she found that, although a nightdress was entered in Miss Constance Kent's list, no such garment could be found in the basket. The next day she came to the house and informed Mr. Kent of the discrepancy. Mr. Kent was exceedingly angry, for these disputes were continually taking place, and he threatened to sue her for the loss of the garment.

Whicher suspected Constance of the murder, and thought if she were arrested she would speedily be brought to confess. In this he was mistaken, for Constance remained sullen and reserved, and all attempts to extract a confession from her utterly failed. She was discharged, and so great was the indignation felt towards Inspector Whicher for arresting a young girl on such trivial evidence that he was obliged to retire from the service.

In October the nurse was re-arrested, and this time actually charged with murder ; again she was discharged. But suspicion was still directed against her, although now another member of the family was felt to be heavily implicated. She must have had, people said, a lover in her room that night. Now supposing that the child, waking suddenly, recognised—his father, what would be likely to follow ? A hand would be pressed on the child's mouth in an attempt to stifle its cries, and, whether intentionally or not, death from suffocation would probably be the result. The wounds would then be inflicted to disguise the motive for the crime.

The London press, indeed, had from the first pointed to Mr. Kent as the culprit, and there were certainly many circumstances to justify this suspicion. For some reason he was thoroughly unpopular in the neighbourhood, and had the reputation of never being able to keep female servants long in his employ. On the strength of this the public did not hesitate to accuse him of profligacy. A curious story that told heavily against him was that a woman who met him on his way to Trowbridge on the morning of the crime, before he had heard of the discovery of the body, stated that he told her that his child had been carried off in a blanket. How, it was asked, did both he and the nurse know that the blanket was missing ? A letter appeared in *The Times* on October 22nd, voicing the suspicions of the public.

Sir,—It seems to be the general opinion that the murder was committed by, or with the connivance and aid of, some inmate of the house. Now most of the inmates of the house were relatives of the murdered boy. In examining the evidence against various possible culprits it is therefore necessary to discard the arguments which have been pretty extensively pressed—that the boy's father, mother, or sister could not have been his murderer, because they were his father, his mother, or his sister. We know that parents have murdered their children, and sisters their brothers, since the world began, and will do so again before the world ends, and it remains to be seen whether a crime of that atrocity has now been committed.

Great stress has been laid upon the fact that Mrs. Kent is supposed to have been a light sleeper, and that she was in a peculiar state of health that rendered her morbidly watchful; but, as there is no doubt that some person removed the boy from the room next to her without being heard by her, it is clear that she slept sound enough on the night of the murder not to hear what was done; therefore her alleged wakeful disposition proves nothing.

It did not appear clearly in the evidence whether Mrs. Kent was asleep or awake when Mr. Kent first retired to bed, nor did it appear whether she had any means of knowing at what precise time he came to bed. She stated that he had not left her side *for more than a quarter of an hour* during the night. How did she know that? Did he leave her side at all? At what time, and for what purpose?

No traces of the murder have been discovered on the premises—no bloody clothes or knife have been found. Yet there was a pool of blood on the floor of the privy, and it seems hardly possible that such an act could be committed without leaving some stains on the clothes of the murderer. Ought we not, therefore, to ask which of the inmates had the best opportunity of disposing of such evidence of crime before the police arrived—before any search took place—before there was any suspicion of murder at all? Mr. Kent is stated to have left the house in his carriage to seek a policeman who lived at a distance. What sort of carriage did he travel in—who ordered it—who prepared it—who saw Mr. Kent enter it—did he leave the premises alone, or accompanied by a servant—

whom did he meet on his journey—is the precise road he took known—has it been searched thoroughly—what sort of horse did he drive—was it a spirited animal that would not stand while its master absented himself for a short time, or a quiet, dull beast?

The nurse's conduct, to say the least, appears suspicious; it was undoubtedly grossly negligent, yet Mr. Kent has shown no *animus* against her. He did not even dismiss her from his service after the event.

On the other hand, the nurse described the murdered child as a nasty little tell-tale, and, openly avowing her suspicions of Constance Kent, has spoken highly of Mr. Kent's character for kindness to his children. Between Mr. Kent and the nurse there is clearly no ill-will.

Everything tends to indicate that the murder was committed early in the night. Had it been committed before Mr. Kent went to bed, and had he had a share in it, any noises in the house would have excited no suspicions in the inmates, and would have been easily explained by him had they disturbed any of the family. In that case, the dog would not have barked, there would have been plenty of time to arrange the bedclothes, and to prepare any bloody clothes for removal in the carriage in the morning. Why did Mr. Kent lock up the policemen? The men are said to have been sent to protect the family; against whom, or what, and how could they do so if they were locked up?

It is for the interest of Mr. Kent, if he is innocent, and for the interest of justice, if he is guilty, that these questions shall be publicly met and dealt with.

COMMON SENSE.

And there the matter rested until five years afterwards, when it was heard that Constance Kent had surrendered herself for the murder of her half-brother. She was at that time staying in a convent at Brighton, and it was to her confessor that she first admitted her guilt. The proceedings were short, and before she disappeared into penal servitude she made a detailed confession, from which the following is an extract[1]:

" A few days before the murder she obtained possession of a razor from a green case in her father's wardrobe, and secreted it. This was the sole instrument which she used. She also secreted a candle with matches, by placing them in the corner of the closet in the garden, where the murder was committed. On the night of the murder she undressed herself and went to bed, because she expected that her sisters would visit her room. She lay watching until she thought that the household were all asleep, and soon after midnight she left her bedroom and went downstairs, and opened the drawing room door and window shutter.

" She then went up into the nursery, withdrew the blanket from between the sheet and the counterpane, and placed it on the side of the cot. She then took the child from his bed and carried him downstairs through the drawing-room. She had on her nightdress, and in the drawing-room she put on her goloshes. Having the child in one arm, she raised the drawing-room window with the other hand, went round the house and into the closet, the child being wrapped in the blanket and still sleeping, and while the child was in this position she inflicted the wound in the throat. She says that she thought that the blood would never come, and that the child was not killed, so she thrust the razor into its left side, and put the body, with the blanket round it, into the vault. The light burnt out. The piece of flannel which she had with her was torn from an old flannel garment placed in the waste-bag, and which she had taken some time before and sewn it to use in washing herself.

[1] A letter written by Inspector Whicher to a friend soon after he retired from the service, describing in detail Constance's probable actions on the night of the crime, was in a remarkable degree substantiated by this confession. The brilliant detective (Whicher), whose apparently far-fetched theories turn out to be correct, and his blundering colleague (Foley), whose stupidity acts as a foil, made their first appearance in literature in *The Moonstone*, and have figured in almost every detective story ever since.

" She went back into her bedroom, examined her nightdress, and found only two spots of blood on it. These she washed out in the basin, and threw the water, which was but little discoloured, into the footpan in which she had washed her feet overnight. She took another of her nightdresses and got into bed. In the morning her nightdress had become dry where it had been washed. She folded it up and put it into the drawer. Her three nightdresses were examined by Mr. Foley, and she believes also by Mr. Parsons, the medical attendant of the family. She thought the blood stains had been effectively washed out, but on holding the dress up to the light a day or two afterwards she found the stains were still visible. She secreted the dress, moving it from place to place, and she eventually burnt it in her own bedroom, and put the ashes or tinder into the kitchen grate. It was about five or six days after the child's death that she burnt the nightdress.

" On the Saturday morning, having cleaned the razor she took the opportunity of replacing it unobserved in the case in the wardrobe. She abstracted her nightdress from the clothes' basket when the housemaid went to fetch a glass of water. The stained garment found in the boiler-hole had no connection whatever with the deed. As regards the motive of her crime it seems that, although she entertained at one time a great regard for the present Mrs. Kent, yet if any remark was at any time made which in her opinion was disparaging to any member of the first family she treasured it up and determined to revenge it. She had no ill-will against the little boy, except as one of the children of her stepmother. She declared that both her father and her stepmother had always been kind to her personally."

But Constance's confession is far from satisfactory, and leaves many of the mysterious circumstances of the murder unexplained. Why did not the child bleed more if she killed him in the way she described? How could she have *stabbed* him through the blanket with a razor ? Why did she take the piece of flannel with her, and why did the housemaid not recognise it ? What happened to the shift found in the scullery, and to whom did it belong ? Was the confession an authentic one ? Was pressure put on her by her confessor to give herself up ? Was everyone round her so convinced that she had murdered her brother that she came to believe it herself ? Or did she in the religious atmosphere of the convent, conceive the idea of sacrificing herself in order to dispel the cloud of suspicion that hung over her father ?

There are still some who wonder if she ever committed the crime at all.

33. AN ENCOUNTER WITH A SEA-MONSTER IN THE ATLANTIC OCEAN

From a letter written by M. Sabin Berthelot, the French consul at Teneriffe, to the Paris Academy of Sciences, which subsequently appeared in the Academy's printed "Transactions."[1]

On the 2nd of December [1861] the steam despatch-boat *Alecto* dropped anchor in our roads on her voyage to Cayenne. This ship had encountered at sea, between Madeira and Teneriffe, a monstrous polyp swimming at the surface of the water. This animal measured from 16 to 18 feet in length, without counting the eight formidable arms, covered with air-holes, that encircled its head. Its colour was brick-red; its eyes, placed level with the top of its head, were prodigiously developed and glared with a frightful fixity. Its mouth, like a parrot's beak, was nearly a foot and a half in width. Its body, fusiform, but much swollen towards the centre, presented an enormous mass, whose weight might be computed at about 4,400 pounds. Its fins, situated at the posterior extremity, were rounded into fleshy lobes of a very great size.

It was on Nov. 30th, about half an hour after noon, that the crew of the *Alecto* descried this terrible cephalopod swimming alongside. The commander immediately stopped his vessel, and manœuvred to catch it. A slip-knot was made ready; muskets were loaded and harpoons prepared, all in haste. But at the first bells the monster dived underneath the vessel and quickly reappeared on the other side. Attacked anew with the harpoons, and after receiving several discharges of musketry, he disappeared

[1] Quoted by J. G. Lockhart in *Mysteries of the Sea*.

twice or thrice, each time showing himself a few moments afterwards at the surface, agitating his long arms. But the ship continued to follow him, or rather checked her course according to the animal's movements. This chase lasted for two or three hours.

The captain of the *Alecto* grew anxious at all costs to capture this novel kind of foe. Nevertheless, he durst not hazard the lives of his sailors by lowering a boat, which this monster would have readily capsized by seizing it with one of its formidable arms. The harpoons aimed at it penetrated its soft flesh, and flew back without inflicting any mortal injury. Several balls had hit in vain. At length it received a shot which seemed to wound it seriously, for it immediately vomited a great quantity of froth and blood mixed with glutinous matter, which diffused a strong odour of musk. It was at this crisis that the sailors contrived to catch it with the running knot, but the rope glided along the mollusc's elastic body, and only stopped when near the extremity at the junction of the two fins. They attempted to haul it aboard, and already the greater portion of the body was clear of the water when its enormous weight drew the rope right through its flesh, and separated the hinder portion from the remainder of the animal. Then the monster, released from its bonds, fell back into the sea and disappeared.

34. THE COURTSHIP AND MARRIAGE OF TOM THUMB AND LAVINIA WARREN

Extracts from New York newspapers quoted in a pamphlet printed in 1865.

Dec. 23*rd*, 1862.

There is a little lady at the St. Nicholas Hotel who bids fair to throw the career of Tom Thumb entirely in the shade. This miniature queen of the Lilliputs is but 32 inches high,[1] 21 years old, and of excellent form. Her dresses are magnificent, being clothed at the rate of 2,000 dollars per outfit, and sparkling with jewels and splendour.

Miss Warren is beautifully developed in physical form, and has great mental aptitude. Her size is so small that a baby's chair is quite large enough for her to sit upon! She has rich dark, waving hair, large, brilliant, and intelligent eyes, and an exquisitely modelled neck and shoulders. Her bust would be a study for a sculptor, and the symmetry of her form is such that, were she of the average size, she would be one of the most handsome of women.

Miss Warren left her pleasant home in the country with the firm determination to visit Europe and gratify her inclination to travel. While in Boston she was introduced to Mr. Stratton (General Tom Thumb), but the meeting was of short duration, and nothing transpired to indicate the course that love was taking, save the interchange of glances. The mother of Lavinia, who

[1] This is incorrect, for Lavinia was only 24 inches high. Her parents were exceptionally tall, and six of their eight children took after them. The remaining two, Lavinia and her sister Minnie, were dwarfs. Before going on exhibition, Lavinia had taught in a school, where in spite of her diminutive size she was always able to maintain strict discipline.

was present, looked upon Mr. Stratton as a rival to her daughter, and made him the subject of criticism. She thought he was proud and aristocratic; besides, he was cultivating a moustache, which was very offensive to her. When the little "Queen of Beauty" arrived at the St. Nicholas Hotel in New York, she was visited by the *élite* and *literati* of Gotham; the newspapers gave graphic and truthful pictures of her charms and accomplishments, and among her many admirers was Mr. Stratton, whose eyes had been entangled with hers at their first meeting in Boston.

Whatever may have been her emotions, with true womanly secretiveness, she kept them to herself, saying little or nothing about the little beau, who was now completely smitten by her. When she made a contract with Mr. Barnum to appear before the public, Mr. Stratton found peculiar attractions at the Museum; and, turning his back upon Bridgeport[1] and making the Museum his headquarters, he watched for opportunities to secure the society of Miss Warren. Emboldened by the encouragement which he met in his career of courtship, he courageously but courteously "popped the question," to which Miss Warren replied that she loved him, but could not agree to marry him without the consent of her parents; and "You know," she added archly, "that mother objects to your moustache." "I will cut that off, and my eyes also, if that will induce you to give an affirmative answer to my question." Little was said, but a great deal was understood, and no time was lost in ascertaining the opinion of the parents of Miss Warren. The report was favourable. Their marriage became the topic of conversation in all circles of society, especially in fashionable conclaves; the *crême de la crême* sought opportunities to see the prospective groom and bride, and endeavoured to secure an invitation to be present at the nuptials.

On Tuesday, the 10th of February, 1863, the grand

[1] Tom Thumb's country house, where he lived during periods of retirement from public life.

national event of the season transpired. The interior of the church was crowded with a gay assemblage of the youth, beauty, wealth and worth of the metropolis.

To the diminutive Stratton-Warren bridal pair the ordinary arrangements of the chancel would have been far too Brobdingnagian. The chancel rail would have towered above their heads, and the chancel steps would have proved heights beyond their powers to scale. Therefore, a neat platform was erected in front of the chancel, to the right of the pulpit, carpeted like the aisles, six steps leading to it, and spanning the three ordinary steps which suffice for ordinary-sized mortals.

After sundry false alarms and consequent stirrings and settlings, finally the bridal cortège appeared. The bride was given away at the request of her parents by the Rev. Dr. Putnam of Middleboro, and the words of the service were repeated with audible distinctness by both the bride and groom, each seeming to realise the solemnity of the hour. Their manner was marked by that courtly ease and self-possession which can only be obtained by intercourse with the world and indifference to crowds. The benediction was pronounced by the Rev. Dr. Taylor, Rector of Grace Church, whereupon the General saluted his wife with an honest kiss, the last of nearly *three million* pressed in public upon the lips of his lady admirers.

. . . .

On the 5th of December, 1863, Mrs. Stratton gave birth to a female infant, weighing at the time of its birth but three pounds. It is now a fine healthy child of about a year old, and weighs about 7¾lbs. It accompanies them on their present tour, and is looked upon by the millions who visit this most remarkable family with as much interest as its Lilliputian parents, its wonderfully small hands and feet being especially objects of curiosity.[1]

"*Morning Post,*" *London, Thursday, November 24th,* 1864.

An intimation having been conveyed to General Tom

[1] The baby died of meningitis at the age of two and a half.

Thumb and his family that the Prince and Princess of Wales would be happy to receive them, the General and his wife, with her sister, Miss Minnie Warren, proceeded to Marlborough House shortly before 7 last evening.

After the formal presentation to their Royal Highnesses had been made, the Prince of Wales and the Duke of Cambridge entered into conversation with the General, while the Princess of Wales bestowed much attention on the pretty little infant, who was uncommonly "good" on the auspicious occasion, although her bedtime had arrived. Her Royal Highness also conversed with Mrs. Stratton and her sister, who, as well as the General, were highly delighted with the affability shown by their Royal Highnesses. The interview lasted for about a quarter of an hour, when the Prince and Princess of Wales, with the Duke of Cambridge and Prince Arthur, retired, having previously expressed the great pleasure they had derived from the interview—a pleasure which, it need scarcely be said, was felt in the highest degree by the General and his party.

The private reception held yesterday afternoon at Cataldi's Hotel, Dover Street, the last of the series, was attended by a numerous and fashionable company.

It is understood that General Tom Thumb, who has attained high masonic honours, will be specially invited to attend a grand lodge next week, under the patronage of the Grand Master, the Earl of Zetland.

35. THE TRAGEDY OF CHARLOTTE OF MEXICO

THE Empress Charlotte[1] was on her way to Rome, and signs of nervous exhaustion could plainly be seen on her face. Her attendants did all they could to spare her unnecessary fatigue, but her tortured brain gave her no peace, and her restlessness was painful to watch. Three months ago, she had left her husband in desperate peril to come to Europe in a last hope of procuring help; her mission had so far been an utter failure, and the news that reached her from Mexico threw her into even greater agitation. She arrived in Rome late at night, and, as she stepped from the train, dressed in black, her beautiful young face looked haggard with exhaustion.

Only two years had passed since she had induced Maximilian to accept Napoleon III's offer of the Mexican throne. They left their Austrian home full of enthusiasm and hope for the future, and, although on their arrival in Mexico, they were rather taken aback to find that only a small area of the country had been pacified, and that the national treasury was empty, they relied on Napoleon's pledge "to secure the re-establishment of peace in Mexico and to consolidate the new empire." After two years the situation had grown worse instead of better, and, at the moment when they needed Napoleon's help most, he announced his intention of withdrawing his troops and leaving them to their fate.

[1] Charlotte was the daughter of Leopold I of Belgium. Thus she was first cousin to Queen Victoria.

The editors' thanks are due to Count Corti, author of *Maximilian and Charlotte of Mexico*, for his courtesy in lending them a Press-cutting of an article which appeared in a Viennese newspaper at the time of the Empress's death, from which this account has been written.

Charlotte went first to Paris. She failed to move Napoleon with her prayers, and only irritated him with her reproaches. Worn out with anger and racked with anxiety, she had come to Rome in the hope of persuading the Pope to intercede for her husband.

Her first interview with Pius IX lasted an hour and a half. What took place between them never transpired, but when she emerged from his study her eyes were black with despair.

Early in the morning, a couple of days later, she summoned Señora del Barrio, her lady-in-waiting, and announced her intention of going for a drive. Her attendants called a cab, and when it arrived the Empress ordered the driver to take them to the Vatican. Señora del Barrio tried to draw her attention to the fact that she was not correctly dressed to enter the presence of the Pope, for according to papal etiquette a mantilla was necessary, and the Empress was wearing a hat. " You know that Emperors and Empresses determine etiquette and are not accustomed to be bound by it," replied the Empress. These words greatly alarmed the lady-in-waiting, for they were uncharacteristic of her mistress, who in matters like these was usually the pattern of propriety.

Although it was only eight o'clock when they arrived at the palace, the Pope consented to see her. Her unconventional headdress was remarked by his suite with painful surprise, but the Holy Father politely pretended not to notice it. Breakfast was served, and he spoke kindly to the Empress, for he could see that she was in great distress. Suddenly she put three of her fingers into her cup of chocolate, and announced that it was poisoned, and that she would starve rather than touch it. The Pope ordered another cup. When this appeared she ignored it, and, after a while, drank out of the first as if nothing had happened.

As she sipped, she talked of Mexican affairs. She spoke calmly and reasonably, yet at such interminable length that the Pope grew impatient, for urgent business awaited him. Charlotte did not appear to notice his inattention, and at last they were obliged to tell her that she must go. She replied that she would not leave the Vatican, as murderers were waiting for her outside the gates. They assured her that her fears were groundless, but all their arguments failed to convince her. She did not wish to take up the Pope's time—he might go on with his duties—she would not in any circumstances leave the Vatican before night. It was suggested that to pass the time she might like to visit the Vatican library. She accepted the invitation, insisting, in spite of what she had previously said, on being accompanied there by the Pope. He could not refuse, and reluctantly complied with her wish. As she was admiring one of the magnificent volumes, however, he succeeded in slipping away unobserved.

Lunch-time drew near, and fresh attempts were made to persuade her to go. She would not stir. Luncheon was served to her, and Cardinal Antonelli, the secretary of state, and her lady-in-waiting kept her company at table. The Empress would eat only from the plate of Señora del Barrio. During the meal she talked sensibly and freely. So the day wore on. Little was said at dinner, and she watched with fear and suspicion the servants who waited at table. After dinner, they hoped that at last the time for her departure had come. She announced most decidedly that she did not intend to leave the Vatican. Murderers surrounded her at the hotel, and only here was she safe. They were greatly embarrassed. No woman had ever stayed the night at the Vatican, and, when they realised that they could not persuade the Empress to go, there was general consternation.

In his kindness and sympathy, however, the Pope ordered that two beds should be made up in the library. He directed that it should be furnished with the most beautiful furniture and the most precious candlesticks, as befitted the dignity of an Empress. Charlotte was so worn out that she had to be carried to bed, and all that night, while her lady-in-waiting sat by her side, she slept the deep sleep of exhaustion. The next morning, Charlotte did not remember at first where she was, but when she had been told she was delighted to know that she was in the care of the Pope.

After breakfast, he tentatively suggested that she might like to take a drive, secretly intending to send her home in his carriage. She preferred to remain in the building. In the end it was the Cardinal who hit upon a ruse to get her out of the palace. The Sisters of the Vincent Convent near by were asked to invite her to visit their orphanage. The Mother Superior arrived and played her rôle to perfection. The Empress, after having exacted from her a promise that no attempts would be made to murder her, got into the papal coach with the Sisters.

During the drive, the Empress held her handkerchief in front of her face so that she might not be recognised. By the time they arrived she seemed rather calmer. She made an inspection of the convent, and displayed her usual tact in complimenting the Sisters on the general cleanliness. All went well until they descended to the kitchens. The Sister-in-charge there offered the Empress some ragoût. Once more she became violently agitated. "Poisoned, poisoned! You have not polished the knife!" cried the Empress in terror, and loudly accused the Sisters of complicity in an attempt to murder her. Then she threw herself down on the floor in the middle of the kitchen and thanked God aloud for her preservation. For a moment she recovered her composure, until her eyes fell on a pot of soup that stood simmering on the fire. Before she could be prevented she plunged her hand into the boiling liquid and, seizing a piece of meat, she began to gnaw it voraciously. Only in this way, she said, could she satisfy her hunger, for she knew that this at least was not poisoned.

The Empress's hand was badly scalded, and as it was being bandaged she fainted with pain. While she was still unconscious they carried her to her carriage, and told the coachman to drive quickly to her hotel. On the way she recovered consciousness, and, drawing back the curtain of the coach, she screamed loudly for help. When they drew up at the hotel she refused to get out, and they were obliged to carry her in, struggling violently, under the curious gaze of the crowd that had collected before the door.

Ten days later her brother, the Count of Flanders, took her back to Miramar, where she had spent the first happy years of her married life. She could do nothing more to save her husband, and he was left to face his enemies alone. When, some months later, news of his execution reached Europe, Charlotte, now hopelessly insane, had forgotten him, and was thinking only of the murderers whom she saw lurking in every corner of her room.

36. THE *MARY CELESTE*

From the United States Consul at Gibraltar to the owner of the "Mary Celeste," December, 1872.

The American brig *Mary Celeste* of New York was brought into this port by the British barque *Dei Gratia*. The *Mary Celeste* picked up on the high seas on December 5th abandoned. Brig in perfect condition, but was taken possession of by Admiralty Court as a derelict. Fate of crew unknown.

Extract from report made to the British Board of Trade.

Early on the morning of December 13th, part of the crew of the British vessel *Dei Gratia* . . . brought into this port a brigantine, which they stated they had found on the 5th of that month, in lat. 38.20 N., long. 17.15 W. at 3 p.m. sea time, totally abandoned and derelict, and which they supposed from the log to be the American brigantine *Mary Celeste*, bound from New York for Genoa. . . . The Master of the *Dei Gratia*, who had arrived on the evening of December 12th, made his claim for salvage. . . . But the account which they [the crew] gave of the soundness and good condition of the derelict was so extraordinary that I found it necessary to apply for a survey.

Extract from report of survey in the " Gibraltar Chronicle," January 30th, 1873.

As regards the cargo—it consisted of barrels marked as containing alcohol, all of which were well stowed and in good order and condition, except one which had been started. As regards the exterior of the hull below the water line—it did not in any part exhibit the slightest trace of damage, nor was there any appearance that the vessel had come into collision with any other ship, nor that she had struck on any ground or rock, nor, in short, that she had sustained any injury whatever, the hull, the copper with which it was covered, the keel, stern-post, and rudder being all in good order and condition As regards the interior of the ship—a very minute survey showed most clearly that not only had the vessel not sustained any accident, but that she could not have encountered any seriously heavy weather. The whole of the hull, masts, and yards were in good condition, and the pitch in the water-ways had not been started, which must have been the case if bad weather had been experienced. The deck-house, made of planking and six feet in height above the deck, was perfect, there not being a crack in the planking nor even in the paint. The seamen's chests and the clothing found on board were perfectly dry, some razors even being quite free from rust. Moreover, a small phial containing oil for use with a sewing machine was found in a perpendicular position, which, together with a thimble and reel of cotton discovered near it, had been upset if the ship had been subject to any stress of weather. Spare panes of glass were also found stowed away and unbroken. All the articles of furniture in the Captain's cabin, including a harmonium, were in their proper place and uninjured by water, the music and other books being also dry. Finally, the conclusion arrived at by the surveyor is that there exists no apparent reason why the vessel should have been abandoned.

But in addition to these facts a sword was discovered which, on its being drawn out of its scabbard, exhibited signs of having been smeared with blood and afterwards wiped; further, the top-gallant rail had marks on it apparently of blood, and both bows of the vessel had been cut, to all appearance intentionally with some sharp instrument. No Bills of Lading, nor Manifest were found on board. The effects found in the Captain's cabin were of considerable value and proved that a lady and a child had been on board. The ship's log, which was found on board, showed that the last day's work of the ship was on the 24th November. . . . The vessel, apparently, had held on her due course for ten days after, the wheel being loose all the time. The Captain, B. S. Briggs by name, is well known in Gibraltar and bore the highest character.

" *Maritime Register.*"

There were no boats on board when she was found.

" *Gibraltar Chronicle*," *January 4th*, 1873.

We have been favoured with a copy of a report made by Captain Shufeldt, United States ship *Plymouth*, after a visit paid by him to the derelict *Mary Celeste*. Captain Shufeldt, with everyone who has examined the ship, is of the opinion that she was abandoned by the Master and crew without sufficient reason, probably in a moment of panic.

Captain Shufeldt altogether rejects the idea of a mutiny, because there is no evidence of violence about the decks or in the cabins, and, with regard to the damage about the bows of the ship, he considers that it amounts merely to splinters in the bending of the planks, which were afterwards forced off by the action of the sea, and not in any way betokening any intention of wilfully damaging the vessel. It will be observed that the opinion of Captain Shufeldt, with regard to the marks on the ship's bows, is in direct contradiction to that expressed by the surveyors here.

37. THE TICHBORNE CASE

THE story of the Tichborne case has become such a classic that we do not propose to follow it through all its various ramifications. Instead, we quote an article which appeared in the *Daily News* on March 3rd, 1874, when, after more than three years of the most costly litigation known in English law, it was announced that the claimant to the Tichborne estates was an impostor, and had been sentenced to fourteen years' imprisonment for perjury.

"It seems already half a lifetime since paragraphs from the Australian newspapers brought us the intelligence that there had arrived in Sydney a man who, though entitled to a baronetcy and £25,000 a year, had, for many years, led the life of a slaughterman and butcher, concealing his true name and position. The tale was startling, but it found faith. Sir Roger Charles Tichborne, long believed to be dead, had at last come out of obscurity and retirement and, with his wife and family and retainers, black and white, was about to set sail for England to claim his own again. Then lovers of romance got down their baronetages, and there found it recorded that Roger Charles Tichborne, eldest son of Sir James and Lady Tichborne of Tichborne, in the county of Hants, born in 1829, was 'lost at sea, off the coast of South America,' in the spring of 1854. But the Australian butcher had declared that this was all a mistake. Wrecked he had been, but not lost; on the contrary, he was alive still and weighing nearly twenty stone. Even at that early time there were paragraphs in the papers mentioning the *Osprey*; and the story of the rescue was abroad—in a rude and imperfect state, it is true, but sufficiently complete to satisfy, to some degree, while it whetted the public appetite for particulars. The statement then was that 'when the *Bella* went down, Sir Roger and a dozen others escaped in the long-boat, and after all but four or five men had been washed overboard, the *Osprey* had picked up the survivors.' It was also announced that Andrew Bogle, an old negro servant of the family, who happened to be at Sydney, had recognised the gentleman.

"About the beginning of the year 1867 English journals began to take up the wondrous tale. It was reported that a member of the family, entering the chapel attached to the mansion near Alresford, one Sunday morning, had been startled at seeing the old black domestic, who had left Tichborne with a pension many years before, who now reappeared, bowed with age, and with grizzled locks, but not to be mistaken by any who had known him in the past. Then it was told how an enormous individual, and had called himself Mr. Taylor, had—quite apart from a gigantic 'R.C.T.' upon his portmanteau—been utterly unable to conceal his identity from gossips in the Swan Hotel in the little town of Alresford. There he had attempted to maintain his incognito by shunning the coffee-room and living in a private chamber. Old tenants and old neighbours, however, knew him. The farmers around had hung about the hotel doors only anxious to satisfy themselves 'whether his knee turned in' and his 'eye-brows twitched.' One enthusiastic person, having obtained by particular request what, in his excitement, he called 'a full-faced view of his back' at once 'slapped his thigh' and declared that he would 'swear to the gentleman all over the world.' Then the Australian—forgetting his thirst for privacy in the enthusiasm of the moment —'recognised many persons' and even reminded them of little incidents of past years. There was, it is true, a jarring note in the form of a sturdy old village blacksmith, who had spent his life at Tichborne, and who, being asked by the gentleman, 'Should you think I am Sir Roger?' had been so far forgetful of decency and good manners as to answer, 'No, I'll be d—— if you are.' But his questioner had at once reminded him of how, once upon a time, when a little boy, Roger had set a dog upon the blacksmith's cat—an old tom—and how the blacksmith had run after the boy to chastise him with a flail. But some people are by nature sceptical, and old Etheridge soon came to be known as the one infidel in a whole neighbourhood of believers.

"When, three weeks later, there came news from Paris that the Dowager Lady Tichborne[1] had thrown her arms as far as they would go round the long-lost wanderer, and had declared in the presence of his attorney, that 'the back of his head was like his father's,' and 'his ears exactly like his uncle Edward's,' the bells of Alresford rang a merry peal; the joyful news was confirmed that Tichborne House, which, since the death of Sir Alfred, had been let to a stranger by the trustee of his posthumous son, was going again to be inhabited by one of the old race, who had been great folks in that part for nine hundred years. Old Etheridge, indeed, was still obstinate and while shoeing horses in his grimy old smithy was accustomed to grunt out rude observations. But then, what did Alresford care for what old Etheridge said?

"Among the most conspicuous of the converts in Alresford was Mr. Hopkins who, in conjunction with his intimate friend, Mr. Baignent of Winchester, began to busy himself very early in the matter. Mr. Hopkins had been solicitor to Sir James Tichborne, but the family had ceased to employ him. He had also been a trustee of certain Tichborne properties; but had been removed from that position by the late Sir James, at which he had expressed himself greatly chagrined. Roger Tichborne had never been his client; and letters of Roger have been brought to light in which he expresses considerable dislike towards Mr. Hopkins. But Hopkins had been despatched to Ireland in 1850 by Sir James to obtain his son's consent to settlements on coming of age. He made

[1] Lady Tichborne's recognition of the Claimant as her son is one of the most curious features of the case. She died in the summer of 1867, and in her he lost his most valuable supporter.

an affidavit of his 'belief' that the Claimant was his 'old client.'

"Converts make converts, and success, according to the proverb, begets success. Busy Mr. Baignent, who knew even less of Roger than Mr. Hopkins, but who kept an eye upon all matters connected with the Tichborne genealogy, went about industriously spreading the report that the family solicitor had recognised Sir Roger. Then Col. Lushington, the tenant of Tichborne House, who had never seen Roger, and had no connection with the family beyond hiring their house, with the old pictures, at a yearly rent, was so convinced that he invited the Claimant and his wife to stay with him. But he has explained that it was the 'knowledge' shown by the Claimant of the family pictures which had satisfied him. The Claimant did not tell him that when he came down under the fictitious name of Mr. Taylor, he had sent old Bogle to ask the housekeeper at Tichborne to let him look over the old place, or that he then gave the old black instructions to observe the positions of the family pictures. Bogle, however, has admitted this, and that he at once made a report to his new master on the subject. Hence the Claimant's knowledge of the pictures was certainly not so conclusive as it appeared to Col. Lushington.

"More than that, Col. Lushington's ill-advised step necessarily tended to increase that 'knowledge' which, however obtained, it was clear that the Claimant knew how to use. Few weeks, indeed, could have elapsed before the Claimant was familiar with every part of the house in which Roger Tichborne had passed so many days with his aunt and uncle and their daughter, Miss Doughty[1]; and he necessarily became acquainted with the park and the country round.

"A few examples of this kind are as good as a hundred.

[1] Roger's uncle had been left a fortune by an old Miss Doughty on condition that he adopted her name in lieu of Tichborne. As he had no son, Roger was his heir. It was this younger Miss Doughty to whom Roger had been so devoted, and it was her refusal of his offer of marriage that led to his going abroad.

Having once established that it was a system with the Claimant, aided by his numerous supporters, to pick up facts connected with Roger Tichborne's career, and to pass them off upon people as genuine recollections, it is hardly necessary to do more in order to disperse all arguments founded on 'knowledge,' than to show, not only that facts were picked up, but that they were industriously sought for. Doctors' Commons furnished Mr. Holmes, the defendant's attorney, with the copious information contained in Roger Tichborne's will, which had been proved in what appeared the certainty of his decease. After this the Claimant's attorney applied to the Horse Guards, and obtained copies of records of all leaves of absence granted to Mr. Tichborne when serving as cornet and lieutenant in that regiment in Dublin, Cahir, Waterford, Clonmel, and Canterbury, in the years 1849–1853. Mr. Norris, the dowager's solicitor, was employed to obtain from Stonyhurst a list of all the professors and heads of that celebrated Jesuit College during Mr. Tichborne's three years of study there.

"It is easy to see that 'knowledge' of this sort was likely to increase at a sort of compound interest. Undoubtedly, the Claimant did display, soon after this time, a good deal of knowledge, not only of the movements of the Carabineers in Mr. Tichborne's time, but of the anecdotical gossip of that regiment; so much, indeed, that several officers, unable to account for the fact, not only came to the conclusion that no impostor could have known so much, but began to find traces in the face and features of the Claimant of their old brother officer. They, however, were certainly not aware that some months before venturing to approach any single officer among Roger Tichborne's old associates, he had taken into his house, Carter, the regimental servant of Mr. Tichborne, besides Sergeant M'Cann and Sergeant Quin, late of the Carabineers. Carter was a coachman, and he had left another employment to go into the Claimant's service; yet it is admitted that the Claimant had at that time neither horses nor carriages. It is certain that the

Croydon household was at that period greatly overstocked with male servants. Bogle was living there, but then he was a martyr to rheumatics, and unable to do anything—unless it was to chat about old times. Carter may, therefore, have been useful in some honest way; but why Quin? why M'Cann? not to speak of Moody, Dunn, Fry, and the numerous others who, though not quartered in the house, were certainly in the Claimant's service?

"Still, in the first six months after the Claimant arrived it could not be denied that he had won over a great number of other persons, especially in Hampshire and in the neighbourhood of Poole, where the Tichborne family had property. They knew that he was an illiterate man; but then they were told by Mr. Baignent and Mr. Hopkins that it could be shown by Roger's letters that he made mistakes in grammar, which was quite true, but a high authority has justly pointed out that these errors were rather such as a foreigner[1] would make than such as are peculiar to an unlettered Englishman. Then they knew that the Claimant's habits and manners were not those of an English gentleman. But Mr. Baignent was positive that Roger Tichborne's chief associates were servants and stable-boys, which was an entire mistake, though not at that time very easily disproved.

"But while the system of converting Carabineers and Alresford and Poole folks was in full operation, and volumes of affidavits were carefully circulated among hesitating witnesses, there were some who were aware of the full flavour of the fact that the Claimant held studiously aloof from all persons who had known Roger Tichborne intimately. Upon this point his family could be under no mistake; for there was not a solitary member of the numerous Tichborne and Doughty families who received a visit, or was even allowed, except by a ruse, to see him for some months after his arrival. There was his dear friend, Mr. Gosford. About Roger's feelings towards that gentleman there has been, and could be, no dispute. The Claimant has positively asserted, that

[1] Roger Tichborne spent his boyhood in France.

besides making him his executor, he confided to him a secret of the most delicate kind[1]; and, moreover, intrusted him with a duty demanding the most devoted friendship and the highest prudence and discretion. Yet the man calling himself Roger Tichborne left Mr. Gosford to track him out at a hotel at Gravesend, and when his old friend arrived there, rushed up to a room, locked himself in, and refused to see him.

"The Claimant had been in England four months when that famous interview at Croydon between him, Mr. and Mrs. Redcliffe and Mrs. Towneley was brought about, not spontaneously, but by arrangement between the attorneys, so that the names of the parties coming were known beforehand. At that interview the Claimant addressed Mrs. Towneley, whom Roger had known intimately, in the words, 'How do you do, Kate?' evidently mistaking her for Mrs. Redcliffe, while he not only addressed Mrs. Redcliffe as Lucy, but continued to converse with both cousins under that evidently mistaken impression of their identity. Yet Mrs. Redcliffe was in her maiden days that Miss Doughty for whom Roger had so strong an affection.

"The scientific probing by Sir John Coleridge of the Claimant's ignorance of Roger Tichborne's life in all its relations and experiences, though not showy, or designed for popular amusement, was in fact masterly and complete. It was this long cross-examination which finally exploded the Claimant's pretence to be Roger Tichborne, and furnished the sure foundations of that criminal indictment which has brought the Claimant to a convict prison.

[1] Before leaving England, Roger gave his friend a sealed packet. Here was an opportunity for the Claimant to prove his identity in a manner that could not have been disputed. It was not until he heard that the packet had been destroyed that he ventured to describe its contents. It was a provision, he said, for Miss Doughty, whom he declared he had seduced. It then appeared that Roger had given a duplicate of the paper to his cousin, and, though she had also destroyed it, her statement that it had consisted of his written promise to build a church in the event of his marriage with her was unreservedly accepted.

"Long before this time, however, the Tichborne family had discovered abundant evidence that the man claiming to be the dowager's son was, in fact, the son of Orton, the Wapping butcher. An accidental discovery by a gentleman sent out to make enquiries in Wagga-Wagga[1] led to a search, in the month of September, 1867, in Wapping, where, by exhibiting the photograph, the gentleman prosecuting the enquiry found, not what he expected, but something still more startling. It was on showing it to the landlady of the Globe public-house that he was informed by that lady that she did not remember any neighbour or neighbour's son in former years like that; but did well remember a stranger of vast bulk making enquiries about Orton and other old inhabitants of Wapping on the previous Christmas-day, the very day, in fact, of the Claimant's arrival. This mysterious person, she said, was the very original of the photograph. Further evidence was then found that the Orton sisters, who had been very poor, had suddenly become prosperous; and, moreover, that Charley Orton had confided to a friend in the butchering trade that he had a brother who was entitled to a large property, and had promised him £5 a month at once, with a future prospect of £2,000, 'when he got his estates.' Charles Orton confessed the whole affair when the payments became irregular; and the Claimant, who at first denied all knowledge of Wapping, was finally compelled to admit his visit to make enquiries on the Christmas-eve, his allowances of £5 to Charles, besides allowances to the Orton sisters, for which he could give no satisfactory or consistent explanation. The Commission sent out to Melipilla, in South America, to examine the folks whom the Claimant had admitted to be old friends of his there, resulted in their deposing that they only knew him as Arthur Orton; and his old employer's widow in Australia not only said the same, but produced evidence of the fact in the shape of ledgers of her late husband.

"In a case of disputed identity it is not by a man's

[1] The Claimant's home in Australia.

knowledge of what he might have learned, but by his ignorance of what he must have known if he were the true man, that he is to be judged. For example, what number of anecdotes about the life in the regiment could weigh against the admitted fact that the Claimant's mind on the subject of his life in Paris was a mere blank? How can we explain this save on the assumption that, being ignorant of France and the French language, he had found it impossible to get hold of old servants or others who could instruct him as Carter, Bogle, and M'Cann could undoubtedly do with regard to Tichborne, Ireland, and Canterbury?

"The Claimant's 'feats of memory' give the key to the extraordinary amount of support which he obtained. There are, indeed, plenty of witnesses,[1] who affirmed that they remember the face, the walk, the upper part of the face, and what not; but in every case it is evident enough that what had really impressed them was that the Claimant was able to remember something which they remembered."

[1] The Claimant called over a hundred witnesses who swore they recognised him as Roger Tichborne.

38. THE HOME LIFE OF BRIGHAM YOUNG

From "Wife No. 19,"[1] *by Ann Eliza Young* (1875).

BRIGHAM YOUNG's habits are quite simple, and he is very regular in his mode of living. At three he dines, and it is then that he meets his family for the first time in the day. Dinner is served at the Lion House, and the appearance of Brigham Young's family at dinner is very similar to that at a country boarding-house, when the gentlemen are all away at business in town, and the wives and children are left together.[2] At a third table, running across the head of the long dining-room, Brigham sits with his favourite wife by his side. At a long table, running lengthwise of the room, all the other wives are seated, each with her children about her. At the sound of the large dinner bell, they all file in, seat themselves quietly, grace is said by the "presiding patriarch" from his table, and the meal goes on. The family table is plainly spread, and supplied with the simplest fare, while the smaller one is laden with every delicacy that the markets will afford. These, however, are only for the president and his favourite wife, and the rest of the

[1] In calling her book by this title, Ann Eliza flattered herself, for she was really only Wife No. 27.

[2] Brigham Young always contended that he practised polygamy solely as a sacred duty. "Some of these my brethren," he said in a sermon, "know what my feelings were at the time Joseph revealed the doctrine; I was not desirous of shrinking from any duty, nor of failing in the least to do as I was commanded, but it was the first time in my life that I had desired the grave, and I could hardly get over it for a long time. And when I saw a funeral, I felt to envy the corpse its situation, and to regret that I was not in the coffin, knowing the toil and labour that my body would have to undergo; and I have had to examine myself, from that day to this, and watch my faith, and carefully meditate, lest I should be found desiring the grave more than I ought to do."

Some of Brigham Young's Wives

p. 224

family must be satisfied merely to look at them, and enjoy the dainties by proxy.

After dinner they see no more of him until "family prayers." At seven o'clock the bell is rung, and the wives and children gather in the large Lion House parlour. Brigham sits in the centre of the room at a large table, on which is an ornamental "astral" lamp. The wives and their respective families are ranged around the room, in the order in which they appear at the table. When all are seated, Brigham reads a few passages of scripture, all kneel down, and he makes a long prayer.[1] He prays with great unction, and, I suppose unconsciously to himself, some of his patronising manner slips into his appeals to the Throne of Divine Grace, until his petitions always seemed to me to be very much like advice to the Deity rather than entreaties for the Divine blessing. If he chances to be in a good humour, he chats a little while before leaving the room, but if not, he goes away directly prayers are over, and that is the last that is seen of him by the household until the next day at dinner.

The Lion House, where most of the wives live, is a long, three-storied house, at the very left of what is known as the Prophets Block. Next to the Lion House is a

[1] Brigham Young once gave this advice in a sermon: "Get your wives and children together, lock the door so that none of them will get out, and get down on your knees; and if you feel as though you want to swear and fight, keep on your knees until they are pretty well wearied, saying, 'Here I am; I will not abuse my Creator nor my religion, though I feel like hell inside, but I will stay on my knees until I overcome these devils around me.'" And on another occasion when he was discussing prayers: "Let me tell you how you should do. If you feel that you are tempted not to open your mouth to the Lord, and as though the heavens are brass over your head, and the earth iron beneath your feet, and that everything is closed up, and you feel that it would be a sin for you to pray, then walk up to the devil and say, 'Mr. Devil, get out of my way'; and if you feel that you cannot get down on your knees for fear you will swear, say, 'Get down, knees'; and if they don't feel right when they are down, put something under them, some sharp sticks, for instance, and say, 'Knees, come to it.' 'But I dare not open my mouth,' says one, 'for fear that I shall swear.' Then say, 'Open, mouth, and now, tongue, begin.'"

low building, which is used as the "Tithing Office." Here all the clerks have their desks, and receive visitors from the Saints who come on church or personal business. Adjoining that is Brigham's private office, where he receives his own visitors. At the extreme right is Bee-hive House, a large building, which has always been used as Governor Young's official residence.

Lucy Decker has always had the care of it, and has lived there with her children. No wife was ever permitted to share her husband's apartments there, until the reign of Amelia was opened. She has lived there since her marriage, and has been virtually recognised "head of the harem."

Amelia is a woman of about forty years of age. She did not wish to marry Brigham, but he wished to marry her and that settled her fate. He was a most ardent and enthusiastic lover, and during all the time that his suit was in progress, his carriage might be seen standing before the door of her parents' house several hours at a time every day. He promised her anything that she might desire, but promises had no weigh with her. He then had recourse to "revelation"; he had been especially told from heaven that she was created for him, and if she married anybody else she would be for ever damned. The poor girl begged, pleaded, protested, and shed most bitter tears, but all to no purpose.

"Amelia, you must be my wife; God has revealed it to me. You can't be saved by anyone else. If you marry me, I will save you, and exalt you to be a queen in the celestial world; but if you refuse, you will be destroyed, both soul and body."

This is the same argument he used to win me, and the one he has always in reserve when everything else fails to secure his victim. Of course, she yielded; what else was she to do?

Since the marriage, Amelia has ruled with a hand of iron, and she has her lord in pretty good subjection.[1]

[1] Brigham Young in his sermons advised his brethren to practise indulgence towards their wives. All the same, he considered himself the master

She has a terrible temper, and he has the benefit of it. On one occasion he sent her a sewing machine, thinking to please her; it did not happen to be the kind she wanted; so she kicked it downstairs, saying, "What did you get this old thing for? You knew I wanted a 'Singer'." She had a Singer at once.

I was once present when she wanted her husband to do something for her; he objected, and she repeated her demand, threatening to "thrash him," if he did not comply. She was not obliged to ask him again. I know he is afraid of her and that she holds him now through fear, rather than love. She accompanies him to the theatre, and occupies the box, while the rest of the wives sit in the parquet.

With the exception of some drives I never went anywhere with him alone; for, with the exception of Amelia, and occasionally Emmeline, he never went with only one wife, but took two or more.

The first winter that I was married to him, the Female Relief Society, to which I then belonged, gave a ball, and all the ladies were to invite the gentlemen. I ventured to ask Brother Young. He was my husband, and whom else should I invite? He accepted my invitation, apparently with much pleasure, and arranged to call for me on the appointed evening to take me to the ball. He was punctual to his appointment, but when he arrived he was accompanied by another wife. I said nothing, however, and was as cordial to the other wife as I should have been had she accompanied him at my express invitation.

Surprised, as everyone was, by my suit for divorce against Brigham Young, no one was more astonished

of his home. "I do not believe in making my authority as a husband or a father known by brute force," he said, "but by a superior intelligence—by showing them that I am capable of teaching them. . . . I shall humour the wife as far as I can consistently; and if you have any crying to do, wife, you can do that along with the children, for I have none of that kind of business to do. Let our wives be the weaker vessels, and the men be men, and show the women by their superior ability that God gives husbands wisdom and ability to lead their wives into his presence."

than the Prophet himself. He would have looked for rebellion from almost any other wife sooner than from me, I had been so quiet and acquiescent during all my married life with him.[1]

From an article in the "North American Review," March, 1890, by Susa Young Gates.

My father, Brigham Young, had fifty-six living children, all born healthy, bright, and without "spot or blemish" in body or mind. Thirty-one of the number were girls; twenty-five were boys. Seven died in infancy, three in childhood, seven more since reaching maturity. What bright memories we cherish of the happy times we spent and the benefit of our father's tender watch-care, supplemented by the very sweetest mother's love ever given to mortals! Forever thinking of us and our welfare, father was particularly anxious about our education.

In 1868, the best stenographer in the territory was engaged by my father to come twice a day, one hour before school, two after, to teach all his children the useful art of phonography. No need to dwell on the seventy or eighty eager pupils who crowded the schoolroom for the first week or two, or the slim company of seven who faithfully clung to those troublesome lines and curves during the whole two years' course. A black silk dress had been promised by father to the girl who should first report his sermon in full. It was won—it would not become me to say a little unjustly—by a dear recently dead sister.

How pleasant were the seasons of evening prayers when ten or twelve mothers with their broods of children came from every nook and corner of the quaint, old-fashioned, roomy house at the sound of the prayer bell!

Sometimes after the prayers, especially on Sunday

[1] The case came up for trial in April, 1877, and the marriage was declared illegal. After this, Ann Eliza became a recognised authority on Mormon polygamy, and gave lectures on that subject all over the United States.

Brigham Young's Ten Tallest Daughters

p. 228

evenings, the girls would be requested to sing and play, or we would all join in a hymn. Father would kiss the children, dandle a baby on his knee with his own particular accompaniment of "link-e-toodle-ladle-iddle-oodle," surprising baby into round-eyed wonder by the odd noise; then a good night and we would all separate.

After the girls began to "grow-up," beaux naturally appeared on the scene. The long parlour, which was prayer room, reception room, music room and best room, was usually filled on Sunday evenings with a quietly gay crowd of young women and their "beaux." Music and laughter, jest and repartee, filled in the evening till the clock struck ten. Then promptly, if the adieus had not already been said, the young people were apt to be startled by the sudden appearance of the President, loaded with hats of all shapes and sizes; each young man would be asked kindly and pleasantly to select his own, and the good nights were exchanged in the ensuing hurry and embarrassment.

One night there happened to be about eight or ten couples, most of whom were already engaged lovers. Now, as walking in the street was out of the question, and as the parlour was the only resort, it was found to be a very unsatisfactory place for a lover, who would, if he could, whisper sweet nothings, or even venture to steal an arm about his sweetheart. I never knew who made the proposition on that particular Sunday night, but certain it was that in the course of the evening the one large lamp on the centre table was discreetly lowered a trifle, while around it in a close barricade stood a small army of books.

Very charming, no doubt! But some stray wind carried a whiff of what was going on in the parlour to the President's ear. Less than a quarter of an hour of the happy gloom had been enjoyed before the parlour door quietly opened, and on the threshold, lighted candle in hand, stood father. Without saying a word he walked slowly and deliberately up to the first couple, holding his candle down in their faces, looked keenly at them, then, to the next couple, repeating his former scrutiny, and so on, around the room. Not a word said he, but, pulling down the scandalised books, and putting them gravely in their places, he turned on the full blaze of the lamp and walked quietly out of the room.

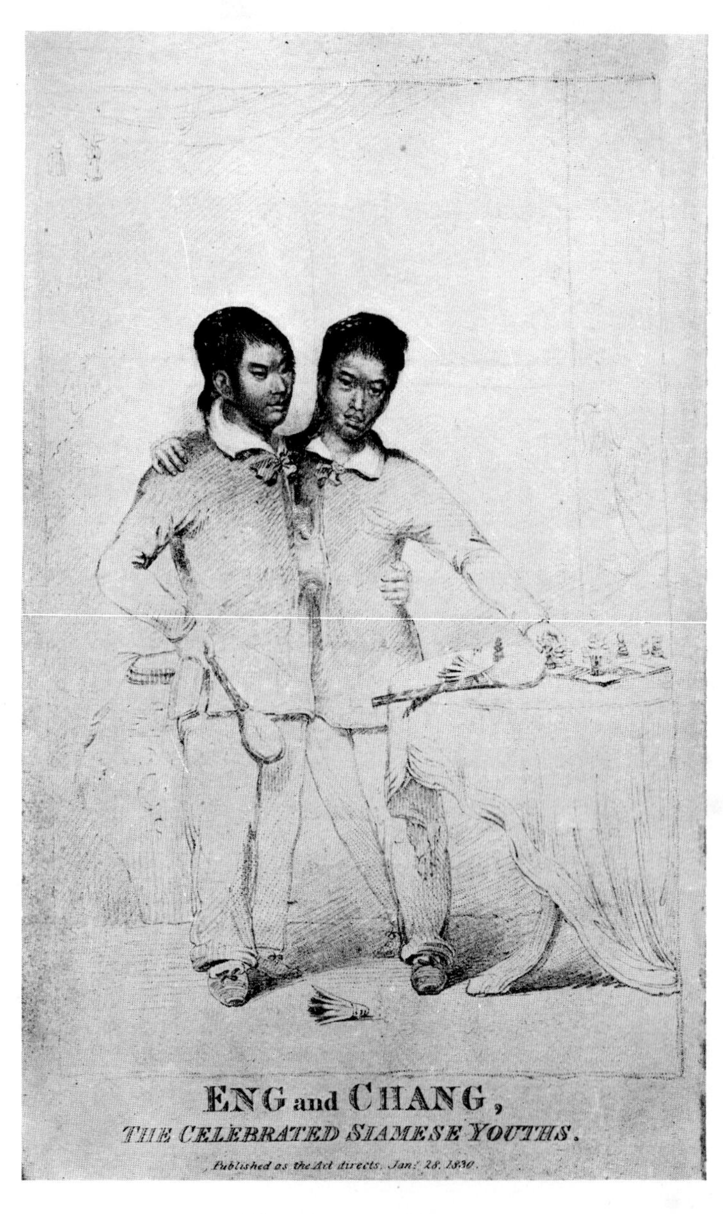

THE SIAMESE TWINS

As they first appeared in England at the age of 19

p. 231

39. THE SIAMESE TWINS

The "Annual Register," 1874.

THESE remarkable twins, who were well known as a "sight" in London some years ago, have just died at their home in North Carolina. They were born in Siam, of Chinese parents, in 1811, and were therefore 63 years of age at the time of their death. From birth their bodies were united in a singular manner by a band of flesh, stretching from the end of one breast-bone to the same place in the opposite twin.

At first, this connecting band seemed to have united them face to face, but constant traction had so changed its direction that they stood partially side by side. Its length was about two inches; below, nearly four; from above, downwards, it covered three inches; and its greatest thickness was one and a half inches. It was covered with skin, and when the centre was touched, both felt it; but on touching either side of the median line, only the nearest individual was sensible of it. The connection between the Siamese twins presented many interesting points in regard to physiology and pathology; for although they formed two perfectly distinct beings, they appeared most frequently to think, to act, and move as one individual.

The twins were purchased of their mother at Meklong, a city of Siam, and were taken to America by Captain Comm, and Mr. Hunter in 1820. After realising a competence by the exhibition of themselves in various countries of Europe, the Siamese twins settled in one of the foreign cities of America, where they were married to two sisters, and had offspring. Owing to domestic quarrels, however, two houses were found necessary, each living with his wife a week at a time alternately. They were, it is asserted, ruined by the disastrous civil war in America, and in 1869 re-appeared in Europe for exhibition. In anticipation of the probable death of one of them before the other, it was then proposed to separate them by dividing the ligature which connected their bodies. The matter formed the subject of much discussion among eminent surgical authorities in this country and in France, and various opinions were expressed as to the probability of the operation being performed without endangering the life of the twins. The proposal was ultimately rejected, and Chang and Eng returned, undivided, to North Carolina, to end their days in peace.

The American papers give the following account of their last days: "Some time after taking up their abode in Mount Airy, the twins purchased a second plantation about two miles from the first, and erected a dwelling upon it, to which Eng removed his family, Chang's family remaining at the old homestead. It was their custom, and the plan was never departed from, to spend three days at each house.

On the Thursday previous to the death of the brothers they were at Chang's residence, and the evening of that day was the appointed time for a removal to Eng's dwelling. The day was cold, and Chang had been complaining for a couple of months past of being very ill. On Friday evening they retired to a small room by themselves, and went to bed, but Chang was very restless. Some time between mid-night and daybreak they got up and sat by the fire. Again Eng protested, and said he wished to lie down, as he was sleepy. Chang stoutly refused, and replied that it hurt his breast to recline. After a while they retired to their bed, and Eng fell into a deep sleep. About four o'clock one of the sons came into the room, and, going to the bedside, discovered that his uncle was dead. Eng was awakened by the noise, and in the greatest alarm turned and looked upon the lifeless form beside him, and was seized with violent nervous paroxysms.

No physicians were at hand, and it being three miles to the town of Mount Airy, some time elapsed before one could be summoned. A messenger was despatched to the village for Dr. Hollingsworth, and he sent his brother, also a physician, at once to the plantation, but before he arrived the vital spark had fled, and the Siamese twins were dead."

From the "Philadelphia Medical Times," 1874.

The father of the Siamese twins being a fisherman of the labouring class, the boys lived in one of the floating houses of the country, and soon became famous swimmers, spending much of their time in the river. It was the peculiarity of their movements in the water which first attracted the attention of a Scotch merchant, Mr. Robert Hunter, and finally led to their leaving their native country in quest of fortune. Chang was the left of the pair and was much smaller and more feeble than his brother Eng. They were different in form, tastes, and disposition; what Chang liked to eat, Eng detested. Eng was very good-natured, Chang cross and irritable. The sickness of one had no effect upon the other, so that while one would be suffering from fever, the pulse of the other would beat at its natural rate. Chang drank pretty heavily—at times getting drunk; but Eng never felt any influence from the debauch of his brother. They often quarrelled; and, of course, under the circumstances, their quarrels were bitter. They sometimes came to blows, and on one occasion came under the jurisdiction of the courts.

After one of these differences, Chang and Eng applied to Dr. Hollingsworth to separate them; Eng affirmed that Chang was so bad that he could live no longer with him; and Chang stated that he was satisfied to be separated, only asking that he be given an equal chance with his brother, and that the band be cut exactly in the middle. Cooler counsels prevailed.

40. CANNIBALISM AT SEA

"The Times," September 8th, 1884.

THE *Montezuma*, from Punta Arenas, arrived at Falmouth on Sunday, bringing in Captain Dudley and two men of the yacht, *Mignonette*, which left Southampton on May 19th and was struck by a heavy sea and foundered on July 5th in 27 S. 10 W. Those on board had been twenty-four days in a open boat 13 feet long. On July 29th, the crew were picked up by the *Montezuma* after having drifted and sailed 1,000 miles in their boat.

September 13th.

Captain Dudley described their sufferings in a letter addressed to his wife, written while on board the punt on the back of the certificate of the chronometer. "July 6th. We had five minutes to get into the boat, without food or water; July 9th. Picked up turtle. July 21st. We have been here 17 days; have no food. We are all four living, hoping to get a passing ship. If not we must soon die."

September 8th.

A Reuter telegram from Falmouth states that a boy who escaped with the crew died from privation and his companions were compelled to eat his body to sustain life.

A further telegram states: The survivors state that they were out of the track of vessels and that they did not see one during the whole of the twenty-four days. To make a sail, three of them joined their shirts and placed them on a pole together, and thus for days they sailed before the wind. The weather was at times tempestuous, but it was remarkable with what ease the little craft rode over the waves. The boy, who was a native of Southampton, was about seventeen years of age and previous to his death was very bad through drinking salt water. They said that they could not possibly describe their sufferings and even now, although they have been on board the German barque nearly forty days, and were treated exceedingly well, they feel the effects of the exposure and privation.

September 9th.

At the Falmouth Police Court yesterday Thomas Dudley, Edwin Stevens, and Edward Brooks were brought before the mayor and charged with murder.

Thomas Laverty, sergeant in the Falmouth Harbour police, said he heard the Captain telling the Collector of Customs in the Longroom that the boy Parker was lying in the bottom of the boat with his arm over his face. The Captain, after offering up a prayer to God to forgive him for anything he was about to do, said to the boy: "Richard, my boy, your time has come." He then took out a small knife from his pocket and put it into the boy's neck, killing him instantly.

The "Annual Register," 1884.

During the trial it transpired that the Captain had just time to secure two tins of what he supposed was preserved meat and got into the punt before the yacht went down. Their situation then was this: there were four of them in a boat 13 ft. long with no water and only two one-pound tins of preserved turnips. For five days they lived on one of the tins of turnips. They then succeeded in capturing a turtle which was floating on the water. After the turtle and the remaining tin of turnips had been eaten, they passed nine days without any food whatever and no water. The lad Parker drank sea water. At the end of nineteen days the Captain suggested that they should cast lots as to who should be killed for food for the rest. Brooks considered that they should rather die together. By this time Parker was in the last stage of exhaustion. The Captain and the Mate discussed the killing of Parker who was evidently the nearest to death of the four. Brooks declined to be party to such an act. The Captain and the Mate nevertheless decided to kill him. . . . Brooks was unable to resist taking his share. For five days they subsisted on the boy's body before they were sighted by the *Montezuma*. When that vessel came alongside they were too exhausted to get on board and had to be lifted out of their boat.

41. JACK THE RIPPER

In the early hours of August 7th, 1888, the first of a long series of crimes was committed—a series which was to startle and mystify the whole world. At the time, the news that an unknown woman had been found murdered in Whitechapel naturally aroused little interest.

She was discovered lying in a pool of blood on the landing of a common lodging-house, and on her body were counted over thirty deep stabs. Presently she was identified as a prostitute who lodged a few streets away. The woman had neither friends nor enemies, she was middle-aged and bedraggled, and nobody could imagine why the murderer had attacked so miserable a creature.

Three weeks passed, no arrest was made, and the affair was nearly forgotten when history appeared to repeat itself. On the last day of the month, another woman of the same class was found stabbed to death in a Whitechapel street. The body had been mutilated, and it was observed that in the way the vital parts were attacked some rough anatomical knowledge had been shown. Like the other, this woman had no particular enemies, but gangs of street bullies used to persecute women of her kind, and the police were inclined to suspect them of these crimes.

A week later, a third prostitute was found dead in Whitechapel, and this time she had been mutilated in a way that clearly displayed the skill of a doctor or a slaughterman. By now all three murders were recognised as the work of one man—a criminal of a very different stamp from the ordinary Whitechapel rough.

During that year there happened to be an extraordinary outbreak of crime, and the first two murders passed almost unnoticed among the many that were daily reported in the Press. But the uniformity in the details of these three tragedies could not fail to attract attention. One account would do for them all. The victim was a middle-aged woman, widowed or separated from her husband, barely subsisting on her earnings as a prostitute. On the night of the crime, she was drunk and penniless. The murderer was a stranger to her until a few minutes before he seized and killed her noiselessly, within earshot of at least half a dozen people. Then, careless of detection, he proceeded to mutilate her body.

The last case, however, differed from the rest in one startling detail: a certain organ had been deftly removed from the woman's body. No meaningless cuts had been made, but there in a public street an operation had been neatly performed that must have taken at least fifteen minutes.[1]

A motive for the crime was suggested by the Coroner. He had been told, he said, by the sub-curator of the pathological museum of one of the largest hospitals in London that "some months ago an American had called upon him, and asked him to secure a number of specimens of the organ that was missing in the deceased. He stated his willingness to give £20 apiece for each specimen. He stated that his object was to issue an actual specimen with each copy of a publication on which he was then engaged." His request was refused, but it was known that he repeated it to another institution. In the coroner's opinion, the murderer was another Burke, who killed in order to sell to the doctors. The story of the American, however, was never corroborated, and the theory was briefly dismissed by the *Lancet* as "fantastic."

Whatever or whoever the murderer was, he had disappeared, and the police had not the slightest clue to work upon. Descriptions were collected of the dead women's

[1] The anatomical knowledge shown on this occasion has given rise to the legend that the murderer must necessarily have been a doctor. But a detailed account of the mutilation of the body appeared in the following week's *Lancet*, and it is apparent that a slaughterman would have been equally competent to perform the operation.

companions on those nights. They differed hopelessly. No one figure stood out as the culprit.

If the West End was startled by these crimes, Whitechapel quickly became panic-stricken. So far he had apparently selected his victims, but would he continue to discriminate? There could be no feeling of security while such a monster was at large. Among the ordinary roughs and street-walkers there was a conviction that he was not one of themselves, and they gave the police all the help in their power to capture him. They showered information that was well-meant, and would have been most useful had it been in the remotest degree accurate. A house-to-house search in Whitechapel was planned and carried out by the police, with the perfect good-will and co-operation of all the inhabitants. Nothing whatever was gained by it. As usual, advice came from every quarter.

"The unfortunates who are the objects of the man-monster's malignity should be shadowed by one or two amateur patrols," said the *Star*. "They should be cautioned to walk in couples. Whistles and signalling system should be provided. We are not sure that every London district should not make some effort of the kind, for the murderer may choose a fresh quarter now that Whitechapel is being made too hot to hold him."

"The pupils of the dead woman's eyes," suggested a letter-writer to the *Daily Chronicle*, "should be photographed, on the chance of the retina retaining an image of the murderer."

Whitechapel bristled with policemen, whose work was rendered infinitely more difficult by the swarms of amateur detectives from the West End. Medical students and newspaper reporters paraded the streets unconvincingly disguised as women, and in every corner there lurked assassin-hunters in tennis-shoes or goloshes. "It seemed at times as if every person in the streets were suspicious of everyone else he met," said *The Times*, "and as if it were a race between them who should first inform against his neighbour." On one day alone, a dozen men were arrested on suspicion, and the excitement in the neighbourhood was so intense that large crowds gathered outside the police-stations whenever a man was brought in—even on the most commonplace charge quite unconnected with the murders.

"It is not considered possible that another murder can be committed in the Whitechapel district with impunity," said a daily paper about this time, "for the whole neighbourhood is thoroughly roused, the women of the class from which the late victims were taken are suspicious of every stranger, and the streets are nightly patrolled by large numbers of plain-clothes constables."

Only a few days afterwards, on October 1st, these headlines blazed from the pages of the *Star*:

THE MURDER MANIAC SACRIFICES MORE WOMEN TO HIS THIRST FOR BLOOD

TWO VICTIMS THIS TIME

BOTH WOMEN SWIFTLY AND SILENTLY BUTCHERED IN LESS THAN AN HOUR

Each crime was typical of the series, except that in the first case the body was not mutilated. The murderer had been interrupted at his work, and, had he been one minute later, would almost certainly have been caught.

Louis Diemshütz was driving into a courtyard in Berner Street at 1 a.m. when his pony shied at something on the ground. He dismounted and struck a match. There he saw the body of a woman with the blood still flowing from her throat. In the shadow of the wall, or perhaps behind the gate, there must have crouched a man, listening to the other's exclamations of horror. Diemshütz, however, did not stop to look round him, but ran indoors to summon help. A dance was being held in the room overlooking the yard, and soon the men and women came rushing out in answer to his cries. They searched the courtyard, but they were too late. It was empty, the streets were silent, and the murderer was already on his way to Mitre Square looking out for another victim.

At 1.30 P.C. Watkins was passing through Mitre Square on his beat. "I looked carefully in all the corners, as I always do, turning my lantern in every direction. I heard no sound but the echo of my own footsteps. I am positive nothing was wrong and nobody was there. At 1.45 I passed through the Square again. I flashed my lantern everywhere, and in the south-western corner I saw the body of a woman lying with her throat cut and her body mutilated."

An hour later, another policeman picked up a blood-stained fragment of an apron a few streets away. It had been torn off the woman in Mitre Square by the murderer and had apparently been used to cleanse his hands. Above the spot where it was found these words were written in chalk: "The Juwes are not the men who will be blamed for nothing." It was hoped that the mis-spelling of the second word would provide some clue, but no amount of research into Jewish dialects revealed anything of importance.

There was, of course, no proof that the words had been written by the same hand that had dropped the apron, and another theory was put forward that seems just as likely to be the true one. For some reason it was generally believed that a foreigner was responsible for the outrages, and then, as now, the population of White-chapel consisted largely of Jews. It may be that the words were chalked by one in anger at the suspicion which had fallen upon his race.

In the absence of any clue, the newspapers could only make wild speculations.

"The theory of madness is enormously strengthened," said the *Star*. "Crafty bloodthirst is written on every line of Sunday morning's doings—everything points to some epileptic outbreak of homicidal mania. A slaugh-terer or a butcher who has been in a lunatic asylum, a mad medical student with a bad history behind him or a tendency to religious mania—these are the obvious classes on which the detective sense which all of us possess in some measure should be kept. Finally, there is the off-chance—too horrible almost to contemplate—that we have a social experimentalist abroad determined to make the classes see and feel how the masses live.

"More important is the discussion as to the possible methods of the murderer. Granting that he has some rough knowledge of anatomy, it is probable that his hands only would be smeared by his bloody work, and that after doing the deed he would put on gloves. He must have done so in order to ensnare the second woman—if, indeed, the two deeds were the work of one hand. He must be inoffensive, probably respectable in manner and appearance, or else after the murderous warnings of last week woman after woman could not have been decoyed by him. Two theories are suggested to us—that he may wear woman's clothes, or he may be a policeman."

The first communication bearing the signature of "Jack the Ripper" was received on Thursday, September 27th. It was addressed to the Central News Agency, and bore the postmark E.C. Reference to the crimes was made in a brutally jocular way, and the writer stated that it was he who had committed them. In the "next job," he wrote, he would "clip the lady's ears off" and send them to the police. It was that Sunday morning that the double murder was committed. On Monday morning a postcard was received dated the previous day. "I was not codding, dear old Boss, when I gave you the tip," it ran. "You'll hear about Saucy Jacky's work to-morrow. Double event this time. Number one squealed a bit, couldn't finish straight off. Hadn't time to get ears for the police. Thanks for keeping last letter back till I got to work again." The writer's pen had been dipped in some red liquid, and on the card were what appeared to be bloody finger-prints. Both the letter and the postcard were reproduced in facsimile on a

THE DAILY TELEGRAPH, THURSDAY, OCTOBER 4,

FACSIMILES OF "JACK THE RIPPER'S" LETTER AND POST CARD.

25 Sept. 1888

Dear: Boss

I keep on hearing the police have caught me but they wont fix me just yet I have laughed when they look so clever and talk about being on the *right* track That joke about Leather Apron gave me real fits......(PART OF LETTER OMITTED)..........

Keep this letter back till I do a bit more work then give it out straight My knife's so nice and sharp I want to get to work right away if I get a chance Good luck

Yours truly

Jack the Ripper

Dont mind me giving the trade name

I wasn't codding dear old Boss when I gave you the tip You'll hear about saucy Jacky's work tomorrow double

The following is the full text of the letter and post-card. The letter, which had the E.C. post-mark and was directed in red ink, ran:

Sept. 25.

Dear Boss—I keep on hearing the police have caught me, but they won't fix me just yet. I have laughed when they look so clever and talk about being on the *right* track. That joke about Leather Apron gave me real fits. I am down on whores, and I shan't quit ripping them till I do get buckled. Grand work, the last job was. I gave the lady no time to squeal. How can they catch me now? I love my work, and want to start again. You will soon hear of me with my funny little

FACSIMILE OF "JACK THE RIPPER'S" LETTER

p. 242

the kidne I took from one woman, prasarved it for you, tother piece I fried and ate; it was very nice. I may send you the bloody knif that took it out if you only wate a little longer. Catch me when you can, Mr. Lusk."

Suspecting a practical joke, Lusk took the package to a pathologist, who, after making an examination, told him that the kidney must have been taken from a woman's body within the last three weeks. Now it is true that the left kidney had been missing from the body of the woman murdered in Mitre Square, but the pathological condition of the kidney makes it unlikely that it belonged to her body.

From the internal evidence of all four letters, it seems improbable that the writer of the letters committed the crimes. At this distance of time, it may be thought equally improbable that two lunatics, each of so abnormal a type, should be simultaneously at large. But it is remarkable to read in the newspapers of those weeks how many dozens of lunatics and half-wits were attracted into the limelight by the publicity given to the murders. After the publication of the first letters, hundreds of others signed by the same name were received all over England. Innocent men by the score confessed to the crimes and surrendered themselves to the police. Others flourished knives in public places, announcing themselves as Jack the Ripper—thereby running grave risks of being lynched. The wave of crime that year seems to have been coincident with a wave of hysteria and madness.

Weeks went by, and no more tragedies occurred. Suspense was renewed at the week-ends, for it was noticed that the murders had all occurred then. This gave rise to the theory that Jack the Ripper, as he came to be called, was a sailor, whose duties brought him to England at regular intervals. It was suggested that he was employed as a butcher on one of the cattle boats that called at London every Thursday or Friday, and left for the Continent on Monday or Tuesday. On the other hand, there was a persistent rumour of a well-dressed man of about thirty-five, who had been seen in the poster, and copies were exhibited on hoardings throughout England. No one came forward to identify the writing.

It was about this time that a large section of the Press began its agitation for the use of bloodhounds, and Sir Charles Warren, the Chief of the Police, added to his long list of blunders by giving way to the public demand. On October 6th, it was announced that arrangements had been made for the use of bloodhounds in the event of another murder. After this, daily trials were held in the London parks, and on two occasions Sir Charles public-spiritedly took the part of the hunted man. A week later, the report that the hounds had been lost in Tooting proved, unfortunately, too good to be true. It seems incredible that their use in a densely populated area, where the scent of blood would almost immediately be dissipated, could ever have been seriously intended.

On the 12th of October, another communication was received from "Jack the Ripper." It was addressed this time to George Lusk, a member of the Whitechapel Vigilance Committee, which had been formed for the purpose of organising means of protection.

"I write you a letter in black ink," it ran, "as I have no more of the right stuff. I think you are all asleep in Scotland Yard with your bloodhounds as I will show you to-morrow night. I am going to do a double event, but not in Whitechapel. Getting too warm there. Had to shift. No more till you hear of me again.—Jack the Ripper." This was followed by a postcard. "Say Boss, you seem rare frightened. Guess, I'd like to give you fits, but can't stop time enough to let you box of toys play copper-games with me, but hope to see you when I don't hurry too much. Bye-bye, Boss." All these letters had been written by the same hand, and the writing, though obviously disguised, resembled that of a clerk.

A few days later, Lusk opened a gruesome parcel. It contained a portion of a human kidney. With it was a letter. "From Hell—Mr. Lusk. Sir—I send you half

I was not codding
dear old Boss when
I gave you the tip
you'll hear about
saucy Jacky's work
tomorrow double
event this time
number one squealed
a bit couldn't
finish straight
off. had not time
to get ears for
police thanks for
keeping last letter
back till I got
to work again.
Jack the Ripper

, and it was, therefore, known to a very few
sons on the Sunday. On Monday morning,
the first post, the Central News received a

handwriting may be recognised by some
part of the post-card is to a great e
cipherable, but the reproductions a

FACSIMILE OF "JACK THE RIPPER'S" POSTCARD

p. 244

company of the murdered women. He looked like a foreigner, it was said, wore brown kid gloves, and carried a black, shiny bag.[1] Before long, everyone who carried a bag answering to that description was in danger of being arrested, and soon those bags went definitely out of fashion.

Gradually, the excitement subsided, and Whitechapel was beginning to breathe more freely, when, on November 9th, the sixth and last of these murders was committed.

At a quarter to eleven on Friday morning, the landlord of a house in Miller Court sent a man to try and collect some money from one of his tenants whose rent was long overdue. Her room was locked, and he looked through the window. What he saw made him almost faint with horror. The woman had been killed, and cut to pieces. Portions of her naked body lay strewn in every part of the room. Whatever doubts there may have been for the sanity of the man who committed the first five murders, it is beyond any dispute that the mutilation of this woman was the work of a madman.[2]

His amazingly good luck held to him to the end. Not a sound had been heard that night by the other occupants of the house. Two windows, each without blinds, looked out on to the court, and for at least an hour he must have worked, in full view of any passers-by, in a room illuminated by the fire he had made in the grate of old clothing or papers.

Telegrams were hurriedly despatched that morning to Sir Charles Warren for the bloodhounds. All that day the police waited for an answer. None came. Sir Charles had resigned—driven from office by this latest proof of

[1] It was because Neil Cream answered to this description that many people identified him with Jack the Ripper. As a matter of fact, he was safely in prison in Canada at the time.

[2] The word " dissection " has often been used to describe the mutilation of the body. To anyone who has the vaguest idea of what is meant by this process, its use in this instance is misleading. The body was disembowelled and hacked to pieces by a hand which showed no trace of any surgical skill whatever.

his incompetency—and his successor seemed anxious to bury the episode of the hounds in oblivion.

Although there was no immediate diminution of crime in general, there were happily no more of these particular tragedies. Jack the Ripper vanished from the scene as mysteriously as he had appeared. It is open to conjecture, however, since homicidal mania usually culminates in suicide, whether one of the unidentified bodies taken from the river that year may not have been the answer to the riddle. On the other hand, the proximity of the docks may be equally significant.

An article appeared that autumn in the *Fortnightly Review* in which Dr. Savage discussed homicidal mania in relation to these crimes. The section which dealt with the automatism which often follows an epileptic fit is especially interesting. In this condition, he said, the sufferer often commits brutal and apparently purposeful crimes. "It is almost certain that the epileptic criminal is ignorant of his act, which may have been started by some impression or thought at the moment of the onset of the fit; he is started like an automaton by this impression." In some cases "epileptic fits are as regular in the inception and development as possible, so that the same muscles are affected in the same order in every fit." He instanced the case of a French lady who would rattle off a volley of oaths in exactly the same order and to the same extent each time she was in this condition. At the end, Dr. Savage gave his own opinion on the matter.

"First, the murders may not have all been committed by one man. There is a fashion in murder, or rather, there are epidemics of similar crimes; or, again, the imitative action may come into play. I do not think that any epileptic or drunken maniac would have so cunningly selected his victims and avoided detection, and the failure to identify anyone is in favour of there being only one agent. A mere lust for blood would not have been satisfied by the selection of victims. The skill with which the murders were perpetrated, and the skill of the mutilation, point to someone with some anatomical knowledge. This might be possessed by a butcher or someone who had medical knowledge; but there are so many nowadays with mechanical knowledge of the body, in the form of post-mortem room and anatomy room porters, that to suppose the murders to be the work of a medical man is, to my way of thinking, going too far. The cunning of the evasion, the ferocity of the crimes, the special selection of the victims, seem to me to depend either on a fiendishly criminal revenge, or else upon fully organised delusion of persecution or world regeneration."

The theories are never-ending, and no one of them is entirely satisfactory.

42. THE MYSTERIOUS DISAPPEARANCE OF MALCOLM MACMILLAN

The "Daily Chronicle," July 30th, 1889.

"*Constantinople, July* 24.

"THE fate of Mr. Macmillan is shrouded with mystery. Briefly, the circumstances are as follows: Mr. Macmillan, who is a son of the well-known publisher, came to Constantinople about three weeks ago on a pleasure-trip. On the 11th inst. he left for Broussa with Mr. A. Hardinge, one of the secretaries of the Embassy here. On the 13th, attended by a servant, they started to ride up Mt. Olympus. Arrived at the second plateau of the mountain, they dismounted, and after lunching, set out to walk to the summit, leaving the man in charge of the horses. The mountain has two peaks, one higher than the other. After climbing for some distance the travellers separated, Mr. Hardinge making for the higher peak, while Mr. Macmillan ascended the lower, with the intention of following his companion afterwards. Arrived at the summit, Mr. Hardinge saw Mr. Macmillan on the lower cone, and waved his handkerchief to him. Mr. Macmillan began the descent, and he was last seen about half-way down the smaller cone. Finding that his friend did not come, Mr. Hardinge came down, and went to the place where he had last seen him. There was no trace of Mr. Macmillan. He was not to be found, and Mr. Hardinge and the servant, after searching in all directions, returned to the town and telegraphed to the British Embassy at Therapia the news of Mr. Macmillan's strange disappearance.

"His relatives in England were informed, and telegraphed that no expense was to be spared to find the lost man. Mr. Block, dragoman of the Embassy, organised search parties, sending out seventy men in various directions, and offered a reward of £500 for Mr. Macmillan living, and £25 for his body. Two hundred men have been engaged in the search. All has been fruitless.

"The man who accompanied the travellers says that he was within earshot of Mr. Macmillan all the time, and that when he last saw him he was about half-way down the peak.

"Conjecture is rife as to the fate of Mr. Macmillan. There are numbers of Circassians and others who would not hesitate either to kill or carry off any traveller. But they are businesslike gentry, and, if they had him alive, would almost certainly ere this have named the ransom they demanded. Had he been killed the murderers would probably have "found" the body and claimed the £25. The guides state that there are on the mountain no crevasses or fissures into which a traveller could fall; and even had there been his body must have been discovered by the searchers."

No trace was ever found of the missing man, and no satisfactory solution to the mystery has ever been put forward.

43. THE MAN WITH THE TRIANGULAR TEETH

From "The Naturalist in La Plata," by W. H. Hudson (1892).

My last case relates to a singular variation in the human species. On this occasion I was travelling alone in a strange district on the southern frontier of Buenos Ayres. On a bitterly cold mid-winter day, shortly before noon, I arrived, stiff and tired, at one of those pilgrims' rests on the pampas. The wretched mud and grass building was surrounded by a foss crossed by a plank drawbridge; outside of the enclosure twelve or fourteen saddled horses were standing, and from the loud noise of talk and laughter in the bar I conjectured that a goodly company of rough frontiersmen were already making merry at that early hour. It was necessary for me to go in among them to see the proprietor of the place and ask permission to visit his kitchen in order to make myself a "tin of coffee," that being the refreshment I felt inclined for. When I went in and made my salutation, one man wheeled round square before me, stared straight into my eyes, and in an exceedingly high-pitched reedy or screechy voice and sing-song tone returned my "good-morning" and bade me call for the liquid I loved best at his expense. I declined with thanks, and in accordance with gaucho etiquette added that I was prepared to pay for his liquor. It was then for him to say that he had already been served and so let the matter drop, but he did not do so: he screamed out in his wild animal voice that he would take gin. I paid for his drink, and would, I think, have felt greatly surprised at his strange insolent behaviour, so unlike that of the usually courteous gaucho, but this thing affected me not at all, so profoundly had his singular appearance and voice impressed me: and for the rest of the time I remained in the place I continued to watch him narrowly. Professor Huxley has somewhere said, "A variation frequently occurs, but those who notice it take no care about noting down the particulars." That is not a failing of mine, and this is what I noted down while the man's appearance was still fresh in memory. He was about 5 feet 11 inches in height—very tall for a gaucho—straight and athletic, with exceedingly broad shoulders, which made his round head look small; long arms and huge hands. The round flat face, coarse black hair, swarthy reddish colour, and smooth hairless cheeks seemed to show that he had more Indian than Spanish blood in him, while his round black eyes were even more like those of a rapacious animal in expression than in the pure-blooded Indian. He also had the Indian or half breed's moustache, when that natural ornament is permitted to grow, and which is composed of thick bristles standing out like a cat's whiskers. The mouth was the marvellous feature, for it was twice the size of an average mouth, and the two lips were alike in thickness. This mouth did not smile, but snarled, both when he spoke and when he should have smiled; and when he snarled the whole of his teeth and a part of his gums were displayed. The teeth were not as in other human beings—incisors, canines, and molars: they were all exactly alike, above and below, each tooth a gleaming white triangle, broad at the gum where it touched its companion teeth, and with a point sharp as the sharpest-pointed dagger. They were like the teeth of a shark or crocodile. I noticed that when he showed them, which was very often, they were not set together, as in dogs, weasels, and other savage snarling animals, but apart showing the whole terrible serration in the huge red mouth.

After getting his gin he joined in the boisterous conversation with the others, and this gave me an opportunity of studying his face for several minutes, all the time with a curious feeling that I had put myself into a cage with a savage animal of horrible aspect, whose instincts were utterly unknown to me, and were probably not very pleasant. It was interesting to note that whenever one of the others addressed him directly, or turned to him when speaking, it was with a curious expression, not of fear, but partly amusement and partly something else which I could not fathom. Now, one might think that this was natural enough purely on account of the man's extraordinary appearance. I do not think that a sufficient explanation; for however strange a man's appearance may be, his intimate friends and associates soon lose all sense of wonder at his strangeness, and even forget that he is unlike others. My belief is that this curiosity, or whatever it was they showed in their faces, was due to something in his character—a mental strangeness, showing itself at unexpected times, and which might flash out at any moment to amuse or astonish them. There was certainly a correspondence between the snarling action of the mouth and the dangerous form of the teeth, perfect as that in any snarling animal; and such animals, it should be remembered, snarl not only when angry and threatening but in their playful moods as well. Other and more important correspondences or correlations might have existed; and the voice was certainly unlike any human voice I have ever heard, whether in white, red, or black man.

I have never been worried with the wish or ambition to be a head hunter in the Dyak sense, but on this one occasion I did wish that it had been possible, without violating any law, or doing anything to a fellow-creature which I should not like done to myself, to have obtained possession of this man's head, with its set of unique, and terrible teeth. For how, in the name of Evolution, did he come by them, and by other physical peculiarities—the snarling habit and that high pitched animal voice, for instance—which made him a being different from others—one separate and far apart? Was he, so admirably formed, so complete and well-balanced, merely a freak of nature, to use an old-fashioned phrase—a sport, or spontaneous individual variation—an experiment for a new human type, imagined by Nature in some past period, inconceivably long ago, but which she had only now, too late, found time to carry out? Or rather was he like that little hairy maiden exhibited not long ago in London, a reproduction of the past, the mystery called reversion—a something in the life of a species like memory in the life of an individual, the memory which suddenly brings back to the old man's mind the image of his childhood? For no dream-monster in human form ever appeared to me with so strange and terrible a face; and this was no dream but sober fact, for I saw and spoke with this man; and unless cold steel has given him his quietus, or his own horse has crushed him, or a mad bull gored him—all natural forms of death in that wild land—he is probably still living and in the prime of life, and perhaps at this very moment drinking gin at some astonished traveller's expense at that very bar where I met him. The old Palæolithic man, judging from the few remains we have of him, must have had an unspeakably savage and, to our way of thinking, repulsive and horrible aspect, with his villainous low receding forehead, broad nose, great projecting upper jaw, and retreating chin; to meet such a man face to face in Piccadilly would frighten a nervous person of the present time. But his teeth were not unlike our own, only very much larger and more powerful, and well adapted to their work of masticating the flesh, underdone and possibly raw, of mammoth and rhinoceros. If, then, this living man recalls a type of the past, it is of a remoter past, a more primitive man, the volume of whose history is missing from the geological record. To speculate on such a subject seems idle and useless; and when I coveted possession of that head it was not because I thought that it might lead to any fresh discovery. A lower motive inspired the feeling. I wished for it only that I might bring it over the sea, to drop it like a new apple of discord, suited to the spirit of the times, among the anthropologists and evolutionists generally of this old and learned world. Inscribed, of course, " to the most learned," but giving no locality and no particulars. I wished to do that for the pleasure—not a very noble kind of pleasure, I allow—of witnessing from some safe hiding-place the stupendous strife that would have ensued—a battle more furious, lasting, and fatal to many a brave knight of biology, than was ever yet fought over any bone or bony fragment or fabric ever picked up, including the celebrated cranium of the Neanderthal.

44. THE ARREST AND TRIAL OF CAPTAIN DREYFUS

In September, 1894, the French Intelligence Department received from one of their spies an unsigned letter, apparently from a French staff-officer, promising certain military information. This had been found at the German Embassy.

The War Office, to maintain its prestige, was anxious to find and punish the traitor immediately. Before long, two of the Staff came forward and denounced a certain Captain Dreyfus. This officer was an Alsatian Jew, the first of his race to overcome the French prejudice sufficiently to be given a place on the Staff. His accusers were rabid in their hatred of Jews, and his Semitic origin, combined with his home in Alsace, seemed to them conclusive of his guilt. Comparing his handwriting with that of the incriminating letter, they fancied they saw some resemblance. On reporting these suspicions to their superiors, one of the two officers, Colonel du Paty de Clam, was instructed to hold a preliminary enquiry. Accordingly, he wrote to Captain Dreyfus requesting him to present himself on the following Monday at the War Office for a general inspection. He expressly commanded him to appear in mufti.

"The hour," wrote Captain Dreyfus in his book, *Five Years of my Life*, "seemed to me very early for the general inspection, which ordinarily takes place in the evening, and the order to appear in civilian dress also surprised me.

"As I arrived at the War Office a short time in advance, I strolled for some moments before the building, and then went up to the offices. Upon entering, I was received by Commandant Picquart, who seemed to be waiting for me, and who at once took me into his private room. I was surprised to see none of my comrades, as officers are always assembled in groups at the general inspection. After a few minutes of trivial conversation, Commandant Picquart conducted me to the private office of the Chief of the General Staff. My surprise was great upon entering. Instead of meeting the Chief of the General Staff, I was received by Commandant du Paty de Clam, in uniform. Three persons in civilian dress, who were completely unknown to me, were also present. These three men were M. Cochefort, Chief of the Secret Police, his secretary, and M. Gribelin, Keeper of the Records. Commandant du Paty came up to me, and said in a trembling voice, 'The general is coming; whilst you are waiting, as I have a letter to write and have a sore finger, will you kindly write it for me?' However singular this request, made under such circumstances, I at once assented. I sat down, at a little table already prepared, and Commandant du Paty seated himself close to me, following my hand with his eyes. After first directing me to fill up an inspection form, he dictated to me a letter in which certain passages recalled the incriminating letter, which I heard of afterwards, and which was known by the name of the '*Bordereau*.' In the course of the dictation the Commandant said sharply, 'You tremble.' I did not tremble. At the court-martial of 1894, he explained this brusque exclamation, saying that he had noticed that I did not tremble during the dictation, and that he had therefore endeavoured to shake my assurance. This vehement remark surprised me greatly, as well as the hostile attitude of Commandant du Paty. But as there was no suspicion in my mind, I supposed he was finding fault with my handwriting. My fingers were cold, as the temperature outside was chilly, and I had only been for a few moments in a warm room. I therefore replied to him, 'My fingers are half frozen.'

"As I continued to write without emotion, Commandant du Paty tried a further manœuvre, and said to me violently, 'Be careful; it is a serious matter.' Though surprised at conduct as rude as it was unexpected, I said nothing, and simply endeavoured to write better.

"As soon as the dictation was finished Commandant du Paty rose, and, placing his hand on my shoulder, exclaimed in a loud voice, 'In the name of the law, I arrest you. You are accused of the crime of high treason.' Had a thunderbolt fallen at my feet the effect produced upon me could not have been more violent. I stammered a few disconnected words, protesting against an infamous accusation which nothing in my life could justify.

"Then M. Cochefort and his secretary rushed upon me and searched me; I did not offer the slightest resistance, but cried to them, 'Take my keys, open everything in my house. I am innocent.' Then I added, 'Show me at least the proofs of the infamous act which you pretend I have committed.' 'The charges are overwhelming,' they replied, but refused to give me any information concerning their precise nature.

"I was then taken to the military prison in the Rue du Cherche-Midi by Commandant Henry, accompanied by an officer of the Secret Police.

"On my arrival at the prison I was locked in a cell whose grated window looked upon the yard used by convicted felons. I was placed in solitary confinement, no communication with even my family being permitted. I had at my disposal neither paper, pen, ink, nor pencil.

"The men who brought me my food were always accompanied by the sergeant of the court and the warder, who alone possessed the key of my cell, and even they were forbidden to speak to me.

"During the seventeen days that followed, I underwent numerous interrogatories by Commandant du Paty, who was invested with the functions of officer of Judicial police. He always came late in the evening, accompanied by his clerk. He dictated to me fragments of sentences quoted from the incriminating letter, showing me rapidly in the uncertain light, words or fractions of words taken from the same letter, asking me at the same time if I recognised my handwriting. Apart from that which has been recorded in my various examinations, he made all sorts of veiled allusions to facts concerning which I understood nothing and then withdrew with a theatrical flourish, leaving my brain filled with insoluble riddles.

" At last, on the fifteenth day after my arrest, Commandant du Paty showed me a photograph of the incriminatory letter, since known as the '*Bordereau*.'

" I had not written this letter; I was not its author."

Forzinetti, the head of the military prisons of Paris, into whose care Dreyfus was entrusted, printed his impressions of the case in the *Figaro* three years after. He described how, one day in October, 1894, he received a secret despatch from the Minister of War, ordering him to prepare an officer's cell. He was informed that Captain Dreyfus would be brought that morning, and gave various instructions as to the care of the prisoner.

" One of these instructions," wrote Forzinetti, " was that I should intern the prisoner most completely *au secret*, and see that he had by him neither knife, nor paper, pen, or pencil.

" He was also to be given the ordinary fare of condemned prisoners, but this instruction was not carried out because I pointed out how irregular it was.

[I was] " ordered to take all precautions which I should consider necessary to prevent Dreyfus' incarceration being known inside or outside the prison.

" Towards mid-day Captain Dreyfus, in civil dress, arrived in a cab, accompanied by Commandant Henry and a police agent. . . .

" A few moments later I went to Captain Dreyfus. He was terribly excited. I had before me a man really out of his mind, with bloodshot eyes. He had upset everything in his room. I succeeded with some trouble in calming him. I had an intuition that this officer was innocent. He begged me to allow him writing materials so that he might ask the Minister of War to be heard by him.

"From the 18th to the 24th of October, du Paty came to interrogate the prisoner. Before seeing Dreyfus he asked me if he could not enter the cell noiselessly with a lamp in his hand strong enough to cast a sudden glare full on the Captain's face, for he wished to take him by surprise in such a way as to nonplus him. I replied that it was impossible.

"After October 27th, du Paty came nearly every day to subject the prisoner to fresh interrogatories and writing tests; he had never any other aim than to extort a confession, against which Dreyfus incessantly protested.

"Till the very day when this unfortunate man was before the magistrate who got the case ready for the court-martial, he only knew he was accused of 'high treason,' but of what sort of high treason he had no idea.

"The 'instruction' was long and minute, and during its course Dreyfus was so sure that he would not be committed, much less condemned, that he often said, 'What compensation shall I demand? I shall ask for the "croix" and send in my resignation.'

"A few minutes before he appeared before his judges he said to me, 'I hope now that my sufferings will soon be over, and that I shall soon be back in the bosom of my family.'

"Unfortunately it was not to be so. After the verdict, Dreyfus was brought back into my room, where I was waiting for him. When he saw me he exclaimed with a sob, 'My only crime is that I was born a Jew. This is what a life of honest, hard work has brought me to. Oh, why did I ever enter the military school, why did I not resign as my family wished me to?'

"The next day his counsel, Maître Demange, when he entered the room opened his arms and clasping him to himself said, 'My child, your condemnation is the greatest infamy of the century.'"

In January, 1895, Dreyfus was publicly degraded, expelled from the army, and sentenced to imprisonment for life on the Île du Diable in French Guiana.

In the summer of 1896, the real authorship of the *bordereau* was discovered. Fragments of a suspicious telegram-card addressed to a staff-officer, called Esterhazy, fell into the hands of Col. Picquart, the head of the Intelligence Department. He made investigations, and the first glance at that officer's handwriting was enough to convince him that here was the writer of the *bordereau*. He reported his discovery to Commandant du Paty and his own superiors, but they one and all refused to take any steps in the matter. Dreyfus was to bear the blame whether he was guilty or not. From now onwards, du Paty, with Lieut.-Col. Henry, the second-in-command to Picquart, deliberately conspired together to shield Esterhazy and prevent a re-trial of Dreyfus.

Now the court-martial had been held *in camera*, and the public was in complete ignorance of the facts. Had the War Office kept silence nothing more could ever have been done for Dreyfus, but in their desire to quiet all suspicions they published information which proved invaluable to his friends.

Their first step was to inform the public in an anonymous article in the *Éclair* that Dreyfus had been convicted, not on the *bordereau*—for that would not have been enough—but on at least four documents which had been shown secretly to his judges. These papers were in Henry's keeping, and, in order to make Dreyfus's guilt more apparent, he now forged a series of letters mentioning Dreyfus by name, and pretended that they had been amongst the letters produced at the trial.

A week or so later, the conspirators made their greatest blunder; they published a facsimile of the *bordereau*. For a year Esterhazy was safe, and then his stockbroker, on seeing a copy for the first time, recognised his client's handwriting. He communicated at once with Dreyfus's solicitor. Acting on the latter's advice, M. Mathieu Dreyfus, brother of the convicted officer, wrote an open letter to the Minister of War announcing the discovery. A court-martial of Esterhazy necessarily followed, but good care was taken to secure his acquittal, and Dreyfus continued to languish on the Île de Diable. Meanwhile, Picquart, who remained the one honest man at the War Office, was sent to the war in Tripoli, and was succeeded in office by Lieut.-Col. Henry.

During all this time nothing else but the Dreyfus case was thought of in France. The fate of Dreyfus had long ceased to be the main issue; it was a struggle between the army and the people, the anti-Semites and the others; civil war seemed imminent. In 1898, Zola's famous denunciation of the War Office appeared in the *Aurore* in the form of an open letter addressed to the President to the Republic. He was arrested, convicted of libel, and had to fly the country. But the grand climax came a little later, when it was heard that Henry had confessed to forgery. On the morning following his arrest, he was found dead with his throat cut from left to right, and from right to left. It was described by the authorities as suicide.

After this, a re-trial was inevitable. It was held at Rennes in '99, and all Europe was dumbfounded to learn that Dreyfus had again been found guilty. Soon after this, however, he was graciously pardoned by the President of the Republic and set at liberty. It was only in 1906 that full reparation was made to him.

45. THE DRUCE-PORTLAND CASE

In 1864, Thomas Charles Druce, a prosperous tradesman with an upholstery business in Baker Street, died and was buried in Highgate Cemetery—or so it was said, for many years later these facts came to be contested.

Early in 1898, Mrs. Anna Maria Druce, widow of his third son, Walter, found out that her husband's parents had only been married four months before his birth. Walter was thus Mr. Druce's oldest legitimate son, but his father, not apparently attaching any importance to this, had left the bulk of his property to Walter's eldest brother, Herbert. By a curious coincidence, soon after this discovery some amazing facts came to Mrs. Druce's knowledge, which, if she could prove their truth, were now very much to her son's advantage. The burial in '64 had, it appeared, been a mock one, and her father-in-law had lived on for many years under the name of Dr. Harmer. Herbert had been party to the conspiracy, and the will in his favour had been the price of his silence. This, if established, would render Mr. Druce's will invalid and entitle her son, as his father's heir, to the whole of the estate. Nor was this all; she discovered that Druce was a name taken by the fifth Duke of Portland, who for many years had lived a double life, and, in short, her son Sydney was heir to the Portland dukedom as well.

In March, 1898, *Lloyd's Weekly News* published a statement which had been given to their representative by Mrs. Druce herself.

"The marriage, which took place on October 30th, 1851, at New Windsor, Berkshire, between my late husband's father and mother, and in which their names are recorded as Thomas Charles Druce and Annie May, spinster, was in reality between the Marquis of Titchfield,